Finance, A Christian Perspective

PIERRE DE LAUZUN

Finance,
A Christian Perspective

FROM THE MEDIEVAL BANK
TO
FINANCIAL GLOBALIZATION

Angelico Press

CONTENTS

INTRODUCTION

DEAR READER, DON'T STOP AT THE TITLE—
whether you believe or not. The subject concerns you. Yes, I know:
finance and Christianity, everything seems to oppose these two uni-
verses. One aims to guide us by charity and gift toward eternal life; the
other sees the world through calculations, aiming at profits. Moreover,
the Gospels have severe and even radical passages against money and
its fascination.

And yet. We can begin with the evangelical texts, which show a
relationship between the two: sometimes conflicting but subtle, and,
in a sense, intimate. First, by the very interest the Gospels manifest
in the question of money. Then, by their regular and unexpected use
of parables involving economic and financial life. We also know that
it was in the Catholic context of medieval Italy that the concept of
finance first evolved — starting with the very words of "bank" and
"finance." And we know that at that time, Christian thought emerged
as the cradle of modern economic reflection.

Surprising? Less so if one considers what connects these two terms.
Finance means credit, trust, investment, betting on the future — all
concepts whose affinity with belief, therefore with faith and hope,
are evident. It is true that the third theological virtue, charity, seems
more incompatible with that association — gift being (apparently) the
opposite of calculation, which is at the center of finance. Yet even
here, you can find an essential common element: there is no finance
without a form of partnership, without a certain human community
in which resources are put by somebody into the hands of somebody
else, in a word, *entrusted*, in order to obtain the desired result.

Moreover, the medium through which finance operates is money.
Money synthesizes the problematic of our desires in its own way,
at least their material realization. People easily believe that it is the
opposite of spirituality. But the issue is not so simple — especially
for an incarnate religion like Christianity, for which this material
thing is not only not bad but enters into the project of salvation.
At a minimum, Christianity could not ignore an activity such as
finance, which is at the center of economic regulatory processes and
therefore of the production and exchange of material goods, and

which arbitrates how resources are distributed in society, and thus the material priorities of the society of human beings — the society in which the Kingdom of Heaven is being prepared.

Exploring the link between these two apparently distant and yet strangely connected realities is an essential task. If only to better understand and orient this protean reality that finance has become: at once the nervous system of our economies, a possible source of disaster through its crises, and a sometimes morbid object of fascination.

However, my aim here will not be to deal with technical measures, except in passing, but rather to address issues that have a moral dimension, considering the logic of the financial system.[1] Even more so because these issues seem to me to be the most fundamental. In these uncertain times, notably with respect to that disconcerting phenomenon finance, which is a risky but indispensable field for action, how can we best direct our activity and that of other people toward the common good? How can we thus renew our perspective on what can be seen as the often-elusive quintessence of this economic medium, money?

But also, for the believing reader, how to place it under the gaze of God, in view of the infinity of eternal life? And, for the non-believer, how to benefit from the only major reflection on economics that is neither utilitarian nor materialistic? We invite both to draw lessons from this original Christian view, at first sight quite different from views that are dominant in our society, but which can speak to every person of good will.

Note: the italics used in the quotations do not necessarily correspond to the original text, but may be employed to emphasize important points in our argument.

---

[1] We will not discuss questions of ethical casuistry or questions about banks or markets (prudential ratios, etc.). We will also avoid discussing issues regarding public finance, money, etc., which are commonly called financial but are, in reality, macroeconomic issues.

FIRST PART

The Gospels and the Old Economy

CHAPTER I

The Starting Point: the Gospels

A CONSTANT REFERENCE TO ECONOMIC AND FINANCIAL LIFE

I have shown in another book[1] the strange affinity that connects Christianity and economic life. It is particularly clear in the Gospels. Passages in the Gospels revealing comparisons with economic life and using it as reference for reasoning are exceptionally numerous. The realities of spiritual life are in fact often explained on the basis of an economic reality: not just a material reality, but a concrete and specific mechanism of economic life. *Most importantly, no other religious text does so.* Of course, the central message is spiritual, but the use of economic life and its logic as a reference is not neutral. This implies that the specific reality and logic of economics should be recognized as legitimate. And as we will see, this is particularly relevant to finance.

Economic and financial calculations

A first range of realities, transposed directly into spiritual life, revolves around the idea of *rational calculation*. The Gospels tell us first to make provision wisely, but not to worry in vain; they tell us that it is rational and commendable to anticipate the future and to organize ourselves accordingly — even though the ultimate meaning of these texts obviously concerns our spiritual dispositions with regard to God's coming return. The classic example is the well-known comparison of the Kingdom of God with the five foolish virgins and the five wise virgins (Mt 25:1–13): the wise virgins await the return of the bridegroom, providing oil for their lamps, as opposed to the foolish virgins, who do not think of it, and will be severely punished. What is approved here is of course foresight, a rational and conscious virtue, not concern or anxiety. Another passage on foresight asks us: "For which of you, desiring to build a tower, does not first sit down and count the cost, whether he has enough to complete it? Otherwise, when he has laid a foundation, and is not able to finish, all who see it begin to mock him" (Lk 14:28–29). It must be done according to rigorous and realistic calculations, as in the example of the house built on rock and not on sand (Mt 7:24–27). And we must invest

---

[1] *L'Evangile, le Chrétien et l'Argent*, Paris, Cerf, 2004.

with patience, but also discernment. This is shown by the parable of the fig tree that gives no fruit: its owner wants to uproot it. The gardener then asks him to wait a year longer while he cultivates it, and fertilizes it with manure, to see whether this improves the result; otherwise it will be cut down (Lk 13:6–9). In other words, he recommends investing—but wisely. We can also see from this example that it may be quite justified to eliminate what is not productive. But we must not rush to eliminate, as is also shown by the parable of wheat and darnel: "Let both grow together until the harvest" and then separate the good grain from the bad (Mt 13:24–30). But the general principle is that one recognizes the tree by its fruit. And the text tells us, if a tree does not yield good fruit, it is cut and burnt. This realistic reasoning is used to make people understand the attitude that a patient God will have toward those people who refuse to give, and to give of themselves. As if His way of proceeding was comparable to that of the peasant with his trees—or of the financier calculating his transactions.

We are then told about *financial arbitrage*: it is the story of someone who has discovered that a given field contained a treasure (Mt 13:44). Hiding this information, he sells everything he has to buy the field; this is the attitude we are recommended to adopt toward the Kingdom of Heaven. In short, everything has to be sold (risked) in order to buy something that is worth more than its price, and therefore whose intrinsic value is higher than the market price, which reflects only the valuation other people give it. This means that they do not have the information to assess accurately the true value of this property: if the seller of the field knew that it held a treasure, the price would rise accordingly and interest in buying it would disappear immediately. This is exactly what is referred to in finance as arbitrage. Another case of risky but rational investment is when, in order to recover one asset, we risk losing all others by temporarily leaving them aside: a shepherd abandons ninety-nine of his sheep temporarily to recover the one hundredth that has been lost (Mt 18:12–14). His behavior is a given. A similar case is the woman who has lost a coin, precious to her, and who seeks it everywhere, all business ceasing (Lk 15:8–10). Here too, the behavior is presented as obvious: Who would not do the same? And it is said she will rejoice greatly if she finds it again. In both cases the value of what is sought is a material thing that justifies complete devotion to that task.

Another point is that of physical or financial *measure*: it is natural in the Gospels to assume that the value of all material things is measured by a figure, usually a price. These notions of measure, number, and price appear regularly in the Gospels; to say that a sparrow has little value (Mt 10:29), Jesus gives us its price on the market (two for an ace—a coin of that time). This implies that it is rational and normal to carry out such an assessment. A final point is that of multiplication and growth: the rationality of all these efforts is in the existence of multiplicative effects; properly utilized, investment and effort yield much more than what has been invested, and often in enormous proportions. This multiplier effect is presented as essentially good. The example given several times is that of a good tree, or seed, which yields a hundredfold (Mt 13:8, 23). Another economic application of this idea is given in the well-known parable of the talents (Mt 25:14–30), of which we shall speak again later: this puts us squarely in finance, since it is about making money by placing it with a usurer!

The natural presence of the market economy

The text is even more at the heart of economic life when it uses the realities of a trade economy as a reference, and in particular, the hoarding or the use of *assets*, financial assets. Cases of treasure hunting, which do not correspond to any investment or productive work, are cited as examples on several occasions. This term "treasure" is characteristic; we ran into it in the example of the man who buys a field and we find it in the comparison that is made between the "treasures" of this world and those of the other. We may also cite the sentence relating the value of a treasure to that of the man who exploits it: a good man derives good things from a good treasure, and a bad man, bad things from a bad treasure. This seems to be a direct extension of the reflections on the good tree that produces good fruit, but this time what makes producing possible is no longer a natural phenomenon, but money. There is no difference here between what is sometimes called the real economy and the financial economy. Finally, need I add that all these texts presuppose the private ownership of the means of production? Let us recall here the case of the Good Shepherd (Jn 10:11–18), who gives his life for his sheep, and with whom Christ is identified. Why this sacrifice? For a reason that is clearly given to us: because he is the owner, whereas the employee has no interest in risking his life since his stake is limited to the wage he receives. The text presents this as obvious.[2]

Remember also that everywhere in these texts what is due is due, including if it is money that has been lent, even with interest. This principle is never questioned, and on the contrary, it is recognized as self-evident. Of course, it is often recommended that the creditor remit the debts, but nowhere is it ever called into question that they are due. Saint Paul, moreover, calls it a precept: pay to each what is due to each: taxes to the one to whom tax is due, revenue to the one to whom revenue is due (Rom 13:7). Furthermore, if it is envisaged to forgive debts, excepting charitable behavior, the only instance presented as "normal"[3] is where a debtor is unable to repay what he owes, meaning that to recover the debts it would be necessary to engage in inhuman acts. In the same way, wage-earning is frequently mentioned and in no way questioned as such, no more than economic inequality. But take care; the consequence is that much more will be required of those who received more, as the parable of the talents shows. This point also reveals an economic calculation: someone who is rich in this world has received much more from the Lord, who therefore expects much more in return.

In short, the underlying logic of what we see is an unequal economy of property and trade, where labor must be remunerated, debts honored, but in a reasonable manner; where money is the yardstick for measuring trade — including labor; where investment is good and must yield abundantly, and where economic calculation is rational and justified by its results. In other words, in the gospel preaching we have all the bases of economic life in a monetary and decentralized market economy, with salaries and financial calculation.

In all these examples, not only does economic rationality escape criticism, but it is transposed to explain and justify by analogy realities of a spiritual order. *This implies a certain relationship between the*

---

2 It goes even further; it compares the mutual knowledge of the sheep and this pastor with that of the Father and the Son: I know my own and my own know me, as the Father knows me and I the Father....

3 For example, we have the parable of the king who settles his accounts with his servants, one of whom owes him an enormous sum of money but cannot repay it. The master forgives him generously but this man has a debtor himself, for much smaller sums, whom he attacks and drags into the courts. This is reported to the king, who sends him directly to the jailers, until he pays back everything (Mt 18:23–35).

rational structures that underpin them. If the economic and financial sphere is judged capable of conveying a spiritual message through comparison, it is evident that at the very least it is not in itself bad, and that the intuitions and reasoning apparent in it are "usable" or "transposable" in the spiritual sphere, at least in the earliest stage. It may even be added that the existence of this analogy implies that in every economic exchange there is at work a distant reflection of our relationship with God. For example, lending is tantamount to entrusting another with assets that allow him to carry out a certain degree of material activity: it is therefore a participative gesture, good in itself—even if it is generally subjectively experienced in a reductive way and sometimes becomes bad. In the same way, a person who employs someone gives him an opportunity to work, that is, to create, that he would not have otherwise. All this is a very distant reflection of the gesture of God entrusting creation to man. This also explains why we can sanctify ourselves by practicing what may be called our social duty (the responsibility arising from our position in society), which for the vast majority of us falls within the realm of economic life: it is because in all these acts we can find a certain reflection of the spiritual order. The explanation of the profusion of economic comparisons made in the Gospels is therefore not limited to the fact that Christ uses a language that is easy to understand: it is also that it is directly placed in a context of life that for most of us is mainly economic, but which we should use for our salvation.

Challenging the economy

Naturally the gospel approach does not end here. In some cases, this economic rationality seems contested or is at least problematic in its own sphere. The Gospels contain two characteristic examples with a financial connotation. The first is the parable of the dishonest steward (Lk 16:1–9). The dishonest steward steals from his master and when discovered, reacts by stealing even more: he forgives the claims of his master on various debtors in order to create a network of friendships that will serve him when his master will have driven him away. The master, when informed of this, praises his steward. Not because of the act itself, which is described as dishonest, but because of the relevance of the calculation, which is judged more astute in its sphere, from this "son of iniquity," than that of the "sons of light" in their own sphere. The second example is the parable of the talents, mentioned above: a master leaving on a journey gives his servants talents (a huge amount of money at the time): five, two, and one. On his return, the first servant explains that he has earned five more, the second two. But the last one tells his master: "Master, I knew you to be a hard man, reaping where you did not sow, and gathering where you did not winnow; so I was afraid, and I went and hid your talent in the ground." The master, of course, praised the first servant: "Well done, good and faithful servant; you have been faithful over a little, I will set you over much; enter into the joy of your master." But he bluntly rebuked the one who had buried his talent: "You wicked and slothful servant! You knew that I reap where I have not sowed, and gather where I have not winnowed? Then you ought to have invested my money with the bankers, and at my coming I should have received what was my own with interest." And not only does he take away his talent, but he gives it to the first one, and then throws out the unfortunate chap. The point is not that the behavior of this master is morally justified in the text. It is that it shows the divine requirement of "results," and a way for us to understand that is a comparison with a particularly greedy investor!

With these parables, the rationality of the economic sphere is thus recognized and used to illuminate spiritual realities. But at the same time, it is associated with behavior that is less clearly justified, and even questionable. In other words, the limits of economy appear. We understand then that whatever its rationality, it does not by itself always give satisfactory results, if we do not add to it a set of considerations that cannot be deduced from its rationality alone. This implies that this economic reality has already been bypassed. However, *even morally objectionable behavior, such as that of the dishonest steward or even the hard and greedy master, can be used to illuminate the attitude of God or of a true believer; there is some analogy with it in their logic.*

THE REVERSAL OF ECONOMIC REASONING
The real investment: eternal life

As we know, far from remaining at this stage, the Gospels call for a radical change of perspective, which leads us well beyond the current economic reality. But at the same time, we are not asked to abandon this economic rationality. Indeed, change results from putting in perspective the realities of this world in relation to those of the other, the world of the Kingdom, which is not of this world, and which is that of eternal life. The main argument used for this is the opposition between lasting and transitory values. The realities of this world are perishable because they are subject to countless physical hazards (predators, diseases, storms) or human ones (thieves, wars, etc.). At any rate, in the best case our fortune can survive — but not us, since we shall die. On the other hand, everything that can be "accumulated" in view of the other world keeps its value eternally. The conclusion is logical: do not hoard in this world, where vermin gnaw and thieves steal; hoard in heaven, where they cannot act. The essential point here is: where your treasure is, there is your heart (Mt 6:19). In other words, *the infinite value of an investment made in view of the other world, because it is eternal, is incomparably preferable to the value of assets in this world, for one day we will lose those.* It is remarkable that the Gospels emphasize this argument, which is expressed in terms of pure economic rationality. What it is showing us is that *economic reasoning, if limited to this world, will leave us immensely frustrated, since the only fruit of all our efforts will ultimately be to lose everything* which, from a rational point of view, greatly reduces the reward of the efforts we have made.

From another angle, it emphasizes a fundamental weakness of "pure" economy, which focuses on the most rational way of producing and exchanging goods, on the basis of a given system of preferences that is limited to this world. In the Gospels, on the contrary, we are told to reflect on what is the true good. From the economic point of view, it can only be what gives you comparatively infinite value and therefore cannot be an asset of this world. *A system of preferences limited to this world is not only distorted, but economically irrational.* Let us add that if investment in the other world is the only real good, it is because it is the only investment that we can make durably in ourselves, in our person. What matters then is to free our hearts from avarice, for even if we possess many things, our life is not among the things that we can possess. The moral is to store up treasures in heaven — in God. We find here again the parable of the treasure hidden in the field; the kind of arbitrage that enabled somebody to sell everything to buy this field is even more justified in the case of the Kingdom, the value of which is infinitely superior to that of any property in this world. *The only real accumulation, the only rational one, is in the other world; this is true out of pure financial rationality, even before any consideration of moral imperative!* Let us note by the way that in doing so, scarcity itself disappears, and the abundance you get then will be without limit. Naturally, the devil seeks to divert us from investing in eternity, redirecting us toward the attractions of immediate material life. He pushes us to make a miscalculation: what he promises remains at the level of this world and excludes the fundamental reality that is God, origin of everything, and the eternal life He offers us.

Wealth and the rich

It is in the light of these considerations that we must analyze the anathema placed by the Gospels on the "rich." We know the terrible statement (Mt 19:24) that it is easier for a camel to go through the eye of a needle than for a rich man to enter the kingdom of Heaven. Even if one admits that the expression is not to be taken literally, the condemnation remains vivid. This perplexed the disciples, who wondered who might be saved. Their lucidity is remarkable: they were poor, but they understood that the term "rich" did not apply here only to opulently wealthy people but to all those who own something and are satisfied with it. Jesus replied that the salvation of these "rich" is impossible for men, but that nothing is impossible with God.

A related question is the abandonment of the riches of this world. In a well-known text (Mt 19:16–22), Jesus asks a wealthy young man about his respect for the Law, and then explains to him that once he has respected the Law, if he wants to be perfect, he must sell all his property, give it to the poor and follow Him — for he will then have a treasure (again) in Heaven. These words sadden the young man, who has great possessions, and he goes away. Again, the choice to make seems radical. Yet other rich people are found in the Gospels, who are not called to make this choice. Nicodemus and Joseph of Arimathea apparently do not give up their possessions, which allows them to play a historical role that would otherwise not have been possible. Even a Zacchaeus (Lk 19:1–10), whose fortune has no commendable source,[4] is saved by donating half of it to the poor and restoring four times the stolen sums: that is a lot, but it does not imply complete destitution. We must emphasize the difference between them and the rich young man: Zacchaeus lived in sin, especially through his financial activity; his conversion involves giving back what has been

---

4 He was chief of the tax collectors, who undertook to raise taxes on behalf of the Government, taking the maximum profit in between.

stolen, and furthermore being generous, but nothing more. On the other hand, the rich young man is not a thief, no blame is attached to him; the question that arose for him was how to reach a higher stage, that of holiness. This required, in his case, abandoning his treasure: no doubt honestly gotten, but something to which he had an excessive attachment. In other words, we must discern two levels of sacrifice: that required to achieve salvation, and that required for attaining perfection. This confirms the existence of several levels of appeal. It appears, then, that a state, that of "being rich," is incompatible with salvation, but that the meaning of the word here is somehow different from that of being rich in the usual sense. The anathema against the "rich" aims at a certain category, those who define themselves *only* as rich, that is to say, whose only wealth (even small), whose only accumulation of riches, is confined to this world. This is what the well-known dictum tells us: "But woe to you that are rich, for you have received your consolation" (Lk 6:24).

The question becomes clearer with several other texts. It is, first of all, the powerful phrase that no one can serve two masters (Mt 6:24), God and Mammon (that is, personified money), for inevitably he will love one and not the other; he will despise one and not the other. This thought is all the more interesting because it does not have its equivalent in other fields of human ambition — power or pleasure, for example: *as if money played a specific role of synthesis of what can turn us away from the right track.* This is consistent with the central role of economic parables and of the language of economics in the Gospels. But if the problem is Mammon, it is not a problem of distribution of wealth: it is the fascination exerted by money, which leads us to make it our master. *It is this abnormal relationship to money that is the problem.* Conversely, the Beatitudes tell us: "blessed are the poor in spirit, for the kingdom of Heaven is theirs" (Mt 5:3). The "poor in spirit" is the one who has understood that the only real assets are in the other world; the "rich man" is the one who has not understood that and who has his reward in this world, obtained by pursuing an objective of this world and succeeding. This often leads him to oppress others. From his narrow viewpoint, this is apparently rational behavior, but it is irrational if you introduce the perspective of the Kingdom of Heaven.

Here we find again our dishonest steward, the one who siphons off the property of his master to provide for his future life. As the text says, "make friends for yourselves by means of unrighteous Mammon, so that when it fails they may receive you into the eternal habitations." Do as the steward does: "divert" the riches of this world to invest in the other. *It is therefore possible to use the riches of this world to attain the other, provided you leave aside the narrow purpose of these goods in this world.* But of course, the same texts remind us that we must remain faithful in matters of money, even if they are in themselves minor, for otherwise it is impossible that we inspire confidence in great issues, which are the only important ones for us. If you are not trustworthy with unrighteous wealth, who will trust you with genuine riches? This makes a clear distinction between respect for the logic of the things of this world in their domain, when they alone are involved, and consideration of what should be our true goals and values.

Hence the importance of gift, which is central to Christianity. And first of all, gifts to the poor. Another text explains, always in terms of economic optimization, that it is better to give to a poor man. Indeed, he cannot give back to us as a rich man could, which constitutes a "credit" for us in the other world. Let us not invite the rich to our homes, for they will return the favor; let us invite the miserable, and our reward will be in the other world (Lk 14:12–14). *Finally, by following through the logic of this calculation, we are invited to go beyond all calculation: the calculation shows that we must give without calculating.*

Do not worry about material life; renounce yourself and follow Him

This seems to lead us to a reversal of the precepts of everyday life such as prudence and calculation: we find here the recommendation of not having any concern for material life, including eating or dressing. (It is not a matter of erroneous thinking, for, as we have seen, economic rationality remains, especially prudence and reasoning.[5]) For, Jesus tells us, God knows what we need. "But seek first his kingdom and his righteousness, and all these things shall be yours as well. Therefore do not be anxious about tomorrow, for tomorrow will be anxious for itself. Let the day's own trouble be sufficient for the day" (Mt 6:33–34). The last sentence is revealing: one can and must do one's job by calculating what is necessary. What is important

5   The maintenance of economic rationality in its own sphere explains why Saint Paul cites among the many qualities demanded of a bishop the ability to manage his family affairs. How could we entrust the affairs of the Church to someone who cannot manage his own (1 Tim 3:2–8)?

is to avoid excessive concern for the things of this world, for that would eventually dominate us, whereas we must concentrate on the only objective that is worth it, eternal life. Since everything comes ultimately from the Father, what is important is to love Him, not to make calculations about His next gift. For the first lesson for the Christian goes well beyond the material question. It is: if you want to follow me, *renounce yourself*. The problem with material wealth is that it makes us withdraw into ourselves through the attachments it arouses. Now we must *renounce ourselves*, take up our cross, and follow Him (Mk 8:34).[6] As it is also said (Mk 8:35–36), "he who wants to save his life loses it; he who loses his life for me will find it. Now what is the use of gaining the whole world if one loses one's life? What can the world give in exchange for a man's life?"

Another paradox: the very fact that all this does not exclude the existence of material rewards in this world. We see it abundantly in the Old Testament. It is also seen in the instructions given to the apostles, where it is said that their toil deserves salary. We can also recall the gestures of multiplication made by Jesus of the loaves and fishes, or the transformation of material goods at Cana. What matters is not to seek these material benefits as such, and especially not to attach oneself to them. For the only true wealth is once again Him. This means that the disciples of Jesus do not hesitate to drink and eat — which is criticized by His opponents. Sending the disciples to preach, He commands them to give as well as to receive gratuitously, not to take any money, provisions, or spare clothes — but He adds at once that every worker is worthy of his food. And He says in Luke (10:7): stay in the same house to eat and drink what is there, for the laborer deserves his wages.

Another key is given to us by the maxim: "*Render to Caesar the things that are Caesar's, and to God the things that are God's,*" one of the best-known teachings of Jesus (Mk 12:17). It is generally applied, and rightly so, to the separation to be established between the political and the religious world. But we must not forget how the phrase

---

6 It will be noted here, to continue with economic metaphors, that to follow Christ is the only way to be ultimately "productive." There is even a direct relationship between the "yield" to be expected of a person and the quality of the bond he has established with God: "Every plant which my heavenly Father has not planted will be rooted up" (Mt 15:13). It is only by staying, if we may say, connected, or grafted onto Christ, that we can produce something worthwhile.

emerges: about a coin. Caesar is the one who mints coins with his effigy. This text can also be applied to economic matters: economic considerations must be given the respect they deserve in their own sphere. After all, Jesus was a craftsman until the age of thirty. Considered in its isolated rationality, this sphere is different from that of God, which is infinitely wider and all-encompassing, and which alone must be the object of our true attention, especially that of our heart. If a conflict occurs, it must be resolved in favor of the only superior consideration, that of the other world. Thus, the merchants of the Temple are mercilessly driven out by Jesus. For He said, "my house shall be called a house of prayer; but you make it a den of robbers" (Mt 21:13).

Conclusion

In summary, there are two horizons to consider. What is vital to the Christian is their structured hierarchy: to recognize that which is really important, the other world, which has, in the most rational way, an absolute priority. This does not exclude concrete preoccupations or material rewards: hence the first level of consideration. But it is precisely because economic logic has such a hold over us that we must make a profound conversion to avoid the fascination of the goods and activities of this world and refocus on the only essential reality, which goes beyond it infinitely. And thus, as Saint Paul says, let "those who buy [live] as though they had no goods, and those who deal with the world as though they had no dealings with it" (1 Cor 7:30–31), *which implies at the very least that we consider truly and intimately money only as a means, without following its law, even in the "reasonable" sense.* This eternal perspective is divine charity, and its manifestation in this world is generosity, or at least solidarity. In contrast to this, you have the hoarding of the miser, focused on material accumulation and its false security. But also, there is *the illusory search for security through the economy, and any idea of closing the economy on itself.* This message proclaims, in short, *the essential incompleteness of the economy.* This will imply in practice that the teachings and recommendations that Christianity proposes spread over several successive levels: it begins with the simple moralization of ordinary economic life, according to rules of natural morality, which can be easily proposed to a non-Christian. Then we have to take into account the dimension of communion in our activities, expressed in particular by gift and generosity. And finally, we arrive at a vocation of absolute poverty and detachment, which is impossible without true faith, and which takes its meaning in the name of that infinite Love that is offered to us in eternal life. This staggered perspective must be kept in mind in order to understand fully what comes next.

CHAPTER 2

Christianity and the Discovery of the Economy

HOW CHRISTIAN ECONOMIC THOUGHT EVOLVED
Ancient Christian conceptions of the economy

It is not surprising in this context that economic and financial considerations are particularly abundant in the Christian tradition. Of course, and this applies to this entire section, when I speak of economic thinking for these epochs, I am referring to the content and object of this reasoning and these activities. I do not infer that there was an autonomous consciousness of what we call economics, much less a separate science like political economy: this only emerged in the eighteenth century. Until then, that which deals with the core realities we call economics was integrated within a broader framework, which was essentially moral or religious, and incidentally political.

The richness of this reflection can be seen notably in the Middle Ages, during which the climax of Christian thought on the matter was achieved. These reflections were then found in books of theology, morality, or canon law. But their origin lies with the Church Fathers,[1] who had already considerably reflected on wealth, money, and work. It is important to note that this reflection emerged against a backdrop of large metropolitan conglomerations, in an economy dominated by the Empire, a strong central power. It was, therefore, not conditioned by a subsistence economy (as some have said) which did not appear until after the great invasions. The main features of this ancient Christian thought are the following: the effective redistribution of wealth was seen as a virtue; the active use of money via redistribution and investment as opposed to hoarding, which was condemned as sterile behavior, typical of infidels; and charging interest on loans was identified as hoarding — hence it was bad. The insistence of the Fathers on the obligation to redistribute wealth links the vocabulary of production or investment with that of distribution and political management. *Wealth is justified in order to distribute it, thus investing in the other*

---

1 See, for example, Todeschini in: Roberto Greci, Giuliano Pinto, and Giacomo Todeschini, *Economie urbane ed etica economica nell'Italia medievale* (Roma-Bari: Editori Laterza, 2005).

world and managing the social fabric in this world. The rich man is saved by feeding others. *To love wealth is bad, but managing it is a duty, and this management is subject to Christian ethics.* Economics appears in one sense as "the enigmatic side of the earthly journey to the hereafter." The repeated condemnation of avarice, as the mother of all evils, is clarified by constantly opposing two sets of alternative terms: individual or institution, family or society, subjective needs or collective utility. The first term of each pair declines into avarice if it is privileged to the detriment of the second, which incarnates the good order of society. Also, the Fathers felt that the experts capable of making this distinction resided in the ecclesiastical world. In general, the Church was seen as the ideal mediator between rich and poor.[2]

The economic thought of the early Middle Ages

From the ninth to the thirteenth century[3] there evolved simultaneously a relatively significant degree of economic growth, which would then become rare before the eighteenth century, and increased intellectual power, which in practice became the realm of the clerics. The corpus of "economic" thought that was elaborated within the Church was more and more considered valid for the entire social body. This began with Carolingian texts relating to the proper management of ecclesiastical property.[4] At the same time the broad prohibition of usury appeared, notably by extending to the laity a rule that was until then applicable only to ecclesiastics.[5] They now perceived the usurer as an enemy of economic public order.

Above all, the influence of monasticism was considerable. It was an autonomous political and economic system, aimed at the prosperity of the monastery and its development, understood as a means of spiritual life. A link was established between discipline or asceticism, and productivity. Weber had already stressed that monks were the first to lead rationally ordered lives. The monastic economy was for the

---

2   Henceforth they defined ecclesiastical wealth as separate, of a different order, but representative of the proper functioning of economic society as a whole.

3   Greci, Pinto, and Todeschini, *Economie urbane*, pp. 161 sqq.

4   In the line of ancient Christian thought these texts tended to define property as public goods (analogous to imperial goods), with a special role in caring for the poor. Their integrity was therefore of major interest; in the name of the poor, they must not be alienated but protected from infidels.

5   Usury was forbidden to ecclesiastics from the imperial era, but the prohibition was extended to the laity only under the Carolingians.

time a rational economy *par excellence*, favoring long-term investments and seeking rationality in accounting. It was therefore a laboratory of economic thought, but a very specific one, with special emphasis on the idea of a separation between collective wealth and individual satisfaction: *abundance, which should characterize the collective, is opposed to privation, which should characterize individual experience.* Expenditure must be rational; the elimination of superfluity leads to productivity.

On this basis, medieval Christian thinking, known as scholasticism, developed into a remarkable thought process that was mostly *non-existent in other religions and civilizations,*[6] and served as groundwork for the economic thinking of subsequent epochs.[7] The emphasis is on Christian morality: what is good, evil, or neutral in economic activity, in the perspective of everyday life, enlightened and guided by the aim of achieving eternal life? A central figure of this reflection is a character whose role was constantly asserting itself at the time: the merchant (in the broad sense of the word). This is particularly true of Saint Thomas Aquinas, whose well-known role is central to Catholic philosophical and theological thinking. In this area as in many others, he is the natural starting point. In his major opus, the *Summa Theologica,*[8] Saint Thomas examined a series of questions posed by market economy, seen from the angle of moral requirements. The notion of justice is at the center of his reflection. The starting point is a moral theory of economic value, with the notion of fair price.

JUST DETERMINATION OF PRICES: THE PRINCIPLES
The analysis of Saint Thomas in the Summa Theologica
This has often been misinterpreted, but it can illustrate how at that time a market was understood. In the first place, Saint Thomas asks himself: Can we sell something for more than it is worth?[9] Even if civil laws allow it, or the buyer has a great need of it, the Gospels tell

---

6 Medieval Islam provided valuable elements, especially on prices, but not an overall thought system like scholasticism. See Ramon Verrier, *Introduction à la pensée économique de l'Islam du VIIIe au XVe siècle* (Paris: L'Harmattan, 2009).
7 Even if it was done in a different spirit. We will draw here on our *Christianisme et Croissance économique*, Parole et Silence, 2008.
8 Thomas Aquinas, *Summa theologica* (Milan: Editiones Paulinae, 1988). In particular *Quaestio 77: De peccatis quae sunt circa voluntarias commutationes.*
9 *Articulus 1. Utrum aliquis licite possit vendere rem plus quam valeat.*

us not to do to someone what we would not want done to us — and *no one wants to pay anything more than the value of an item. So he says, it is not morally lawful.* He then develops why it is a sin, even when there is no fraud. The idea is that a commercial act is carried out for the mutual benefit of both parties, and that justice excludes one from benefitting more or less than the other.[10] The measure for that is the price. Now equality consists in an exact correspondence in the values of what is exchanged. It is therefore *immoral to buy something for less than it is worth, or to sell it more expensively.* It may, however, happen that there is a significant imbalance between the need of one of the parties to the transaction, and that of the other: for example, if the seller is particularly impacted by the deprivation of that good, or if the buyer has a very great need of the thing: this factor will then have to be taken into account. On the other hand, a seller must not exploit a very great desire exhibited by a buyer, because the additional pleasure that the latter expects from the good is not due to the seller, who should not derive a benefit from it.

Let us note the important points in this text. First, it speaks of *moral laws, not of civil laws* (Thomas admits that they should not be concerned with evaluating the reference to "what the merchandise is worth"). Then, in the background, we have what we would call today a *free trade economy*, where both parties agree on a price, independent of any reference to law or custom (otherwise the question would disappear). Finally, the argument turns on one question: how to define precisely what the good considered "is worth." In this analysis, obviously it must be an objective value, depending on the situation in society, and in this respect, it is placed beyond the individual wishes of the buyer and the seller, which, however, may influence it if the need is great.

The point Saint Thomas then examines is whether the seller must disclose the *defects* of the thing to be sold.[11] We get the same affirmative. Let us insist, however, on the guarded response he gives us in the case of somebody selling wheat which he transports to a region that is lacking it. Necessarily he will be able to sell it at a higher price than at home. Should he disclose that? If buyers in the region knew that merchants were coming in with additional wheat, locally the price

---

10   The exchange is considered positive as such because it involves a mutual benefit: each needs what the other offers.

11   *Articulus 3. Utrum venditor teneatur dicere vitium rei venditae.*

would drop. But Thomas explains that the merchant is not *obliged* to inform his customers of this possibility: he is only obliged to take the price he "finds" on the spot, which is the value of this good locally. The objective character of the price is again there; at the same time, we see that this price depends on local conditions. *The Thomistic just price is therefore in no way abstract. It is the equilibrium price locally found in a given place and at a given time.* On the other hand, he tells us that our merchant would be *more* virtuous if he lowered his price or if he delivered the information he has. The fair price therefore does not arise either from an intrinsic characteristic of the thing or exclusively from the personal circumstances of the buyer or seller or from their relationship, but from local and temporal circumstances in a given society. *It is the price as it is settled in a given region, depending on the local characteristics of the market*, which obviously depends on supply and demand, as seen in the example of wheat; is not the pure play of supply and demand as in the liberal era.

Another question he raises is *whether it is lawful to sell at a higher price than one has bought*, that is, to be a merchant.[12] Yes, he tells us. Indeed, the role of the merchant is to buy or sell not because he needs the thing itself, but to make a profit. Aristotle, whom he cites, criticizes this activity, considering that it is oriented toward profit alone (*lucrum*), which in his scale of value is bad. But Saint Thomas says (and the divergence with Aristotle is very important here), even if this is not particularly estimable in itself, it is not reprehensible. Moreover, nothing *prevents orienting this profit to a commendable purpose, and thus making it good.* This is the case with a trader who, taking a reasonable profit, provides for the needs of his family or helps the poor, or acts on grounds of public interest, for example, to supply goods to his country. In such a case, he seeks profit not as an end in itself, but as the remuneration of his activity. *Selling a thing, even in its raw state, for a profit, when prices are just in the preceding sense, is in itself illicit only if that profit is an end in itself.*

He had told us, however, that it was illegal to sell something more expensively than it is worth, or to buy cheaper. How then can one make a profit by buying and selling? The answer is that if someone buys without intending to resell immediately but then resells it, either after modification, or at another time, or another place (he may have transported the thing for this purpose, taking on additional risk), and if the price has changed because of that change of time or location, he does nothing illegal. We find the same idea: if the merchant brings added value to the thing, or plays on exogenous price fluctuations, outside of his will and scope of action, he does nothing abnormal. But in all these cases *profit is a means: it must be related to a purpose other than itself. A great difference of appreciation between this conception and liberalism lies in the moral conscience of the merchant.* We shall find this point throughout the teaching of the Church. This does not prevent Saint Thomas from having a certain distrust of commerce: it has, he says, too often the appearance of vice, or inclines to it. And above all, it makes us sink too much in the preoccupations of this world, taking us away from spiritual realities, something we know about in our time!

Key ideas

How to assess this conception? As Joel Kaye[13] reminds us, ever since Aristotle, the question of equality is at the center of the reflection on justice in exchanges, the problem being how to equalize things that are radically different in themselves. The means of doing this is money, which enables people to establish a proportion between all things and measure them. Aristotle, followed by medieval people, noted that the matter was not about measuring the value of things in themselves,[14] but from a particular approach, that of human need, *indigentia* in medieval Latin. The price of a good therefore does not refer to its nature, but to the extent to which it satisfies the needs of man. But if utility is in this sense subjective, the value will be also. And so, the price will shift and vary according to needs. In the wake of Aristotle, Saint Albert and Saint Thomas took up the idea that value should be considered from the point of view of human need. As Thomas says in his *Commentary on the Sentences*, one cannot compare such diverse things according to their truth, but according to

---

13 Joel Kaye, *Economy and Nature in the Fourteenth Century: Money, Market Exchange, and the Emergence of Scientific Thought* (Cambridge: Cambridge University Press, 1998/2000), pp. 46 sqq.

14 Consequently, as St Augustine already noted, the resulting value may be different from that derived from the hierarchy of beings; it is economic, and not metaphysical: a man will value carrots and peas more than rats and fleas, though the latter are animals, in themselves more elaborate than vegetables.

human need: "*per comparationem ad indigentiam hominum.*"[15] The hierarchy of essences has no place here. Saint Albert notes additionally that the quality thus measured by money is defined *in common*, in the context of the community. This implies an important correction in relation to Aristotle: *it is not the individual need that counts first, but the joint confrontation of estimates and needs.* And our two authors take up the idea of Aristotle that the exchange thus conceived, according to proportional rules, is what links human society. To this was added the legacy of Roman law,[16] which poses the principle of freedom of negotiation, but with one exception: the possibility of rectification of the price by a judge, if, compared to a reference price, it deviates by more than a factor of two in either direction, not more than double, not less than half. It was developed by medieval people around the concept of *laesio enormis* (huge damage). But what is the reference price for this calculation? Justinian's Digest spoke of *common determination*, a price discovered on what must be called a market and evaluated in realistic terms: "*res tantum valet quantum vendi potest*" (a thing is worth the price at which one can sell it). Medieval jurists took up this principle but adding *in common*.

But according to Kaye this poses a theological problem, for then what has to be considered as right is not determined in the framework of a conscious ethical decision. Now, he says, in the conception of that time, all order is the product of the conscious decision of an intelligence. The relativism of prices also contrasts with the static image of the world of the early medieval, hence a resistance to what was seen as a possible relativity of values. But it is true that here Saint Thomas is not considering ultimate philosophical principles: he examines social facts, as we have seen. What has complicated things here, according to Kaye,[17] was the introduction by Saint Thomas of the idea of coercive justice, that of the judge, in order to restore equality. Hence emerged after him a tendency to seek absolute equality, in conformity with certain philosophical tendencies of the time. This is what we will find in the understanding of usury (see below). The question is not so much that of civil law: Saint Thomas admitted that it did not aim at an ideal; he even acknowledged that buyers and sellers try to deceive each other, one seeking to buy at the cheapest

15 Kaye, *Economy and Nature*, p. 70.
16 Ibid., pp. 91 sqq.
17 Ibid., p. 76.

price possible and the other to sell as high as possible. Such latitude is not possible at a moral level. And so, says Kaye, while Saint Thomas had no difficulty with common estimation and market price, he did not say with perfect clarity that in a moral sense the benchmark price is simply that of the market.

It seems to us, however, that it is not a lack of clarity that is at issue here; the question is really complex, with two levels to consider, which are coherent with Saint Thomas's general method. One is that of society and its actual functioning: what matters then is the process through which the price, or rather, a possible range of prices, is determined in common; it depends on the comparison of needs, and is governed by civil laws. The other is that of the personal moral attitude; as we have seen with our merchant who carries wheat from town to town, it implies taking into account the price charged in this place and at that moment. But this is not enough to ensure absolute equity. *At the moral level, there is necessarily a conscious act of seeking justice.* Ideally, we already need that to achieve the common local price, since this price stems from the attitude of each, facing off the other. This is *a fortiori* the case with individual transactions, if there is no clearly established and undeniable reference price, satisfying the requirements of justice. We can better measure the originality of this conception by comparing it with that which followed: as Francisco Gómez Camacho[18] notes, the mental revolution that followed scholasticism eliminated any conception of a hierarchy of values and goals, in favor of physical laws operating in an infinite and neutral space. In the scholastic conception, he says, agents are "price makers": they are responsible for the prices they make and therefore for the market. In the following era, however, the design of the market becomes depersonalized. The design of the price by pure interaction of supply and demand (understood as an automatic mechanism) eliminates all human responsibility. As one sees, one cannot say (as some people assert) that the scholastics eliminated the market; rather, they viewed it differently, because the priorities of the actors were not exactly the same.

There is therefore a dual difference. First, in the conception of what the market is: in one instance, it is understood as being composed of persons morally responsible for their actions, and in the other case, as a

---

18   About Luis de Molina, in Stephen J. Grabill, ed., *Sourcebook in Late-scholastic Monetary Theory: The Contributions of Martin de Azpilcueta, Luis de Molina, and Juan de Mariana* (Lanham, MD: Lexington Books, 2007), pp. 114 sqq.

pure mechanism; and second, in the relationship with this same market, in the case of individual transactions. The idea was that *the determination of price in common on a market, if properly done, offers an unavoidable basis, sufficient in law; it is difficult, however, to establish this as an absolute moral reference.* In the financial market, which is the subject of this book, this seems obvious, given the considerable fluctuation of prices and the fragility of their mode of formation (we will return to this with more detail). The possible discrepancy between Christian references to value *per se* and the relativity of price on the market are such that a later and major author in the person of Nicole Oresme,[19] a lucid and realistic analyst of money markets, expressed in his sermons considerations on the relativity of money and its role, and consequently thoughts on the moral risks it presents, according again to an established Christian tradition. Even if money makes it possible to determine prices through the confrontation on a market, this provides only a partial indication and does not relieve us of our moral responsibility.

Synthesis and consequences

In any case what counts as a reference price is the common estimation, which translates into what we would call a market price; it does not presuppose perfect competition, but at a minimum a reasonable one, and open to all. It was considered legitimate that in this process not only the opinions of competent people are taken into account, but the estimation of all, which takes into account their different appetites for things. It is therefore normal and natural for our authors that prices vary according to time and place. And note this important point: many scholastic authors considered it arbitrary and unjust that political power should change this state of affairs. For example, it is normal for the price to be high in case of shortage, and low in case of abundance. For them, the question of helping the poor is a question apart: we have to help the poor, of course, but not by eliminating the entitlements of sellers. So, if there is a shortage, the price is legitimately high, but solidarity should offset the effect on the poor. The responsibility of political power is also engaged in ensuring the truth of prices, which means that they are based on true transactions. Juan de Mariana[20] vigorously attacked the depreciation of money by princes as injustice. For, he says, the king has no right to tax his

19   Kaye, *Economy and Nature*, p. 149.
20   Grabill, ed., *Sourcebook in Late-scholastic Monetary Theory*, p. 243.

subjects without their consent; the private property[21] of citizens is not at the free disposal of the king. These principles were further developed by the kings of Castile themselves, including Alfonso XI in 1329. Mariana even extended the idea to the institution by the king of a monopoly "not accepted" by the people, which he saw as a form of taxation. This led him[22] to challenge the King's right to change the value of money without consulting the people.

Buying and selling must also be free, like any transaction, provided it is done fairly, because each person is responsible for what he owns. We can therefore always refuse a transaction, even at a fair price. A transaction is invalid where violence, including what we would call cornering the market and monopolization, fraud, or ignorance is present. There must indeed be reciprocity in the exchange, and this is an essential point. That said, again, the profit resulting from better knowledge of the market is legitimate; the knowledge of some, or the ignorance of others, does not change the right price. Joseph in the Bible, who stored during the fat years to resell in lean years, serves as an example. Similarly, whoever assumes that the price is going to rise has the right to buy at the current price, and they who think it will fall have the right to sell, if the price paid is "fair" and they do not manipulate the market.

This notion of fair price was all the more important since, as Laurence Fontaine noted,[23] in the pre-industrial economy bargaining was widespread, because there was constant uncertainty about everything and especially about the merchandise and its quality. Hence the importance of reputation, because researching information was time-consuming. Hence also the geographical clustering of merchants and markets, which facilitated comparisons, and therefore the formation of prices. Hence also the popularity of auctions: "the auction is the most habitual way of trading in the old regime because it allows the community to fix the price, taking into account all uncertainties, and to have it validated. Anything can go to auction." All this incidentally reminds us of the problems posed today by the financial markets, and in particular the question of how to organize the most open, fair and transparent order-matching system. We'll come back to that.

21 Ibid., p. 256.
22 Ibid., p. 260.
23 Laurence Fontaine, *L'économie morale: Pauvreté, crédit et confiance dans l'Europe préindustrielle* (Paris: Gallimard, 2008), pp. 255 sqq.

DEVELOPING THE CONCEPT OF FAIR PRICE

Subsequent development of the debate and refinements

Starting from there, the evolution of medieval thought led to its refinement, but with a non-negligible risk of deviation.[24] Kaye presents here symptomatically the positions of two authors.[25] Henry of Ghent insists on the idea that in every contract the parties must be their own judge, but they must consciously seek to find the delicate balance of equality. He therefore refuses the idea that any price at which a good can be sold is just, for such a price may have nothing to do with the current price or may result from an extreme need of the buyer. This does not prevent him from recognizing the importance of markets. But he insists on the search for the price at which one *should* buy or sell. Kaye confronts this with the analysis of Godfrey of Fontaines, who, on the basis of the same premises, insists on the notion of common estimation (in a market process), which for him is the right price. He even explains that this is a rational price, in accordance with what is expected of a rational creature in natural law, arising from the confrontation of needs. These two positions are not as opposed as it may appear, because their perspectives are different (practical and collective, as opposed to ideal and personal).

The reflection then went further.[26] We find in an inventive author like Peter John Olivi these same ideas of common estimation: according to him, in any commercial contract there is equalization of utility and need between buyers and sellers, within a certain range; he considers the general confrontation of these approaches a rational process. His thesis appeared in Duns Scotus and was emphasized in the presentation that the prominent author Saint Bernardine of Siena made a century later, even though he does not quote Olivi.[27] As regards the determinants of the price, Olivi, taken up by Saint Bernardine,[28] distinguishes three components that determine market

---

24 See in addition Kaye, op. cit.; Alejandro A. Chafuen, *Faith and Liberty: The Economic Thought of the Late Scholastics* (Lanham, MD: Lexington Books, 2003); Giacomo Todeschini, *Richesse franciscaine: De la pauvreté volontaire à la société de marché* (Lagrasse: Editions Verdier, 2008); and our *Christianisme et Croissance économique*, op. cit.

25 Kaye, *Economy and Nature*, pp. 106 sqq.

26 Ibid., pp. 118 sqq.

27 Olivi was, in theology, one of the representatives of the Franciscan "spirituals," who were condemned.

28 Saint Bernardine distinguished three factors: objective value in use

value: the intrinsic quality of the object, the needs or preferences of the people, and scarcity. The price thus becomes a result, qualified as "geometric" or "proportional," based on the aggregation of facts, estimates, desires, and needs. Our authors linked this process to the notion of common good. But what does not appear in this conception, which remains a norm, is the idea that *any* transaction is possible between a willing buyer and a seller: the price must aim at an external reference, an idea of justice, in principle within the community. *It was felt that by common determination, the possible distortions and injustices of bilateral exchanges were overcome.*

In the sixteenth century a well-known theologian like Luis de Molina noted as obvious that the abundance of applicants raises the price.[29] Between two monetary marketplaces,[30] he then finds it reprehensible to require the same nominal value for two amounts expressed in formally similar currencies, if the real value of these currencies on these markets is different. For, he says, "there is no better rule than to consider the current price on the exchange market, and in the exchanges that the merchants practice from one place to another, and to accept this price as fair and accepted by the common estimation of merchants."[31] He then makes a concrete and realistic description[32] of the profit realized by playing on the different values of the currencies, according to places and moments, in particular depending on their local scarcity and demand. He adds: "As the just natural price of things depends on the common estimate in one location, one cannot consider the price commonly accepted for exchanges between one place and another as unjust" provided it is not "manipulated by a monopoly or by fraud."[33] If we remain at the just local prices there is no injustice for, as he said, there was *no fraud against anybody.*

But some go further, announcing future developments. Gérard Odonis believed that free trade, even bilateral, is more reliable than the verdict of a judge, for as he said a just man is better than a good

---

(*virtuositas*); desirability, which is subjective preference (*complacibilitas*); and scarcity. The combination of the three is perhaps the most elaborate state of the medieval theory of value. Let us note that we do not speak here of value based on work, contrary to what is sometimes said.

29 Grabill, ed., *Sourcebook in Late-scholastic Monetary Theory*, p. 183.
30 Ibid., pp. 203 sqq.
31 Ibid., p. 205.
32 Ibid., p. 209.
33 Ibid., p. 227.

law: according to him, the equality that the existence of an agreement implies in itself prevails over the fact that each person seeks an
advantage over the other. In the same line, John Buridan considered
that an exchange is fair even if one of the parties gained an unequal
advantage, because the search for personal advantage is in the very
logic of the exchange. The evolution here is clear: in looking for
tools to obtain order and the equality of a common reference, even
if it is theoretical, we have passed from the common estimation to
the sovereignty of the single agreement, from conscious choice to
an instrumental mechanism. On another level, Henry of Ghent, like
Duns Scotus, insisted on the merchant's right to compensation for
his contribution of competence, diligence, risk-taking, and transport. Olivi also developed the idea of widespread rarity of certain
personal talents, or rarity of talents developed by training people.
Buridan has developed this issue of measuring services, noting that it
depended on people and situations. In the end then, to get the right
price, they would cross two lines of preferences, instead of trying to
level the playing field around a reference. The result would then vary
according to the transactions. The need is not in things, but in the
relation of men to things, and this is measured proportionally. *The
novelty, potentially a threat to the balance of the concept, is the idea
that the simple fact of entering into a process of exchange can suffice as
a guarantee of justice*: there we moved away from Saint Thomas, even
more so when one came to envisage a complete individualization of
transactions. This could have been understood before in the case of
specific transactions, something Saint Thomas admitted already. But
not as a common reference.

The negotiated price and the question of coercion

What remains to be mentioned is the way in which transactions are
carried out, and in particular the risk that violence will determine the
outcome, including a specific form of violence, which is the intensity
of need. A fine analysis of the question is made by Odd Langholm.[34]
As we have seen, beginning with the idea of Roman law, for which the
price of a thing is what someone is willing to pay for it, and without
denying this framework, the original schoolmen placed this within a
normative perspective, aiming at the price that *should* be paid (a fair

---

34   Odd Langholm, *The Legacy of Scholasticism in Economic Thought* (Cambridge: Cambridge University Press, 1998/2006), pp. 78 sqq.

and reasonable price). But this leaves open the question of the transaction process, in which free will and the absence of fraud are required. Freedom was presumed to be impaired if the need was too great, especially in the case of basic necessities. But conversely, if all constraint is excluded, how can we integrate the role of need (*indigentia*)? The main solution used here was once again to promote the collective nature of the need and its public expression, and thus the open public market, provided it functions normally.[35] The idea is to prevent the risk of individual abuse; we see it in cases that are condemned in the textbooks of the time, which generally refer to manipulation of the market. Thus, creating scarcity by cornering the market is condemned as manipulation; likewise, the collusion between merchants and any monopoly.[36] Except in late scholasticism, this implies not simply accepting a price resulting from this or that individual transaction.

The issue is less straightforward[37] if there is not a sufficient market. In this case, negotiation takes place, and the two parties determine the price in common. The idea is present that every transaction involves a form of cooperation on the basis of mutual need: for this reason, Duns Scotus sees an element of gift in any exchange, since one concedes one advantage to the other without balking at the existence of irreconcilable conceptions, the buyer and seller putting justice at a different level. But the question of free will then becomes central, which gives rise to important debates; it is judged that free will can diminish if need is too great, and *necessity can then become a real constraint, altering the validity of the transaction or in any case the price.* The aim was to combat the selfish use of relative strength in bargaining power.[38] Conversely, the disappearance of this idea subsequently meant an increasing depersonalization of the market. In the later phase of scholasticism, the importance of the modalities of the transaction was emphasized (for example, considering who initiated

35 Naturally if it is a question of luxury goods, the constraint is supposed to be much lower, and one acknowledges greater freedom of transaction.

36 It was then forbidden to sell at a higher price to someone who was travelling and just passing by: he had a right to the local market price.

37 Langholm, *The Legacy of Scholasticism*, pp. 108 sqq.

38 Ibid., pp. 125 sqq. In the case of labor (wages), the reference to the market was similarly accepted. Although the exploitation of the need existed, it was also considered that the problem disappeared in an open market, even if this results in very low wages. The role of scarcity was admitted — for example, the higher pay to an architect compared with that to a mason, despite less physical effort.

the sale) and in so doing it was assumed that prices could be different without deducing that the will of the parties has been altered.
From there, the idea of the eighteenth century, that the economy is a
purely natural order, without moral responsibility for people, gradually began to appear, evolving into the modern,[39] purely contractual
conception. It was accompanied by the justification of the pursuit of
selfish interest. Langholm asserts that in every economic act there is
an element of moral responsibility,[40] which modern doctrine denies.[41]

MEANING AND SCOPE OF THE MEDIEVAL CONCEPTION
OF FAIR PRICE

Misunderstandings

This conception is not always well perceived by a whole school,
whether Christian or not. Following Raymond De Roover and many
others, Kaye[42] strongly criticizes those historians who imagine a medieval world with static references, cultivating an ideal of just price
based on the sole value of work and the objective needs of the community. As we have seen, this idea is coherent neither with the texts
nor with facts. But it remains widespread. According to Jacques Le
Goff, for example, the correct price being the one used locally, it is
stable and in conformity with the common good, and then it is "the
exact contrary of what is usually understood by the notion of competition and free play of supply and demand,"[43] adding that among
the great theologians the "notion of fair price that refers to justice is
founded like it on *caritas*." But this sentence opposes two unrelated
terms: certainly, the "just price" tautologically refers to justice, which

---

39   This is found in Hobbes (cf. pp. 147ff.), which eliminates any role for
justice —then there remains no other recourse than charity, but it's outside
the economy.
40   Ibid., pp. 189 sqq. Langholm cites examples given by Nozick, where one
is blocked by the fear of being electrocuted, in one case by a big storm, in the
other because someone threatens that person with an electrical appliance. The
practical effect is the same and the difference may be small for the victim. But
not on the moral level, especially with regard to the one who threatens.
41   But not necessarily practice; as Langholm says, it is possible to argue that
our system works only because this sense of responsibility subsists in the reality
of behavior, despite the theory.
42   Kaye, *Economy and Nature*, p. 88.
43   As Alain Guerreau says, whom Le Goff quotes. See Jacques Le Goff, *Le
Moyen Age et l'argent* (Paris: Perrin, 2010), pp. 226 sqq.

itself supposes a certain spirit of charity to be implemented in its plenitude, despite the two notions being distinct. However, this gives no concrete idea of what prices are. As we have seen, the theory of the determinants of price in the medieval world is a complex question;[44] various considerations were mentioned by authors, such as the objective utility of goods, the needs of consumers, the risks taken by the merchant, or his added value, or scarcity — but rarely the cost of labor. In all cases, both in theory and in practice, they agreed that these factors are combined by a simple method: the confrontation of buyers and sellers, and thus a market (not to be confused with an uncontrolled freedom of supply and demand). The simple fact that, for example, considering the case of high prices in the event of food shortages, Saint Thomas finds it legal for a merchant, who arrives from a low-cost area, to sell at the high price he finds, shows that he takes into account (aggregate) supply and demand in determining the local fair price. All texts find it obvious for a price to rise as scarcity increases, or demand. Of course, then, there was no explicit analysis in the form of a law as such — neither was there economic science as such. But *this does not mean that there was no awareness of these mechanisms that today we call economics.*

Even more characteristically, according to Geneviève Gavignaud-Fontaine,[45] for Saint Thomas the fair price would only result from collective estimates, through corporations, associations, et cetera, and the opinion of experts. And so, she says, "unlike the market price which results from a balance of forces, the fair price is the exercise of an authority." We see nothing of this kind in our authors: Who is that authority? Moreover, apart from the fact that it is questionable to say in general terms that a market price is the result of a balance of forces, a price fixed by someone with political power is an administered price. Nothing guarantees that it will result in something better and more just. Quite the contrary, especially if there is no market, because these authorities then no longer have a reference to use in fixing these prices.[46] What was sometimes observed at the time is, at best, in the

---

44 See also Murray N. Rothbard, *An Austrian Perspective on the History of Economic Thought,* vol. 1, *Economic Thought Before Adam Smith.* Quoted on http://www.lewrockwell.com/rothbard/rothbard212.html.

45 Geneviève Gavignaud-Fontaine, *Considérations économiques chrétiennes de saint Paul aux temps actuels* (Paris: Boutique de l'Histoire, 2009), p. 57.

46 This is the case of totally administered Soviet-type economies. Their limits

context of a market, the setting of minimum or maximum levels, but with the then-recognized risk of creating shortages or encouraging the black market. The Christian Middle Ages did not operate on the basis of systematically administered prices, even if the authorities tried from time to time to set ceilings or price scales here and there, with unconvincing results and without relying on a doctrine.[47] Nevertheless, she adds: "Thomistic doctrine holds, in short, that price does not result from the relation between supply and demand, but from the relationship of justice that is established between the value of things."[48] However, the two terms are not opposed: to speak of value[49] you must have a measure and therefore prices. In fact, it was recognized that price formation depended on the market under consideration (those who have the goods and those who want to buy them, with what volumes, what appetite, etc.) and its dynamics, at a given place and moment. These factors lead to establishing a price, ideally a fair price if it is the fruit of an honest and proper interaction of the whole community on which the authorities might, rightly or wrongly, wish to intervene. In scholastic doctrine there are no prices falling from heaven, originating with some *ex nihilo* estimate that is alien to any market.

Moreover, if one goes to the bottom of things, this results from practical reasons that are unavoidable in decentralized economies, based on property, as was already the case at that time. No one was obliged to make a transaction: if one buys or sells, it means one finds

and irrationality are well known, in particular because of the arbitrariness of prices. This has nothing to do with the economic model of the scholastics.

47   Prices were basically set freely, especially for agricultural prices: one intervened mainly against price manipulations. It is a little different in the case of manufactured products, in fact mostly handicrafts, where prices were easier to fix because this amounted to fixing the compensation of the craftsmen. See for example Kaye, *Economy and Nature*, pp. 26 and 89.

48   In particular, she says, in order to protect the dignity of work: the price would express "an equivalence between the utility of the product and the cost of labor," apparently determined by custom or authority. This leads the same author to analyze subsequent evolution as the fact that "the value of use so near the heart of the Thomists" was challenged by free trade proponents to "profit from exchange value." All this is very far removed from the real economy and real price regimes of those times, as well as from the texts. Gavignaud-Fontaine, *Considérations économiques chrétiennes*, p. 76. Markets have existed everywhere since the Middle Ages and served as a basis for prices; no one thought this was abnormal.

49   And of course, there was no intrinsic or "metaphysical" value of things: this idea was lucidly dismissed from the field of price determination by all authors.

it convenient to buy (demand) or sell (offer) a given quantity of a given product at a given price; *this price must therefore be compatible with supply and demand, understood in a general way*, except to frustrate or steal from one or the other, which is not in conformity with justice. But of course, *there are multiple ways of confronting offers and demands, in terms of the functioning of the market, the terms of the transaction, and personal or collective values*. In particular, it is not sufficient to reflect any convenience, or balance of power, but we have to seek, collectively, what is right. What leads to the determination of a price is then a local confrontation, ideally carried out by responsible and well-intentioned people. But it is a market price, and it is responsive to supply and demand since transactions are made freely.

From a moral point of view, it must be admitted that just as no one has an interest in selling at a lower price than what is available, no one has the right to sell at a higher price than what can be found elsewhere. In other words, it is unfair to sell at a price higher than a price someone may find — with the proviso that reasoning is based on a given time and place. So, it not just to sell outside of the market, except in special cases. In other words, the best way to ensure collective justice according to Saint Thomas and the scholastics is a general matching of prices, in a given place and at a given moment, provided that it is in good faith, without manipulation. More generally, this can be deduced from the social nature of the human being: it is in fact as a community that we must determine what is most just among the various possibilities. Overall price matching on a given "market," one that is defined in time and space, is the best procedure in this respect, provided that this is done in a clear, transparent and open way, and that participants have the right orientation in favor of a just process. Are not real markets often far from this pattern? Of course, but it does not reduce the value of the principle. In any case, at a personal level this does not exonerate anybody of the moral responsibility of seeking the right price, especially if the market does not work well.

The discovery of the economy: trade and the market

In addition to this central question of prices, scholastic economic ideas were amplified and explained later in other areas,[50] at least until the sixteenth century. First there is the issue of money. As noted by

---

50 See our *Christianisme et Croissance économique*, op. cit.; Chafuen, *Faith and Liberty*, op. cit.; Todeschini, *Richesse franciscaine*, op. cit.

Giacomo Todeschini,[51] the importance of money as a representation of things that are important to everyday life and to the life of the city was recognized very early in the Middle Ages. *They were fully aware of the many pecuniary and financial comparisons contained in the Gospels*, including the use in the religious vocabulary of notions such as redemption. But they applied it to a new situation, originating with the impressive economic expansion of the twelfth and thirteenth centuries. Giving a fair value to all traded goods became a major collective issue in a much more active economy.[52] The merchants were then perceived as trade professionals. The idea of their collective function developed gradually, and their profit was considered justified if it worked to the advantage of the Christian community. It was even said that, like religious men, merchants abandon what they have in order to profit more; those two callings were directly compared with each other in the literature of the time. The image of the good merchant, who is successful but knows how to renounce wealth, was also present, exemplified in the remarkable example of Saint Homobonus of Cremona[53] in the twelfth century, besides the innumerable anathemas of preachers against the lure of lucre.

In the wake of Saint Thomas, the Christian thinkers of the time, the scholastics, had a pioneering role in the analysis of the main economic facts, beyond the question of prices.[54] Their modernity is noteworthy, except for the issue of interest rates. Let us pass on the defense of private property: as these thinkers tell us, in view of our present condition, affected by sin, which results in a scarcity of goods and makes it impossible to expect spontaneously altruistic behavior

---

51   Todeschini, *Richesse franciscaine*, pp. 14 sqq.

52   Hence, of course, also the importance of money: see here Jacques Le Goff (*Le Moyen Age et l'argent*, p. 94), which recalls St. Louis's efforts: "to endow the kingdom with a strong currency is essentially due to his desire to have justice also in trade." He notes that while Nicole Oresme in *De Moneta* emphasizes how useful a stable currency is in as much as it is shared by all, there was a general tendency toward the weakening of currencies during the Middle Ages, although this varied from place to place. He notes the frequency of popular revolts against monetary changes, which was rightly considered a fundamental source of injustice.

53   Homobonus Tucenghi, the first non-noble laymen canonized as a non-martyr, two years after his death, by Pope Innocent III, on pressing popular demand: a skillful trader, who was efficient and very generous toward the poor.

54   Again, from a moral and political angle, without individualization of the economic fact.

from all, private property allows us an effective and realistic relationship to material goods, and better relationships among human beings. The scholastics exhibited a remarkable sense of the usefulness of trade, including on an international level through imports and exports. They were aware not only of the utility of distribution, transport, storage, and the value of offering goods that would otherwise be unavailable, but also of the advantage of transferring those goods from where they are abundant to where they are scarce, and to make a living in this way. Our authors made the remark that when a merchant suffers losses because he has miscalculated his business, everyone considers this normal: So why should it not be normal when he makes a profit? They insisted even on the unifying effect of international trade for the world. Profits are considered justified if they are based on purchases and sales at fair prices, completed at risk. On the other hand, they did condemn those who considered profit as their ultimate goal.

All this clearly foreshadows the development of modern economics, except on two points. First, the underlying value system, of course, a difference that persists today. Secondly, the condemnation of interest rates, which was at the time unanimous — at least in principle. This last point represents the greatest divergence between former and current practices. We will examine this issue in more detail below. Let us now evoke the central importance of money in that society and its role.

CHAPTER 3

Money in Medieval Christian Society

THE SCHOLASTICS AND MONEY
Money and the merchant as perceived at that time

In ancient Christian thought, money[1] was fundamentally ambiguous. It could help you improve the management of a property through a rational and quantified method, but it could also threaten your moral integrity if it made you seek immediate opportunities of gain. It multiplied the opportunities of production and of donation, but also of personal appropriation. One point that focused Christian reflection was money's socially and morally undifferentiated nature, hence its capacity to give a benchmark, which was risky because it escaped religious or moral standards, at the same time offering wide possibilities. Hence a complex mindset developed, which was far from the blunt condemnation often understood by historians on the basis of a selective reading of the texts. *It was not money itself that was rejected* but its "improper" use, which covered two things: hoarding (accumulating without use for society), and seizing ecclesiastical goods (that is to say, goods intended for a collective solidarity use).

In the twelfth and thirteenth centuries, the growing role of money and the concomitant growth of the economy, in which ecclesiastical entities participated to a very wide extent, led to a refinement of these analyses. The techniques for the development or mobilization of ecclesiastical or lay wealth were approved if there was no sterile accumulation. The canonical texts intervened even to *protect merchants* against lordly or royal acts, for they were recognized as beneficial. Naturally they knew that merchants were subject to personal temptations, but they were considered fundamentally useful if they could act for the good of the community, of which they were an essential constituent element. If on the other hand they should speculate, monopolize, or manipulate prices, they fell into a form of "usury." *It is*, as Peter Lombard said, *the moral conduct of the merchant that mattered, and especially the danger of aiming at accumulation alone.* Even the pursuit of gain, although ambiguous, is not purely negative, for it can serve the community.

---

[1]   As noted by Todeschini and others. See Greci, Pinto, and Todeschini, *Economie urbane*, pp. 173 sqq.

The most interesting development of this thinking[2] took place from the end of the thirteenth to the beginning of the fifteenth century, in a Franciscan and Dominican context. It is instructive to note the nuances between those schools. The Dominican Saint Thomas, for example, simply said that profit is neutral but can be transformed into something good. Even such an austere Franciscan as Olivi emphasized the beneficial role of the entrepreneurial initiative of the merchant. One of Olivi's contributions[3] was his understanding of the notion of capital and the possible alternative uses of money. The Franciscan school also insisted on the professional skill of the merchant, which determined both his profit and the equilibrium of prices; it insisted on the multiple interplay of merchant initiatives, with their subjective dimension and the role of personal expertise. The role of scarcity, of subjective valuation, and of use value was also stressed, as well as each person's responsibility in the judgment of what is useful and necessary. They therefore insisted on the role of economic agents. On the other hand, the Dominican school legitimized gain by its social utility. For this school, value was rather something given and external, objectively observable and politically controllable.

Be that as it may, in both cases the merchant's proper use of his wealth was recognized to be in the public interest. Money, which can be a passion for the profane, is or ought to be only a tool for the merchant. And in particular they were to be responsible for the process of price discovery. This reflection culminated in the work of Saint Bernardine of Siena; *it urged the construction of a community of faithful constantly attentive to the control of their desires and to the verification of the social utility of their actions.* Hence his conception of the formation of prices, comprising, as we have seen, three references: rarity, utility, and subjective appreciation. He acknowledged the central role of finance in fructification — which he understood in a broad sense, by constant reinvestment and permanent circulation of wealth. He recommended the wide use of public auction procedures, and even the creation of public credit institutes. But he also saw the usurer as an idle and unproductive accumulator. He equally condemned expenditures on ostentatious and useless goods.

---

2   Greci, Pinto, and Todeschini, *Economie urbane*, pp. 203 sqq.
3   Kaye, *Economy and Nature*, pp. 118 sqq.

FRANCISCANISM, POVERTY, AND DEVELOPMENT
OF THE MARKET

In this elaboration, the role of Franciscanism was considerable both theoretically and practically, without being exclusive;[4] it gave a central role to poverty, which gives more meaning to its contribution in the Christian context. We have seen how society in the Middle Ages accepted the value of trade and exchanges, and therefore the role of the merchant. But this was linked[5] to a reflection on poverty. This further led to a reflection on the notion of *want*, which justifies the activity of merchants, because they enable the community to overcome it. On the other hand, the question of *voluntary poverty* is even more important. For Giacomo Todeschini, the apparent paradox is that "it was the most rigorous religiosity that, as such, elaborated a large part of the vocabulary of Western economy."[6] For "Franciscanism progressively discovered the decisive elements of an understanding of the exchange value in deprivation and renunciation." The direct influence of this thinking remained noticeable until the eighteenth century.

The starting point: the strategic role of poverty

Even before Franciscanism (twelfth–thirteenth centuries), people became more sensitive to the poverty of Christ, who is the model for a Christian. It was also noted that it gave an ability to transform things by possessing nothing. *To detach oneself from material goods gives the capacity to manage them best in a collective interest.* At the same time, the notion of common good was developed. Following the Church Fathers, there was increasing friction between the nobility, who too often managed their property from a purely private standpoint, and the voluntarily impoverished managers of Church resources guided by the circulation of wealth in the collective interest and thus in the interest of the poor. They therefore condemned assets that were immobilized for purposes of inheritance. The demarcation between private wealth or its conspicuous use, and public use, was carefully regulated. Saint Bernard criticized what he perceived as a

---

4   The monasteries aside, we must notably mention the role of the other mendicant orders (Dominicans, Carmelites, Servites, etc.), the first especially for drawing up the doctrine, including in economic matters.

5   Todeschini, *Richesse franciscaine*, pp. 20 sqq.

6   Ibid., p. 10.

form of misuse in the splendor of the Cluny monastery; *he argued simultaneously for personal renunciation* and *for collective expansion.* At the same time, a growing distinction was made between passive poverty and voluntary poverty, and the contrast between the opulence of the Cistercian monastery, which was productive because of its renunciation of property, and the sterile passivity of the actual poor was emphasized: *passive poverty* then became the illustration[7] of an inability to see beyond immediate deprivation, whereas through *consented poverty* one can *create* in abandonment to God.[8]

As a continuation of these ideas, Franciscanism seemed to play an essential role in the development of the understanding of economics within the Christian society, especially in Italy, which was then at the heart of economic innovation. The point of departure is not, however, self-evident; it means rediscovering the evangelical paradox. In the teaching of Saint Francis of Assisi,[9] the simultaneous importance of activism, of caring for the poor, and of refusing money is well-known: the primitive Franciscan rule forbade the brothers from contact with money. They considered money incapable of responding to the true needs and necessities of life, nor could it measure the grace received, including in the form of alms; the brothers sought concretely hospitality and work, *before* any alms in cash. But the texts emphasize at the same time the miracles by which all this was transformed into material abundance. Poverty was in this perspective "both a productive renunciation and a total freedom with regard to the restraints of immobilized wealth." The main novelty here is that Saint Francis denied that "money in its monetary form can constitute a credible representation of the reality of the natural and social world," especially in the case of outcasts and dropouts. Behind the univocity of money, he rediscovered multiple meanings and potentials: we must certainly take care of the body and its needs, but away from money. The measure was that of the goods necessary to the subsistence of the brothers, and of the work to be accomplished. This led to a growing distinction between ownership and possession or use. *This refusal to equate money with wealth, but rather equating money with the satisfaction of needs, is a founding principle*

7 Todeschini, *Richesse franciscaine*, pp. 56 sqq.
8 See also here Michel Mollat, *Les Pauvres au Moyen Age*, Editions Complexe, 1978–2006.
9 Todeschini, *Richesse franciscaine*, pp. 81 sqq.

of Franciscanism; it implies a new conceptualization. This is what provided the means of considering the relation between increasing wealth and evangelical precepts. The central intuition is that *to handle material things, detaching yourself is essential, especially from money.* Opting for poverty means reconsidering the whole social and political role of material goods; *this choice of poverty makes it possible to manage reality without appropriating it or getting caught up in it.* It is then more than an ascetic sign: it becomes an administrative criterion, testifying to the perfection of the community. For there to exist a degree of civic solidarity the only solution is to separate use and ownership. In later texts,[10] through their detachment, the brothers appeared in real terms as experts in the use of wealth, and therefore in what is good for society.

Of course, practice was not so simple. As the historians' analysis of these practices confirms,[11] mendicants did indeed start from an ideal of total poverty and precariousness. This ideal had to evolve afterward, especially because of its success, which is always the most difficult threat to manage. However, in spite of some gentrification and of certain ambiguities, these orders kept a strong distinctive specificity. The brothers managed to remain in an urban environment without an income base or a large estate, essentially living on a flow of services like Masses, et cetera, that in its own way inserted them in the trade flow of the city. Hence also their symbiosis with the commercial milieu, and a dependence on municipal power, which was then dominated by merchants.

Franciscanism and the laity

Let us now turn to the relationships of merchants with the brothers. Let us first recall that the reflection on the secular economy pursued by the Franciscans was not the result of spontaneous thinking within this commercial milieu. On the contrary, it was based first on the imperatives of a religious order, particularly as a question of practical morality: How to manage wealth appropriately? The Franciscans met the world of wealth in order to reinterpret it; they discussed the meaning of goods and of what is desirable. They admitted clearly the

---

10   Todeschini, *Richesse franciscaine*, pp. 113 sqq.
11   For example in Nicole Bériou and Jacques Chiffoleau, eds., *Economie et religion: l'expérience des ordres mendiants (XIIIe–XVe siècle)* (Lyon: Presses Universitaires de Lyon, 2009).

principle that, on the laity side, ownership could include a valid use of economic goods: as Saint Bonaventure said, sumptuous garments may be justified as a sign of legitimate power. Their vision of the secular world was as an interplay of intentional actions: to be good, wealth and poverty must be voluntary, intentional, and appreciated according to their actual use, which, according to the tradition, makes every form of hoarding sinful.

It is in this respect that they raised the question of practical morality we raised in the preceding chapter: How to determine the price of objects according to rules that make it morally acceptable, especially according to their utility, which varies over time and involves some forecasting? After having reflected on the relationship between subjective need and price, a man like Olivi[12] also came to distinguish the use of money from ownership: money as a measure of everything only circulates, it has no direct utility in itself.[13] It is purely functional, as a sign of the value of useful goods. Poverty, want, and deprivation are not only a vacuum to be filled, but a tool that facilitates the calculation of values. *Seeking to own money as such has no meaning, but money is legitimate to use if one has in view the (social) use of things themselves,* and voluntary poverty makes it possible to discern that better (Olivi insists on the value of some examples for the faithful, and in particular Christ's model of poverty). In contrast, luxury is an insult to others if it does not correspond to a legitimate social role (hence the sumptuary laws of the era). Such reflection makes it possible to integrate the laity into the Franciscan model: *money makes it possible to set up a measurement of need, necessity, and even superfluity; it is handled in a sphere that is managed by professionals and experts: the merchants, who must detach themselves from its fascination. Money will have meaning if these professionals know how to circulate it for the good of the community, without immobilizing it.* Hence the central importance of the transaction and of the market, which is a social melting pot if it works properly.

Market, trade, and commerce are therefore considered social realities that also contribute to the building of a Christian society. It is the collective interaction of the market as an expression of the

---

12 Peter John Olivi. A remarkable example of an unbending ascetic Franciscan who happened to be one of the best interpreters of economic activity.

13 Except when sociability is lacking (for example with a stranger) because then there is no community.

community that determines values by agreement within it. It depends on the generally recognized utility of things, on their relative abundance, and on their subjective appreciation. Altering the currency is therefore a serious sin on the part of the authorities. *The ascetic traits*[14] *that are expected of the merchant or attributed to him, and in particular the risks he takes, entitle him to account for prices and their formation to others; he is a master of practical economics.* Good reputation is an essential dimension, hence the possibility of trust. Their profit rewards the merchants' contribution as artisans of evaluation and introduces an educational function. Calculation, education, and analysis are essential to achieve this correct measurement. Merchants thus motivated are ultimately at the heart of the civic community (at least that of these Italian cities) and thanks to them one can measure its economic and even religious cohesion and efficiency; through the market they are the mediators of collective life. There is no opposition to the Franciscan friars; on the contrary, people were more willing to give public (and therefore financial) offices to merchants who were members of the secular Franciscan Third Order, for they were more detached than others. Many merchants became Franciscan brothers. The ethical nature of economic exchanges implies constant control by partners, since it involves entrusting the regulation of society to its most reliable members. Hence an ethic of the good merchant, including a religious one: deviating from the price established on a functioning market is a grave sin; conversely, the exercise of a skilled trade brings merit. The analysis of intentions is essential here, as well as the context of the fabric of the city, and religious practices. *There is then a close link between private or public ethics and public happiness, a judicious use of money, and detachment from it.*[15]

---

14 Todeschini, *Richesse franciscaine*, pp. 162 sqq.

15 Giacomo Todeschini emphasizes an undesirable consequence of this conception of a market, entrusted to a minority of competent and virtuous merchants: it is the exclusion of others. Jews, for example, were perceived as external to the common good, although they could be useful. That emphasized the distinction between what is inside and what is outside, between what promotes the growth of the market and what is supposed to block it. What was considered negative is to aim for wealth, independently of the economic and religious equilibriums of the city, and therefore without being integrated into it. Hoarders or luxury enthusiasts are put on the same level as Jews. Hence a serious problem in relation to the initial Franciscan ethics, because this creates exclusion. (*Richesse franciscaine*, pp. 213 sqq.)

A WORLD RADICALLY DIFFERENT FROM OURS?

Challenges: Jacques Le Goff and Bartolomé Clavero

Jacques Le Goff[16] disputes Todeschini's analysis of the relationship between mendicant orders and money. He thinks the recourse to Peter John Olivi is too dominant; he considers Olivi's influence to be limited. Citing Jacques Chiffoleau, he recognizes the relative fidelity of the mendicants to their initial principle: voluntary poverty. But at the heart of this economy of salvation there is, he says, "grace, *caritas*, and gift." He therefore criticizes the idea of economic thought among the Franciscans, for they never perceived the economy as such, nor money as an economic reality. The Franciscan preachers criticized money and focused on charity and love of God. We must then recognize the central place of *caritas* in the Middle Ages (theological charity, divine love); it was a supreme value, both spiritual and social. Its centrality implies the centrality of almsgiving and donation: studies show that the increase in donations followed that of wealth and exceeded that of tax levies. Hence the formidable impulses of charity at the time.[17] Le Goff feels that it is therefore anachronistic to view money at that time as it is seen today. He sees in those writings that hail the modernity of the Middle Ages an error he regularly denounces: not understanding that the people of those eras held views very different from ours.

These positions owe much to Bartolomé Clavero,[18] who made a remarkable analysis of the value system of the Middle Ages. For him the Catholic conception can be summed up in two great principles: a particular principle, that of *justice*, and a more fundamental one, that of *charity*. The first, essentially relating to commutative justice, applies to exchanges and implies equality or, where appropriate, proportionality between the elements exchanged. This may involve a just retribution whenever a real service is provided, but it depends on what this service is "worth," no more and no less. Such an exchange may be the subject of contracts and have legal force. The second is more fundamental and governs society more centrally — or should do so.

---

16 Le Goff, *Le Moyen Age et l'argent*, pp. 200 sqq.

17 Ibid., p. 123. As he recalls, "the great development of the foundations and hospitals was massive and impressive in the thirteenth century. This can be measured by the size and importance of the hospitals built at that time. And the cost of cathedrals could also be highlighted" (p. 46).

18 Bartolomé Clavero, *La grâce du don* (Paris: Albin Michel, 1996). Le Goff wrote the foreword of this book.

When applied to trade between people or between communities, it implies an *a priori* of beneficence: I give to others considering our relationship, within the framework of a society founded on mutual benevolence. These others must then, out of pure gratitude, reciprocate, but it is for them a purely moral duty; it cannot be translated into legal terms and must not contaminate the initial gesture, which must be made without calculating the return (what Clavero calls "*antidora*," a scientific term meaning "counter-gift"). Clavero emphasizes that this second conception is more fundamental than the first.[19] But both exist together. That is to say, morality, or rather the religious faith on which it is founded, is more important than law, and *homo economicus*, the calculating and self-centered individual, has no meaning in this context.

On the basis of these clear and globally fair analyses, at least at the level of collective representations, our authors then proceed to more questionable extrapolations. Clavero, for example, asserts both that at that time the notion of person did not really make sense and that one cannot then speak of "economy," except in the sense of domestic economy (that is, the family), nor of capitalism.[20] The first point falls beyond our scope, but Clavero[21] forgets that the very notion of person is essentially Christian; what did not exist at the time was the individual of the liberal era, considered separately from his attachments and commitments; but they are two different things. On the second point, he again aligns himself with Jacques

---

19   Here we find the theme of gift, developed by Jacques Godbout or the MAUSS (*Mouvement anti-utilitariste dans les sciences sociales*): this point is important. See, in particular, Jacques T. Godbout and Alain Caillé, *L'esprit du don* (Paris: La Découverte/Poche, 2000).

20   He even proclaims aloud the absurdity, contradicted by obvious facts, that Catholicism was as such closed to innovation, not giving enough place to the individual; see Clavero, *La grâce du don*, p. 21. We have shown, on the contrary, in *Christianisme et Croissance économique*, and elsewhere, to what extent the Catholic Middle Ages was a period of intense innovation.

21   Notably, p. 143. Even though it emphasizes the decisive importance of intention in the conceptions of the time and the deep freedom conferred by a vision which essentially recommended totally free gift (here we find the old meaning of the word "liberal" — that is, generous). But all this is inconceivable without the notion of person! And can one seriously maintain that in Catholic doctrine the person did not exist outside the family, even though the Church struggled against the then-dominant vision of a family to defend the concept of marriage based solely on the consent of the two spouses?

Le Goff,[22] who, with Marx and Weber, considers that one cannot speak of "capitalism" before the sixteenth, or even the eighteenth century.[23] The remarkable technique of double-entry accounting was certainly developed at that time (the end of the fifteenth century), but its use was limited. Moreover, according to Le Goff, it was difficult to distinguish bankers in the strict sense of the word. Most money handlers were still merchants, and banking was only just developing. For him the growth of the market at the end of the Middle Ages is more a reorganization of feudalism than the emergence of capitalism. Buying and selling were determined by social logic, hence the absence of a real market for land; we have seen what he thinks of the formation of prices. With Polanyi, he believes that the economy was "embedded in the labyrinth of social relations" and that "before the industrial revolution, like the rest of the world, Europe ignored the domination of the economy over the social; economic phenomena were themselves inseparable from their social context."

It is not my task here to decide from a historical point of view which of these eminent specialists is right, especially about when one can speak technically of "capitalism." But it seems clear to me that these remarks are partly based on a confusion of economics and economic mechanisms, and awareness of them, and moreover, between these two, and the modern conception of economics[24] and its practice. In my view, it is true that full-fledged modern capitalism is only clearly present with the industrial revolution of the eighteenth century. But one cannot deny that there has been a continuous development since the thirteenth century, which was not present in other civilizations in, for example, banking and accounting techniques — of course, despite the fact that they were relatively limited in their influence on society. It should also be remembered that these developments were considerably more visible and socially important in the Italy of the period, which was the center of innovation and development — with real

---

22 Le Goff, *Le Moyen Age et l'argent*, pp. 156 sqq.

23 He believed that what was lacking in the Middle Ages was a regular influx of precious metals, the unification of the market, and the stock exchange: these three only appeared in the sixteenth century. And so, he says, we cannot speak of capitalism: the real mutation took place in the eighteenth century.

24 Dominated by what I call the founding paradigm of political modernity, a paradigm of supposed neutrality as regards essential truths. See on this point my *l'Avenir de la démocratie* (Paris: Francois-Xavier de Guibert, 2011).

bankers like the Medici and many others — than in feudal France or Spain, so near to our authors' hearts. Besides, there is no doubt that at the time there was no political economy consciously considered as a field of autonomous knowledge, as it was viewed by Adam Smith and his successors. Neither is there any doubt that they did not conceive what we call economic acts according to the grid of utilitarian and individualistic values that has dominated this field of knowledge since the end of the eighteenth century. If we say that capitalism is exclusively what works according to this logic, there was none at the time, at least not in a collective conscious and assertive form, and no "economy." But even in a context of values and representations of the human being that differed significantly from those of the modern era, there was *an astonishing awareness of mechanisms that we call economic, whose practice, theorization, and formalization are among the glories of that time*, and were decisive to later development, in particular "capitalism," even though in its evolution it has ultimately abandoned its original values. To see the difference, just compare this with other civilizations.

The medieval value system and the economy

For our purpose the main question revolves around the system of values and doctrinal reflection concerning it. At this level, opposition is not as radical as it may appear between our authors: the centrality of the notion of charity (*caritas*), emphasized by Le Goff and Clavero, is beyond question. So is the prevalence of values and references other than those of a purely economic nature. Nobody says the contrary. At the same time Todeschini by no means relies solely on Olivi and we have seen the formidable theoretical development of scholasticism on economic questions, with leading authors such as Saint Bernardine of Siena, Saint Antoninus of Florence, Nicole Oresme, not to mention the Spaniards, or before them Saint Thomas Aquinas himself. We have also evoked the original and well-thought-out practices of those merchants living in the atmosphere of Franciscanism. If, therefore, the notion of capitalism had to be connected with that of the autonomy of economics in relation to morality, there is no doubt that the birth of capitalism should be placed much later in the scheme of things. However, if we look at the thinking and the technical practice of economics, it is possible to speak of "capitalism" for this early period, for undeniably significant parts of the activity then presupposed the seeds of a nascent capitalist economy. Of course, the essential point is that the system of values remained fundamentally moral, and this economy was entirely viewed from the moral angle and not thought of separately as such; this was to remain the case until the eighteenth century up to Adam Smith, which is in every point the hinge. We are, indeed, at the heart of what we have said: what Todeschini and others have rightly shown is not an economic thought that would be independent from faith and morality, quite the contrary: *it is the emergence, within a society of faith, of concepts that for us belong to economics, but which were inserted in a different way in the field of reflection because they were integrated into a wide and fertile value system.*

If, then, it is anachronistic to consider as "economics" in the modern sense (that is, cut off from moral value) the reflections and practices of the time, it is just as questionable to send them back to an archaic prehistory, on a linear time scale, because you think they were not conscious of these realities. On the contrary, *there was new awareness, albeit still only partial, of these realities that we call economic,* and therefore in this respect a *major innovation* (again, no other civilization has done the equivalent). But *it is in a way that is different from what will be done afterward, for it was based on faith, morality, and social responsibility.* Now this is precisely the characteristic of the Social Doctrine of the Church still today; the first criticism it brings of modern economics is the breakdown of morality and social responsibility. *One of our aims in this book is precisely to contribute to the conception of a system of financial economy, and thus of society, based on an anthropology that is different from that underlying the liberal world, in the light of the Christian tradition,* and, fundamentally, morally oriented. As I emphasize in another book,[25] the mental and cultural factors that enabled the take-off of the West were born in a Christian context and this is not a coincidence; its emergence is evident from the Middle Ages. But it is also clear that the subsequent evolution led to a growing estrangement in relation to these sources, and that the subsequent take-off and rapid growth were characterized by an equally increasing secularization. The question is then whether, apart from its obvious material fruits, this has not been a major regression in other respects, and particularly in relation to

---

25 *Christianisme et Croissance économique,* op. cit.

the preoccupation with *"caritas"* that animated the medieval origins of that movement. This regression seems obvious to me.

There is then that idea that the medieval world was so different from ours that communication with it is impossible, and that therefore we cannot draw from it lessons for today. This is what Clavero[26] and Le Goff assert, on the basis of a monolithic conception, closing each epoch onto itself in an irreducible paradigm. Without taking the point beyond the concrete example provided by our subject, I think the contrary is true. It seems clear to me that *the Middle Ages and the modern era, although based on very different anthropologies, are not in a state of radical incommunicability*. In more general terms, *one can extract oneself mentally from the paradigm that dominates one's world; it is one of the essential benefits of historical research, without which this would be impossible*. And this is why this research is useful to us, and even indispensable: without projecting our conceptions on the past, nor rashly asserting a state of things that we consider archetypal, historical research can provide us the basis for a *reflection on the intrinsic value and goodness or flaws of certain conceptions or references*.

CONCLUSION ON MEDIEVAL ECONOMIC CONCEPTIONS

The issues just mentioned are very important to our research, since the medieval economy was Christian in its inspiration, at least in principle. At this level, it is in line with the evangelical precepts seen in previous chapters, developed with reference to the new specific historical experiences being encountered. First of all, as in the evangelical teaching, it is recognized that in all moral and spiritual considerations of economic activity we progress from level to level. We start with the moralization of ordinary economic life: the prudent merchant who seeks the right price in his transactions, while respecting his commitments toward society: that gives us a lively and direct conception of the *morality of the market* one would seek in vain in another civilization or another epoch, and which no doubt has not since been surpassed. Then progressively, even before the

---

26 Notably without his conclusion, see Clavero, *La grâce du don*, pp. 195 sqq., which excludes every possibility of communication between this period and our own. A conception that is the opposite of those American economists who analyze the Middle Ages with the concepts of modern liberal economy used as such; both are equally false.

stage of true monastic detachment, we arrive *at the ideal vision of an entrepreneur who is paradoxically as detached from his riches as is the Franciscan who has made a vow of poverty, and who generously lavishes his talents (gifts of God) for the good of the community.* And this is *a fortiori* true with regard to giving, according to that virtue of magnificence that is one of the glories of the Christian tradition. Not that this wealth and activity would be suspect by themselves, since their positive contribution is recognized, especially through trade. But wealth will be better used if we are detached, on the model of the mendicant orders. Underlying all is the distinction between *profit* (as surplus, which is good if it benefits the community) and *lucre* or greed (a morbid fixation on money and its accumulation).

We can add two practical lessons. The first concerns their conception of pricing, incorporating a search for fairness in the transaction, and their conception of the market, understood as a place where a process of collective and responsible pricing takes place as an expression of the community, and not as a savage confrontation of arbitrary choices.[27] Of course, such a market is a tool, like money, and it must not dictate choices. The second is our duty to have the appropriate view on how to invest our money: our aim should not be the supposed return of this money, taken in itself, but a human and social act of association between what this money represents, in terms of resources, and the action of people, united in a concrete project, involving a collective stake. The hope of a gain which is a real surplus, ultimately created for the good of all, is the result of that association. We will review all this now, in the case of the controversy over usury.

---

27 The Gospels did not elaborate on this point: the market and prices appear there as fluctuating data (see the parable of the field with its treasure, or the parable of the pearls). But of course, the notions of equity and community are present, as in the whole Bible.

CHAPTER 4

The Debate on Usury: the Data

THE CHURCH'S CONDEMNATION OF INTEREST-BEARING loans is central to our discussion. It was the subject of sarcasm by whole generations of liberal historians, especially in the nineteenth century, who plastered their simplistic schema, i.e., the "Enlightenment" triumphing over medieval "darkness," over a thought whose logic they did not understand. It was then easy for them to attack a conviction that had become incomprehensible. In fact, this issue deserves special consideration and it will prove highly instructive.[1]

DOCTRINAL DATA

In such a creative economy, in which financial capitalism was born, the debate about interest-bearing loans, called usury, seems paradoxical. For while the Christian tradition had long disapproved of usury, it had not been an important theme for a long time. The change came about 1200: it became a major sin, just after heresy, and it was attacked with violence;[2] in principle the Catholic Magisterium condemned "usury" until the nineteenth century. Accordingly, in the seventeenth century, it was emphasized that it is illegal "for the lender to demand something more than the sum lent if he undertakes not to claim this sum for a certain time."[3] As we see, it is the very fact of interest[4]

---

1 I evoked it briefly in *L'Evangile, le Chrétien et l'Argent*, op. cit. The following analysis is substantially updated.

2 Jacques Le Goff (*Marchands et banquiers au Moyen-âge* [Nice: PUF Que sais-je, 2001]) gave a colorful description of this process. But his analysis suffers here again from his bias toward a radical departure from the mentality of the time in relation to ours, making this past experience unusable, whereas it holds a wealth of information for us.

3 Heinrich Denzinger, *Symboles et définitions de la foi catholique* (Paris: Cerf, 1996), Denzinger no. 2062, March 18, 1666. (Hereafter cited as DS.) Again in 1745 the encyclical *"Vix pervenit"* of Benedict XIV condemned the thus defined "usury" (DS 2546 to 2550, November 1, 1745). See, for example, the comments of Fr Pierre Tiberghien, *L'Encyclique Vix pervenit de Benoît XIV* (Paris: Spes, 1914), who brilliantly defends the conception of the encyclical. We thank Mr J. Rouquerol for pointing out this book.

4 For as Thomas Aquinas said: "he who entrusts a sum to a merchant or a craftsman by way of association, does not yield to them the property of his

that is targeted, not the amount (as in the present sense of the word usury). But let us recall that the condemnation was directed only to the pure interest form of a loan, not to the profit of an enterprise, nor to everything resulting from participation in a project with corresponding risks: shares of a ship engaged in trade, or parts of what we would call an industrial or commercial company (the first joint company emerged in Toulouse in the thirteenth century!)—in short, any investment in equity. Similarly, no difficulty arose over the leasing of a building. On the other hand, interest from consumer credit was in principle condemned. Where did this condemnation come from, how was it motivated, and what were the consequences?

The theoretical foundations of condemnation: the Scriptures

Is the condemnation founded on the Scriptures? This is not self-evident from the Gospels, for they do not raise the issue of the lawfulness of interest-bearing loans: they even mention its possibility in several major parables, without condemning it, beginning with the parable of the talents. We find only one text, on which medieval thinkers insisted, a sentence of Saint Luke (6:35): "*date mutuum, nihil inde sperantes*" (lend, expecting nothing in return); they understood it not as a general counsel of disinterestedness, but as a precise legal prescription on the status of interest.[5] But this literal reading of a single text, isolated from the context, is not faithful. The source passage is theological; it encourages us to perform good deeds out of love, rather than with expectation of reciprocation, and it goes on by saying, "love your enemies." It is therefore a general moral precept and not a legal prescription.

The other biblical point of departure for condemning usury is more explicit; it is the Mosaic law.[6] Thus Deuteronomy 23:19–20 says, "You shall not lend upon interest to your brother, interest on money, interest on victuals, interest on anything that is lent for interest. To a

money that remains his own, so that he participates in the commerce of the merchant and the work of the craftsman in their risks and dangers; that is why he will have the right to claim, as a thing belonging to him, a share of the profits." *Summa theologica*, II-II, question 78, article 2, ad 5. The bull *Vix pervenit* also recalls the same doctrine.

5 It should be noted, moreover, that, if the text is understood in that way, there is no reason to target interest more than principal; what we are told is broadly: do not expect *anything*!
6 In three places and in much the same way: Ex 22:25; Lev 25; Deut 23:20.

foreigner you may lend upon interest, but to your brother you shall not lend upon interest; that the Lord your God may bless you in all that you undertake." This being said, besides the fact that the literal validity of the Mosaic law is not self-evident for Christians (many other provisions were considered null and void without hesitation), the context shows that these texts refer to the case of a loan to a poor person who is a "brother" in need asking for help, and to the possible extortion of money in exchange for this "help," where the concept of solidarity should dominate. In this case, reprobation is logical. But its extension to any other form of loan is not self-evident.[7]

The theoretical foundations of condemnation: reasoning

To justify a general condemnation, this reasoning remains the main basis. It is found especially in Saint Thomas,[8] who, after quoting these Mosaic texts, proceeds as follows. He distinguishes between goods that are consumed, like bread, and those durable goods which do not wear out perceptibly, like a house. For the former, he says, the lender can only claim the equivalent of what he has lent, without interest. In fact, a good and the use of that good (its consumption) then merge: one cannot sell or lend separately wine and the use of this wine: he who lends wine is entitled to compensation by receiving what he has lent, that is to say the same quantity of wine. On the other hand, for the second type of property, interest is lawful, for it is possible to distinguish the ownership of the house and its use; and therefore, cede the latter for a time by receiving a rent for that purpose. Returning to money, Thomas considers that it belongs to the first category of goods, for it is an instrument of exchange, which is consumed by spending. The negative conclusion follows:

---

7   In medieval Jewish texts, for a long time, the condemnation that was current among Christians was hardly to be found. They insisted at most on the *practical* disadvantages of lending at interest to Christians, who forbade it. Therefore, they lent with interest. No problem was raised by Jewish theorists; we find nothing equivalent to what we have among Christians, as we shall see, on selling time or on the thing sold twice. This, however, changed afterward, especially in the seventeenth century, when they began to condemn usury, doubtless under Christian influence. See Abriel Toaff and Haym Soloveichik in Diego Quaglioni, Giacomo Todeschini, and Gian Maria Varanini, eds., *Credito e usura fra teologia, diritto e amministrazione — linguaggi a confronto (sec. XII–XVI)* (Rome: Collection de l'École française de Rome, 2005), pp. 104 sqq.

8   The main text is *Summa Theologica* II-II q 78, especially a1.

lending money should not provide remuneration. In *De Malo*[9] he explains to us that

> usury, in fact, comes from the word usage, in the sense that for the use that is made of money, one receives a certain price, as if one were selling the use of the money lent.... The proper use of money is to be spent in exchange for other things: currencies have been invented for the purpose of exchange.... So when you lend your money with the promise that the money will be returned in full, and you want to have a definite sum for the use of the money, it is obvious that you separately sell the use of money and the very substance of money; and the use of money, as has been said, does not differ from its substance; therefore, you sell what does not exist, or twice the same thing, namely money itself, the use of which is spent, and this is manifestly opposed to the notion of natural justice. Therefore, lending money with interest is in itself a mortal sin.[10]

On the other hand, as Jean-Claude Lavigne puts it, other "arguments used by Saint Thomas are the breakup of honest friendship entailed by lending with interest (rupture of a relationship) and the existence of violence in the asymmetry between borrower (seen as one in need) and lender (who benefits)." The idea was in fact widespread that the borrower promises the payment of interest only under duress, in this case an economic constraint.[11] It is a form of ransom to exploit the need of the borrower. Certainly, in a sense any economic

---

9   *De Malo*, question 13, article 4, written about 1266. We also find elements of the reflection of St Thomas on the interest loan in *Commentaries of the Sentences* III, D. 37, a. 6 and *Quodlibet* III, Question 7, s. 2. See Jean-Claude Lavigne in Paul H. Dembinski, ed., *Pratiques financières, regards chrétiens* (Paris: Editions Desclée de Brouwer, 2009), pp. 135 sqq., with many references on loan interest. The corresponding references and citations are taken from this text.

10   According to Odd Langholm, the problem addressed by the condemnation of usury is not what money cannot produce; it is that it *must* not produce: the use that is made is an abnormal one, whereas money is nothing more than a means of exchange. Grabill, ed., *Sourcebook in Late-scholastic Monetary Theory*, p. xiv.

11   The borrower's will is said to be "relative" and not "absolute" according to the Aristotelian tradition; it is analogous to that of the sailor, whom a storm obliges to throw off his cargo to save himself. Langholm, *The Legacy of Scholasticism*, p. 60.

scarcity can be understood as a constraint. But they judged here that an abnormal constraint is brought to light by the mere existence of interest, which presupposes the idea that money is sterile, and that this interest is paid only under violence.

Still other arguments are related to time. According to Dempsey[12] one argument was that the mere passage of time alone does not justify anything; to judge whether a profit is legitimate, it is necessary to examine what happens on a case-by-case basis. But in a pure loan only the passage of time justifies interest, and so it is not justified. On the other hand, it was assumed that the value of money could change over time in the corresponding market (or on the "forex" — foreign exchange market). The great jurist Martin de Azpilcueta[13] rejected the idea that time counts in itself; on the other hand, he said, it is legitimate to make a profit if there has been an increase in the value of money during the period. The scholastics were aware of the effects that were later known as the quantitative theory of money, or the impact of money supply and demand on prices. But of course, for them this would not justify interest in itself. If there is a change in value, then it is not produced by the passage of time; it is an external cause, a fluctuation in the money market, which depends on the circumstances of time and place, and the responsibility of participants.

The moral background of hostility to usury

We shall see later what we ought to think of the substance of these arguments.[14] To better appreciate them, it is essential to situate them in the moral context of the Middle Ages.[15] It was then felt vital to classify properly the new phenomena induced by the development of the economy. Also, conversion to poverty, at the heart of mendicant orders, played an important role in this evolution. Usury in the strict sense came to be seen as the form of economy that is

---

12 Grabill, ed., *Sourcebook in Late-scholastic Monetary Theory*, pp. 121 sqq.
13 Ibid., p. 67.
14 It should be noted, however, that this condemned only naked interest: in modern words, the renting of money and the remuneration of the capital of the bank. The reasoning does not seem to preclude paying for costs like banking overheads, or even the cost of risk, in the form of provisions for future losses. See the case of the "mounts of piety" below.
15 Greci, Pinto, and Todeschini, *Economie urbane*, pp. 177 sqq.

typical of infidels; it was classified with hoarding, monopolizing, not working when one could, or avarice that neglects social utility. It was perceived as diabolical in that it involves using the power of money in front of the need of the other, excluding all social and productive activity, and outside of the market. Believing that, as Sylvain Piron[16] says, they vituperated mostly against a fantasized usurer, who lives without working, sells time and is enriched by the substance of others.

But as we have seen, all this did not imply a general condemnation of money. Amassing was a crime if its purpose is to amass even more, but "the desire to obtain a gain, a fair wealth, from the timely sale of what one possessed" was freely admitted. Moreover, the ductility of money, highlighted at the time, was also related to positive moral judgments: to use it effectively is to circulate it in a useful or creative way, especially in real investments. Furthermore, there are positive financial or monetary comparisons with money throughout the religious language.[17] And as Todeschini[18] said, when they said that a usurer sells time, which is the property of God, the interest as such was not even condemned, since there were examples of lawful interest. What was denounced was basically the attitude of those who indulged in it, understood as refusing to be inserted in the context of exchange and charity that the society of the Christian faithful is (or should be). Hence the central opposition between the merchant and the usurer, between hoarding or ostentatious expenditures paid by debts, and a productive and useful economy in which we constantly reinvest. In the end, *they contrasted living money with dead money, private and useless money with money that animates the collective economic life.* The usurer is somebody who has not learned the lesson of exchange; he sells money instead of investing it: "the public usurer did not perceive the difference between the sale of money and the investment of wealth quantified by money."[19]

16 Sylvain Piron in Quaglioni, Todeschini, and Varanini, eds., *Credito e usura*, pp. 74 sqq.
17 See the extreme examples of the Host, or of Eternal Life, compared to money!
18 Todeschini, *Richesse franciscaine*, op. cit.
19 Ibid., p. 31.

ECONOMIC, LEGAL, AND SOCIAL PRACTICE
The influence of practice

We will now examine what happened in practice. In his analysis, Jacques Le Goff little develops the theoretical dimension, although he recalls the understanding of usury[20] as robbing time, which belongs only to God, and the fact that it is a sin against justice, one of the great themes of the Middle Ages. But for him the main reality is the opposite: "money profoundly modified the conception and practice of time in the Middle Ages." As he notes,[21] "from the end of the twelfth century onward, the increasing sensitivity of city dwellers to the value of time can be observed. We see the idea that time is money. Above all, the thirteenth century emphasized the economic and monetary value of labor, including manual labor. The protection of merchants was now justified by their usefulness and by the reality of their work. More generally, work was rehabilitated; the creative man was exalted as a collaborator of God; and the importance of the risk taken by merchants was recalled." He even thinks that the interest-bearing loan[22] "was gradually and under certain conditions rehabilitated during the thirteenth century and especially in the four-teenth and fifteenth centuries." The idea of justice led to the con-ception of a reasonable level of interest. There would therefore have been an adjustment to the reality of the facts. This analysis — on the whole correct, especially for commercial activities — seems to me to miss certain points that are essential for our purpose, especially with regard to trade activities, for the distinction remained in principle and therefore so did the condemnation, at least theoretically.

The central role of the practice of trade

In the context of a thinking that enhances the value of the cir-culation of money for the common good, the notion of sterility of money[23] was assessed not abstractly, but in relation to transactions and their usefulness, either for the management of ecclesiastical property, or in the trade or craft industry. And therefore, in order to characterize the usurer, especially the publicly declared one, they referred to custom; what was condemned was the prospect of seeking

---

20 Le Goff, *Le Moyen Age et l'argent*, p. 102.
21 Ibid., p. 57.
22 Ibid., pp. 109 sqq.
23 Greci, Pinto, and Todeschini, *Economie urbane*, pp. 194 sqq.

profit without foundation, not oriented toward public utility. For example, among those who lent to maritime businesses, they distinguished between those who were certain to recover their funds (this was considered usury) and those who assumed a share of the common risk, which was lawful. *Commercial risk became a central criterion of justification.* Money at risk was considered to be legitimately compensated, as contractor risk. For example, in the case of forward sales, if a mechanical increase of the forward price was applied at the outset, it was usury, but not if there was real doubt as to the future value of the goods (*vendita sub dubio*). So again, the price criterion was the value of things as agreed jointly: to depart from it meant usury. Hence the need, if necessary, for experts who knew the prices on the market.

An interesting case is the contract called "cens," indicating purchase of the future benefits of a property over a period of time, popular among religious institutions: if it was for life or in perpetuity, equality was no longer possible as the price paid had a limit, while the purchased flow was unlimited or almost so. At first, some people concluded that it was usurious. But others felt that since there was a doubt about the future reality of that fruit, it was outside of usury. Finally, Innocent IV analyzed this transaction as the final sale of total future cash flows, which was no longer a loan. The reference was then the price in use for this type of contract at the time of the signature; if this price was a proper one, there was no usury. After all, in the sale of any land, the total of future benefits in perpetuity inherently exceeds the price paid if no discount enters into the calculation, and no one found fault with this. Likewise in the leasing of public resources: the Franciscans analyzed these operations as the commercialization of future money mobilized in the direction of the collective interest, within an institutional framework; they therefore considered it lawful, especially since the product remained risky.

Ways of taking into account the economic reality

Notions of Roman law that were taken up at the time were used to conceptualize the legitimacy of payments aimed at compensating for what could have been gained elsewhere with the money lent (*lucrum cessans*), or what was lost in the process, including any delay (*damnum emergens*),[24] or to provide an indemnity for the risk taken

---

24 St Thomas Aquinas said: "In his contract with the borrower, the lender may, without any sin, stipulate an indemnity to be paid for the prejudice he suffers

if it was certain (*periculum sortis*),[25] besides of course the remuneration of a job or service. This normally justified a loan if it financed a productive activity or was linked to it, since two possible productive uses of money were compared, and/or the vagaries of economic life were taken into account. Olivi asserted that the merchant's money could generate interest, which could be assessed; at the end of the thirteenth century, credit extended by merchants could legally produce a legitimate rate of interest. It was recognized in the same way that the case of banks, which developed at the time, was different, since at any time they needed to be able to honor deposits; they needed to be able to borrow and repay quickly, and it was normal to pay for this availability. It should be noted that in all these examples the issue is about multiplying opportunities of participation in economic life. We have seen that the flow of wealth was thought to be like the flow of blood: money must circulate. But it was not a question of making the most of an amount of money one owned. It was recalled that in their financial activities, merchants had to remain detached. They were supposed to lend only to people who knew what money was, and to do business only with professionals. In such cases, by definition that sterility of money that was so condemned was absent. But again, it was condemned if it revolved around a private strategy, disconnected from the community and therefore from the market, according excessive devotion to money in consumer-oriented relationships, and seeking to accumulate it without reference to a collective good.

The position of lawyers

All this was reflected in legal texts. There are two levels to consider here: civil law and canon law (law of the Church). The analysis of the legal provisions[26] of Italian cities shows the possibility of taking into account the costs of proceedings to recover one's money, and in cases

---

by depriving himself of what was in his possession; this is not selling the use of money, but getting compensation." *Summa theologica*, II-II, q 78, a 2, ad 1.

25 Cardinal Ostiense, for example, a great canonist, recognizes default interests by relating them to the time lost by the lender, at least if he is a merchant, for the time of commercial transactions has a measurable value. But this was not considered true by everybody.

26 Patrizia Mainoni in Quaglioni, Todeschini, and Varanini, eds., *Credito e usura*, pp. 137 sqq.

where it was a commercial activity, assessing interest was possible;[27] an allowance was made for default interest charges, but often a period of time was set out, before which charging interest was not possible. But this situation remained uncertain: in Milan, preaching against usury and pontifical offensives in the same direction led to changes in laws: around 1396, in practice charging interest became possible only if there was a commercial contract (exchange and deposit), or in canonical cases, and at very low rates. Usury had a complex place in medieval civil doctrine,[28] although wider than in canon law. For the great jurist Bartole, interest could be charged on a dowry, or if there was a delay.

A great humanist canonist like Azpilcueta[29] still saw Saint Luke's passage ("lend, expecting nothing in return") as a norm and not as a counsel for improvement; at the same time, he noted that interest is universal, that it goes even beyond what civil law admits (12 percent), its frequency in fairs, et cetera. He added that if the rate is low, one cannot speak of mortal sin. His concrete analyses are subtle, as in the case of the "company contract" (in which someone brings capital, another labor, and they share the benefits) which he considers lawful because there is no abandonment of ownership, unlike in the case of a loan (and one can also lose one's capital). Like other authors, he also accepted charging interest if there is *lucrum cessans* or *damnum emergens*, in the case of default interest, or a forced loan. But in practice this was not so simple and the debates continued; for example, when a lender claimed interest on the basis of a commercial activity that he *might* have had: it was inadmissible for De Soto, acceptable to Azpilcueta, provided that there really was a commercial activity from which the money was subtracted. He justified,[30] in the name of *lucrum cessans*, taking into account the delays, since the loss of business is greater as time passes. But at the same time, he linked this authorization with the confirmation of the actual existence of a flow of activity, and extended it when the money in question was placed in reserve as a precaution. Moreover,

---

27 See also here Le Goff, *Marchands et banquiers au Moyen-âge*, in particular p. 93.
28 Diego Quaglioni in Quaglioni, Todeschini, and Varanini, eds., *Credito e usura*, pp. 253 sqq.
29 Christian Zendri, ibid., pp. 277 sqq.
30 Grabill, ed., *Sourcebook in Late-scholastic Monetary Theory*, p. 57.

the doctrine said that the *lucrum cessans* must be equal to the profit thus lost; our author added that it must be calculated on the basis of the expectation of an alternative gain. Therefore, an element of risk had to be maintained.

All these considerations ultimately led to great flexibility, and in most cases merely required a certain moderation in the amount of interest. It was acknowledged, as Bartolomé Clavero[31] reminds us, that merchants were in a specific situation and needed a specific law with much wider margins of action. But the principle still existed and required a case-by-case examination. Hence the sometimes-difficult growth of banking.[32] Also, if it were concluded that there had indeed been wrongful usury, reparation implied full restitution of the interest charged,[33] although in practice making restitution proved complex; in doubt, they required wrongdoers to pay over their gain in alms. In addition, it was sometimes difficult to specify the notions of *lucrum cessans* and *damnum emergens*, which, logically, could justify any form of interest, at least in a commercial context. Moreover, in the set-up of operations, lawyers sought obstinately to maintain an element of uncertainty[34] and the existence of a community of gains and losses between the parties.

But in reality, things could go quite far. In addition to contracts with questionable canonical validity, the famous "triple contract"[35] closed the loop: it was used to lend interest while respecting the letter of the doctrine. Azpilcueta[36] was in favor of it, unlike Domingo de Soto, on the grounds that each of the three contracts that composed it was lawful, and yet the legal hazard had disappeared, excluding the

---

31 Clavero, *La grâce du don*, pp. 145 sqq.

32 Ibid., pp. 120 sqq. and 149 sqq.

33 Unlike prostitution, in which the act that was condemned was distinguished from its recompense, which was judged to be due. F. Ceccarelli in Quaglioni, Todeschini, and Varanini, eds., *Credito e usura*, pp. 10 sqq.

34 See also Clavero, *La grâce du don*, pp. 109 sqq.

35 This is a "company contract" between an entrepreneur and an investor, including sharing in the benefits of a company; the entrepreneur insures the profits to the capital provider, for a certain sum; the contributor of capital sells the future profits, against a given sum.

36 Azpilcueta also believed that interest can be claimed if the money is "rented" for another use: to be "shown" or to serve as collateral (security deposit), as there is no transfer of ownership of that money, but lease of its use. Grabill, ed., *Sourcebook in Late-scholastic Monetary Theory*, p. 35.

counterparty risk of course, and we are left with pure credit bearing interest. One finds here in an implacable way the limits of the reasoning that founded the condemnation: *if indeed (as do our canonists) we accept the legitimacy of insurance* in the form of a fixed price paid to cover a hazard, *by extension we can give security to what is risky*, by paying a fixed amount of money, and we can then transform the risky profit resulting from participation in a business into a legally insured gain; we can also sell future profits for a given sum; combining them, we manufacture an interest rate. The fact that this is possible also shows that interest has its place in a complete logic of financing, in addition to risk-taking proper.[37] To avoid this, it would have been necessary to reject insurance itself, or the sale of future flows of money, and more generally all that gives an operator any guarantee on the future. But our medieval friends, fortunately, did not go in that direction.

The mounts of piety

The foregoing considerations were more difficult in the case of consumer credit. In the case of the poor, given the social importance of credit, it is understandable that people were not satisfied with the foregoing considerations and wanted to take action to provide practical solutions to fragile borrowers. Saint Antoninus of Florence and Saint Bernardine of Siena thus distinguished between alms and honest loans; they stressed that credit could help people to recover and can be more effective than charity. This point of view has always been present, albeit as a minority one; it is partly at the origin of the spectacular development of the "mounts of piety"[38] at the end of the medieval period, very important not only for private financing but also for the economy in general.[39] These institutions, based on the then-widespread practice of pawnbroking, with very moderate interest charges, were genuine banks for the population concerned, which

---

37   In modern terms, the total profit of a profitable operation is sufficient to pay for both economic risk-free financing (interest-bearing loans) and remuneration covering the risk (profit).

38   A public lending institution, mainly by pawn-lending to craftsmen and other people of limited resources.

39   Greci, Pinto, and Todeschini, *Economie urbane*, pp. 217 sqq.; Maria Giuseppina Muzzarelli in Quaglioni, Todeschini, and Varanini, eds., *Credito e usura*, pp. 182 sqq.; Paolo Prodi, *Christianisme et monde moderne* (Paris: Hautes Etudes Gallimard Seuil, 2006), pp. 421 sqq.

often pledged during a certain period those of their assets that were not immediately useful, so as to finance their business cycle. Combining economic strength and wealth generation, they were typically both charitable institutions (through solidarity) and real banking entities (it was often the only safe place to put one's money). This credit was supposed to be profitless and curative, but the poor receiving support were not overly poor. The character of *public initiative* is constant in the mounts: there was always at the origin of their creation churchmen, a municipal decision, and a pontifical approbation; all of them were very aware of the novelty of the initiative.

However, the complexity and diversity of the problems they posed must be mentioned. Countries of Catholic culture, in particular, recognized the necessity of these loans, but the preoccupation with charity predominated, and they often refused to resort to the money market, even though it was necessary for their refinancing as donations were not sufficient. Hence a problem: the first mount, in Perugia, had to start by borrowing (with interest) from the Jews! The ambiguity then continued: most of the Italian mounts were unable to obtain authorized remuneration for deposits, and so it was gratuitous on this side, at least at first. Then came deposits at 4 percent, to finance loans that were at 5 percent and more. In Northern Europe, the use of capital markets was more widespread. The other crucial question was billing: cost or interest. Very quickly they saw that donations were not sufficient to cover the costs.[40] In the end, it was agreed to charge interest both to cover costs and risk, and to raise funds; the bull *Inter multiplices* of 1515 (Leo X)[41] and the fifth Lateran council confirmed this: a preference was given to gratuity, but the possibility of covering expenses was acknowledged. Thereafter the mounts played a considerable role in the development of interest-bearing loans, in the framework of a public mission at rates of 5 to 15 percent. The interest demanded depended on who was borrowing (the rate could be very low, for example, in the case of a ruined artisan). Sometimes as in Florence they were used by nobles—and even by King Philip II. Their range went from small personal loans, to production loans or loans to municipalities. It should be noted that the mounts were particularly widespread in Italy, in the most developed area of the country. In short, it was *a*

40 Especially since the link with hospices upset their finances.
41 The text of the bull is in Prodi, *Christianisme et monde modern*, pp. 421 sqq.

remarkable case of the creation of a financial institution for reasons that were largely disinterested. The contribution to the population was very important. Their great handicap was the link with social assistance, hence their relatively high cost, and their loss of competitiveness, compared to private lenders where these were not practicing usury in the present sense of the term.[42]

CREDIT AND SOCIETY

The central role of interpersonal credit, its link with social networks

In the case of interpersonal credit, it is useful to broaden our horizon further by situating it in the economy and society of the time. Laurence Fontaine[43] produced a remarkable synthesis of the historical reality of credit in the pre-industrial European economy. This was for many an economy based on uncertainty, an informal one, without large financial institutions and with little money circulation. Borrowing was then a vital necessity for many;[44] intermediaries were ubiquitous. Pawning was tolerated and widely practiced, even by prominent persons. But this did not exhaust the meaning of indebtedness, which in this respect was very different from our own. For it was also a sign of belonging to the community; it was rooted in networks, family, or corporate entities that featured organized forms of solidarity and contingency reserves, very often present in neighborhoods.[45] One could not easily refuse credit to a relative, or if one was a public figure: *there was a mentality about the obligation to lend.* This indebtedness was therefore often chronic; it created a reciprocal link and, depending on the case, power or solidarity. The social role of the debt was much superior to its economic role: it ensured the permanence of social ties, but

---

42 Let us note already the affinity of this problem with a modern one, microfinance, with the same ambiguity on the positioning between charity and a special form of credit.

43 Fontaine, *L'économie morale*, pp. 255 sqq.

44 Most of these loans were intended to accommodate due dates related to taxes, weddings, pre-harvest financing, delays on rent payments, etc. From the creditor viewpoint, food shops were particularly exposed, especially bakers; lenders knew that they would often never be repaid. The role of religious communities was also important, to increase the incomes of their estates and make the dowries of nuns more productive.

45 Inter-personal ties were predominant, followed by those related to work, or to village-based clientelism.

also of dependence. Hence indebtedness and even over-indebtedness was rather widespread, but at the same time practices of leniency were equally frequent: one often did not go to recording officials about debt immediately. Initial debt maturities were rarely adhered to; over-indebted persons were generally not driven from their homes and could live out their lives there, et cetera. Lenders often lost money, given the weakness of their borrowers' assets. It was an economy where it was easy to borrow; there was no stigmatization attached to credit until the end of the eighteenth century; it was even a part of an aristocratic existence. But as security was low, fortunes included many claims that were more or less certain. In the case of commercial credit, it was difficult to treat it rationally, particularly because of the lack of information; the difficulty of having the necessary information pushed lenders to limit themselves to a narrow circle of well-known partners. In the event of a crisis, the risk of propagation became high, without any payer of last resort. Hence speculative trends and frequent panics, accompanied by large fluctuations in the short term.[46]

Trust, virtue, and social values

In a society where credit was vital but not regulated, and uncertainty was general, confidence was essential. Reputation was therefore a major stake and jealously preserved. But it is important to note that it was not based solely on qualities such as calculation, the ability to manage, even probity or fidelity: it also included compassion and gentleness toward debtors. We see it in the books of that time; as Fontaine says: "the purpose of these recommendations is to set up a sense of Christian generosity and compassion that in turn will protect its supporters from the worst setbacks in an unpredictable credit market."[47] So, there calculation and generosity were intermingled. Why this concern for leniency? Besides what we have seen of the role of credit, in which an important element of relationship and the culture of gift were intermingled, and of course Christian concerns, this also results from the existence of two conceptions cohabiting in a complex

---

46 The author here makes a stimulating comparison with the subprime crisis: the resemblance is in the issue of trust: then it was the lack of information that fuelled panic, now it is the excessive complexity of products and institutions: this can amount to the same thing. Fontaine, *L'économie morale*, pp. 426 sqq.
47 Ibid., p. 290.

symbiosis, which Fontaine describes as aristocratic and capitalist. In fact, she said, the aristocrats lent a great deal and were more generous toward their debtors.[48] Lending played an important part for wealthy gentlemen, but they had little choice of their debtors. At each succession, they gave or remitted debts. In short,[49] "credit, because it was embedded in an aristocratic political economy based on interpersonal ties and a culture of giving, was a very uncontrollable activity." Hence the reluctance of many wise minds at the time. The relationship of businessmen with debtors was very different: they demanded every penny and had no sense of duty toward them. In fact, two systems intermingled: "on the one hand, an economy of giving still very alive and, on the other, a capitalist economy very pregnant and that never ceased to assert itself. While each implies totally different practices, they were constantly interacting."[50] Another important dimension[51] was the role of risk and the relationship with God: *"Time belongs to God and the only way in which man can live it is in a relationship of risk and chance and not in a relationship of foresight and calculation."* "Acting with risk is therefore an essential aristocratic modality."[52] Even though the Christian dimension is essential, we are not dealing here with pure Christian values.[53]

---

48 In times of crisis, that kind of morality was relaxed, and the aristocrats also became harder with their debtors.

49 The calculation in rational terms was difficult; we also note the importance of loans between nobles. And merchants could hardly refuse credit to the nobles. Fontaine, *L'économie morale*, p. 100.

50 She notes that this duality is a privileged subject of theater in the sixteenth and seventeenth centuries: see *Le Bourgeois gentilhomme* and *The Merchant of Venice*. Or *Timon of Athens*; friendship was a central aristocratic value, just as giving.

51 Fontaine, *L'économie morale*, p. 238.

52 One sees it especially in *The Merchant of Venice*. "Risk and Love are therefore the major categories of the economy of giving. . . . Even if the gift is self-serving, it must appear as if it were not and this is precisely where time and risk appear. . . . In the aristocratic transaction, both the motives and the expected counterparts must never appear: they must remain indeterminate; for any precision, by reducing the part of risk, would at the same time diminish the love and confidence that is played and replayed in each specific exchange." Fontaine, *L'économie morale*, p. 242.

53 This is also expressed in the passion for gambling, conspicuous in these circles: repaying one's gambling debts was even judged (absurdly) to have a priority over other debts.

Between this conception, which I think it is excessive to reduce to the aristocratic reference, and the capitalist conception (in the modern sense of the term) there was no pure succession, but coexistence and competition in complex and multiple ways. But with the eighteenth century, there was a shift toward the objectification of relations and information, and a questioning of types of behavior that were deemed unreliable (criticism of irresponsible borrowing, etc.). Fontaine[54] notes that "in this context Simmel's analyses of money that frees personal links are particularly relevant because monetary exchange effectively equates things, which are then exchanged independently of personal ties.... While 'the anonymous market of neo-classical models does not exist in economic life,' it nevertheless exists as a social fiction that structures a new political economy: the fiction of impersonal and egalitarian market relations makes possible the existence of a democratic society." But, more than an aristocratic or democratic model, I would speak of a relational model, in which the aristocratic component was of course important, but which also permeated our medieval and Renaissance merchants and even the whole of society, and in which Christianity played an important role. It is the opposite of the characteristic impersonal mode of modern society.

Private loans and the prohibition of usury

In this context of general indebtedness, the prohibition of usury (at least theoretical) played a central role. But as Fontaine notes, despite this prohibition, the diversity of practices was great and even in purely private loans they knew how to make up the perceived interest: inclusion in capital, introduction of a hazard, link with a sale, insurance, lack of term to the repayment of capital (that transforms it into an annuity, which was admitted because in this case there is no return of capital), penalty in case of non-repayment in term, et cetera. In addition, loan counterparties were not always monetary. Her analysis confirms that the repression of usury was very light, on the ecclesiastical as well as the civil side, the latter gradually taking the upper hand. Denunciations were rare because indebtedness served everybody, and it had numerous legal derogations: interest was accepted for money coming from dowries and orphans, for borrowings from the king and others, and of course

---

54 Fontaine, *L'économie morale*, p. 275.

in commercial uses — where as we have seen the concepts of *lucrum cessans* and *damnum emergens* could justify it in most of the cases. When there was accusation of usury, this showed a less personalized relationship and it was aimed in particular at foreigners.

Nevertheless, the ideal of social relations was still founded on a morality hostile to "profit" (more exactly, we should say, to lucre). But the influence of the Church on the debate decreased everywhere from the seventeenth century and especially from the succeeding century. It then ceased to compel society to comply with its standards. On the practical side, it was increasingly pointed out that the ban in fact led to an increase in the cost of credit. The macro-trend, resulting in part from increasing flexibility, perhaps from the greater abundance of cash, was to a decline of then-current interest rates (down to 3 to 5 percent). Ultimately, the notion of a general interest rate became a reality.

CHAPTER 5

The Meaning of the Usury Controversy

HISTORICAL PERSPECTIVE

Historical effects of the prohibition

The practice of interest-bearing lending was ultimately flexible in the case of productive economic activity. There was more hesitation in private lending, but here too, how it was actually carried out was quite complex and diverse. But the condemnation in principle of interest and the related reasoning were maintained during the Middle Ages and the Renaissance. Certainly, some admitted that money is fruitful if it is associated with human labor, or that the future value of an asset is lower than the present value, or even the existence of a specific market for money, which takes into account money's lower value in the future (without suggesting that this results from the pure passage of time). But others criticized these arguments by pointing out that they were precisely what justified an interest rate.

We shall not here mention the contribution of the Protestant world, the best known being that of Calvin. While he accepted the idea of interest-bearing loans, they were subject to strict conditions, showing his affinity with the thinking of scholastic authors.[1] He understood it was necessary to go beyond formal arguments or too rigid readings of the Scriptures; this led him to a frank acknowledgment of the principle of interest in commercial transactions. In fact, he showed that in a sense it is wrong to say that money does not generate money. But this did not lead him to a greater anticipation of industrial capitalism, or to a practice that was very different from what already existed, even if it became clearer. The insistence on justice prevailed also in his considerations on equity return.

As regards the historical impact of prohibition as a whole from an economic point of view, there are, as Laurence Fontaine[2] notes, two theses: for John Noonan, the ban was positive because it diverted capital from consumer loans; for Raymond DeRoover it was negative because it increased the cost of credit and its risks. Without deciding

---

1   See, for example, Édouard Dommen and Marc Faessler in Dembinski, ed., *Pratiques financières*, pp. 171 sqq.
2   Fontaine, *L'économie morale*, p. 412.

this debate, one tends to give partial credence to both, although more to the first: the prohibition of usury understood as an abuse was a good thing[3] at the social level, but also economically, when compared with other civilizations like India, where it was a scourge. Moreover, the inconvenience to true economic development seems to have been minimal. A text by Keynes[4] shows the historical utility of the Church's position to maintain simultaneously a high rate of capital efficiency and relatively low interest rates (whereas in this type of premodern society the latter tend to climb very high, thereby stifling initiative). But at the same time this condemnation undoubtedly dampened the awareness of the reality of the money market and consequently its rationalization. That said, the main issue for us is not this: it is rather in the lessons to be learned from the economic and social model of that time and its value system.

Subsequent evolution of the doctrine

In the case of Catholicism, it should be noted that the condemnation was never explicitly lifted in a doctrinal document, except indirectly, notably in canon law. First of all, instruction was given in the nineteenth century[5] to cease imputing sin to interest loans.[6] Jean-Claude Lavigne[7] then notes the clearest turning point:

---

3   Here again Jacques Le Goff (*Marchands et banquiers*) is wrong when he sees the usurer as the capitalist's ancestor. It is paradoxical to minimize the obvious elements of modernity present in the medieval economy, then to claim that an old-fashioned usurer is the ancestor of capitalism. These persons were present in the Middle Ages, but they were not the usurers in the narrow sense, who were mostly parasites.

4   Quoted by Paolo Prodi in *Christianisme et monde moderne*, pp. 421 sqq.

5   Answer of Pius VIII, August 18, 1830. It considers that in the case of loans to businesses, the question of interest has not been explicitly settled and that confessors can therefore be flexible in the matter. DS 2722–2723.

6   Some social Catholics in the nineteenth or early twentieth century have condemned interest. La Tour du Pin defines it as "the productivity of an object by virtue of its temporary alienation, this object undergoing, during this alienation, neither deterioration nor diminution." This, according to him, makes it possible to take over the work of others unduly, for he denies that money as such is fruitful (Gavignaud-Fontaine, *Considérations économiques chrétiennes*, p. 101). In the same sense, Tiberghien's booklet, op. cit. Similar theses are sometimes defended today. See also Denis Ramelet, "La rémunération du capital à la lumière de la doctrine traditionnelle de l'Eglise catholique," *Catholica*, no. 86 (Winter 2004–05).

7   Lavigne in Dembinski, ed., *Pratiques financière*, p. 153.

In 1917, the code of canon law, in the part that concerns contracts, specifies in relation to the consumer loan or *mutuum*: "If a fungible thing is given to someone and has to be returned in the same form, no gain in respect of the same contract shall be levied; but in the provision of a fungible thing, it is not unlawful in itself to agree on a legal profit unless it appears to be immoderate, or even a higher profit, if a fair and proportionate reason may be invoked" (Article 1543). This is therefore an apparent reversal: a contract may stipulate an interest rate. The word "provision" here seems to oppose that of "ownership" (transfer) to authorize interest; the loan is seen no longer as a provisional abandonment of ownership, but as a service, which can be remunerated. This remuneration must be explained in the contract and cannot be the result of violence by one of the partners against the other. Canon 1547 goes in the same direction by recommending that the funds of "pious foundations" be well managed and therefore placed at interest in serious institutions.

And Lavigne[8] adds: "the new canon law of 1983 follows this evolution. It no longer speaks of prohibitions concerning interest-bearing loans; on the contrary, it demands that ecclesiastical institutions should manage their accounts properly and, in order to do so, place money with interest. The perception of interest has become a criterion of good management and therefore a positive element. The Church has thus entered into the era of management efficiency, represented by the need to remunerate capital and not to let it lie idle." In fact, the rule of management efficiency has existed since the Middle Ages; the new element is the factual recognition of the possibility of a lawful form of interest-bearing lending.

ECONOMIC AND MORAL ANALYSIS
The prohibition of this practice seems odd
All of this leads to the essential question before us: the lessons to be learned from this historical experience. There is indeed something surprising, even enigmatic, in the condemnation of interest. In the context of an economy and a society that were diversified and inventive in economic matters, this seemingly incongruous prohibition

---

8   Ibid., p. 155. Canons 1284, 6°; 1294, 2°; 1305.

contrasts with the remarkable awareness of economic realities that we see elsewhere in that era. And even more so, if we remember that Christianity is unique among religions by its absence of material prohibitions: no food prohibition, no economic ban, except precisely this one. But we have also seen the strong motivating force behind this in the preceding chapters: the ideal of an economic activity oriented toward real added value, which is the fruit of human action and is turned toward a social, community benefit, and that of just transactions, where one pays only one real service and at its right price, and finally, and above all, *the rejection of hoarding, conceived as the selfish and sterile act of people seeking profit only in their money and not in social relations and in work.*

The strangeness of this prohibition lies elsewhere; it is in the consideration that lending money to someone is *never* a service that justifies a remuneration, especially if it is a consumer loan — the consideration that it is the equivalent of making someone pay for what should be free. They refused to see any service there, and they considered that money was sterile if it is alone. From this point of view, we either co-invest — and it is not money alone that produces, but the association of which it is an element — or we lend out of solidarity, instead of simply giving. If you want to justify claiming more than what was supplied, there must be a link with the creation of wealth, in the form of an association (with its risks), aiming at fructification, the result being shared.[9] We can see how this is consistent with its moral basis; we can also see that the condemnation presupposes a certain underlying analysis of the economic operation. But this analysis runs up against experience, even at that time, and further examination shows it is questionable.

Clavero and interest-bearing loans

We shall understand it better with Clavero's help,[10] following on his earlier analysis. He applies it directly to the case of usury: he says that if a loan is considered legally from the perspective of justice, there must be strict equality between what is given and what is received, and "therefore" we can in no case receive more than what we have

---

9 Admittedly, compensation may be capped, resulting in interest, provided the loan is at risk and made to a genuine company. See Tiberghien, op. cit., who thus justifies the principle of bonds.

10 Clavero, *La grâce du don.*

lent. Yet, from the broader perspective of generosity, one has to lend without expecting anything in exchange. But naturally, according to the same principle, *morally* there is, or ought to be, gratitude from the recipient, hence a gift in return (*antidora*), which might then resemble interest, with these two essential differences: first, that it should never be expected or even stipulated, and second, that it cannot be fixed in advance in any way. Hence "usury is above all a mental fact, a behavior that is essentially characterized by its intention." And he quotes J. T. Noonan saying that: "in the Middle Ages the counterpart of loans took explicitly the form of a gift."[11]

This presentation is ambiguous. It replaces, in fact, a conception, that of the epoch, which brings together economic logic and religious morality, by another conception in which economic reality[12] has no place. This is indefensible: in general, there is no valid morality without a well-founded analysis of the reality to which it applies. In this case, we're talking about monetary transactions that must be analyzed as such according to their logic, which is economic in the general sense of the term (even if the term did not then exist), at least in the case of commercial transactions. Concretely, if interest was condemned in lending operations, it was not because economic profit was condemned, as Clavero[13] wrongly says, but because *that specific profit was regarded as unjustified*, and if it was considered unjustified, it is both for moral or religious reasons, and for reasons that we would call economic. We shall therefore make the same remark here as on Clavero's general conception: the doctrine of the time cannot be criticized at the level of the moral structure on which it is founded. The current view that any transaction, any price, any profit is lawful *a priori* if the parties are consenting, is actually morally reprehensible, not only according to the views of the Middle Ages, but according to morality in general. Morality asks us to determine whether we are

---

11 Ibid., resp. p. 8 and p. 17.
12 Understood as a material activity translated into prices. As such, it obviously existed in these societies. But this does not mean they were "economic" in the sense of our political economy, which is a peculiar reading of it; applied to that time, it is actually inadequate and disabling because its origin is in a different anthropological background.
13 Clavero, *La grâce du don*, op. cit., including p. 65: "the very rejection of the idea of naked, purely economic gain constituted a characteristic trait, not only of moral theory, but also of jurisprudence." No: what was refused was gain itself, sought for itself, with no accompanying service.

being fair with somebody else, and this implies a form of equality or proportionality of terms. The problem raised by the doctrine of that time is elsewhere: again, it is in the economic part.

The theoretical reasoning in favor of prohibition

The central point is the preconceived idea of that time (that historians dealing with the question do not sufficiently point out) that any loan (in Latin *mutuum*) is a pure operation of exchange of the same thing in the two directions, involving only the quantities lent and returned: hence the strict demand for equality between them.[14] But in fact, on the contrary, *every loan, by its very nature, contains the provision of a service that, in commutative justice, justifies a remuneration*, especially since resources are drawn that could otherwise beget a lawful product. And therefore, a return in interest is in any case lawful, if not necessary. To recognize it does not exclude the possibility, which can be laudable for appropriate transactions, of operating on the basis of gifts, with the expectation of a counter-gift in the name of charity. But we are then on another level.

Let us take up Aquinas's analysis again, and his distinction between the two types of goods, consumable or not. It seems *a priori* sensible: he who uses a house does not consume it, except for negligible details; we can thus easily distinguish the possession of a house from its use, and this use can be sold separately: this is called rent. On the other hand, the only way to use bread is to make it disappear, and the one who derives profit from it by eating it no longer has that same bread to return. But why can it be inferred from that that the borrower must restore only the same bread, whereas the lender could have sold the bread, invested the money in a productive activity and derived a legitimate profit from it? The biblical idea was that the borrower of bread is hungry; once his hunger is satisfied and his needs met, if he has to return something, it is fair that he gives back bread, no more. This puts us in the case of the provision of means to someone in need; this action is a matter of solidarity. And for the old Christian society,

---

14   Denis Ramelet cited Benedict XIV, who wrote that usury "consists in the fact that someone wants by virtue of the loan itself—which by its nature requires that what is to be given back is equivalent to what has been received—that more should be paid than what has been received" (*Vix pervenit* § 3 / I, DS 2546).

the social bond has to be in principle interpersonal and free. That is indisputable. But why should we *always* regard interest as a sin, and forbid it? Because the other idea that no service or investment was provided came into play.

Certainly, in a consumer loan transaction there is no *production*, but why would not there be any service? If in exchange there must be a form of equality, in the loan what is exchanged is the use of a monetary or monetizable asset for a set period, in exchange for something that has no reason to be limited to the quantity lent. Of course, the lender does not provide any work, but apart from the fact that he delivers a real service, he deprives himself of his property for a period of time, and, as has been said, he could have used it in another, profitable way, which was lawful for the medieval economic culture as it is for ours. If the money was used to build a house and then to lease it, it would allow the creation of a property that would produce a lawful regular income, exceeding its own value. If somebody had built the house and collected the rents, the lender would have received this flow of income. The same if that somebody had invested in a commercial transaction, or in the capital of a company. It is therefore normal that people should be compensated for lending: there is an intrinsic *"lucrum cessans"* because *money is representative of possible alternative investments, and the fact that someone parts with it provides a scarce service that it is fair to pay for.* Moreover, money is also a means of exchange. Where the reasoning of that epoch is again curious is when it was said that when money is spent, it is consumed like bread. But eating bread and spending money are two different things: the money spent does not disappear, it is traded for something else — and it is this other thing that determines the meaning of the spending, since money is a universal means of mobilizing material resources. Furthermore, since the owner can use it in multiple ways, especially productive ones, there is a way to measure the service provided from the point of view of the owner: what money would have produced if used elsewhere.

In his assessment of Aquinas's reasoning, Kaye[15] stresses the importance of this concept of *aequitas*, a measurable equality between the two terms of a commercial transaction, purchase and sale.[16] But he

---

15 Kaye in Quaglioni, Todeschini, and Varanini, eds., *Credito e usura*, pp. 33 sqq.
16 This idea was reinforced by two assertions of the ancient doctrine (see Ramelet, op. cit., and Tiberghien, op. cit.). According to the first, the money

says, with this mechanically understood starting point, coupled with the idea that money is "consumed" in its use, Aquinas has impoverished the analysis of the role of money, compared with Aristotle or certain contemporaries, whose views led to a more nuanced appreciation. Certainly, he said, Aquinas recognized that human law, and not moral law, allows interest-bearing loans, given the practical advantages that it may entail. But as regards theory, according to Kaye, his analysis was more formal than moral, and quite narrow compared to his views on fair price (see chapter 2 on this point). He considered the loan without reference to the actual situation of the lender as well as of the borrower, who may have a legitimate need, justifying a payment to satisfy it, without being in actual shortage.

The object of the loan

This is best understood by considering of the object of the loan. Consider first consumer credit. Here again we must distinguish, by taking up the criterion of the usefulness, including the moral value, of the transaction: if lending to a needy person should not involve interest because it is an act of solidarity, what about a loan to a young couple who settles down and wants to buy appliances to equip their kitchen? By borrowing, they will obtain equipment immediately that will create a degree of well-being for their family, and it will probably allow them to save external expenses.[17] To do this, credit enables borrowers to mobilize now the future flow of wealth that they will be able to create in the future, generally through their salaries. And if it is lawful to lease the income of a city, it must also be possible to do that with the future income of a borrower who creates wealth. There is no reason why this loan would be unlawful,

---

lent becomes property of the borrower, who uses it freely. This is true for the most part, provided that this property remains burdened with the debt contracted. According to the second, the lender has no right to the product that the borrower draws from the investment of that money. But this is true only as regards what is specific of this product. But because the lender could have used his money elsewhere in a profitable way and provided a real service by lending, which therefore costs him (see above), he is entitled to a generic and non-specific remuneration.

17 Similarly, someone who has just got a job, and wishes to make a trip (a pilgrimage for example), therefore anticipates expense. Again, providing for this anticipation is a real service: in some cases, it can be morally better (or neutral) to have something at once rather than to have it later.

and why access to it should not be paid for,[18] since there is a real service coming from the mobilization of scarce resources, and again the money lent could have been invested in a productive activity. For the characteristic of a loan is that one lets someone dispose for a time of a sum of money that is not his. In so doing, it draws on the collectively available capital stock, which could have been used elsewhere and in particular used to produce.

This reasoning, which is compatible with the scholastic conception of economic activities, implies *a fortiori* the possibility of interest-bearing loans to finance productive investments. Let us recall that this is the area in which medieval people ultimately concluded the lawfulness of loans that in one way or another contribute to the creation or commercialization of a future flow of wealth. However, that did not follow the reasoning through to its complete conclusion, but it may be argued that capital goods only produce because someone cares for them, that is, does a job (including entrepreneurial work), and that these activities present a certain hazard. But if we can discuss the comparative degree of risk of the shareholder and the creditor, there is no doubt that the creditor of a company also participates in his own way in the creation of wealth. It may be argued that an association between the holder of funds and the entrepreneur, that is to say shareholding (a form of co-ownership), is better. This is very often true. But why limit licit funding to that case, which gives the investor full financial risk but also full compensation? It may be in the interest of both partners that another form of financing be chosen, which simultaneously reduces the risk *and* the remuneration of the investor. And in order to reduce the risk, the only way is to give priority to the provider of funds in the event of a bankruptcy, a certain guarantee that he will get back at least a part of his capital, and some fixed remuneration; this leads to interest-bearing loans.

---

18 If we examine it closely, it breaks down into what bankers call counterparty risk (the fact that some debtors do not repay), then into the remuneration of the bank's own funds (which are there to cover unforeseen risks and provide security to depositors); then the processing fee, and possibly other risks, such as interest rate risk (the bank's assets and liabilities may not be adequate) or even exchange rates risks. All these costs are in principle justified because they correspond to real services.

The role of time; stagnant economies and growing economies

Here, we have considered mainly the micro-economic level, that of the operators. At the collective level, what was most missing at the time was the prospect of employing money in alternative uses: John Finnis[19] rightly notes that now the existence of an active and liquid financial market makes it possible to know in a more objective way how to compensate a lender for the fact that he could have made an alternate financial investment: there is a global matching of the possible uses of money.[20] As was not possible during the Middle Ages and the Renaissance, the service can now be measured using the money market if it works properly (and morally), because it is the matching of socially available offers and demands of money to be lent or borrowed.

An important point that appears here is the role of time in the economy, what time adds to the collective wealth. In a growing economy, it is clear to all that money allows projects to start and develop, thereby increasing collective wealth; economists have even shown that in theory the interest rate should be equal to the rate of growth, all other things being equal. This means that the average rate at which loans are made is the rate at which the economy grows.[21] On the other hand, in an economy without growth, or rather, which considers itself to be such, as was the case in the past, it is not clearly perceptible. The stock of capital was stable; money only served to replace the existing stock or to organize the transfer of goods between thrifty families and poorly managed families. One might then be tempted to say that the "basic" remuneration of money (excluding risk and expense) "should" be zero. And the only borrowers that remained were the poor or the spendthrift, meaning people who consume now what they will not be able to repay later. We know that charging interest on them does not make sense: we are indeed

19 John Finnis, *Aquinas: Moral, Political, and Legal Theory* (Oxford: Oxford University Press, 1998), pp. 206 sqq.
20 We have spoken up to now of the interest rate as if it were unique. But the remuneration of money is measured in increments, very low for short loans without risk, much higher for equity holdings in new companies. And there is a strong correlation between levels of risk and remuneration.
21 In this case, an interesting point in terms of fairness is that creditors, at loan maturities, get the fraction of the national purchasing power that they had at the beginning, since their assets grow at the same rate as national wealth. This seems fair.

following the assumptions of our authors. This makes prohibition more understandable. That said, even in this case the outright prohibition of interest remains debatable. Because in any case loans are useful to finance repairs or new construction, or for people who start their working lives or for projects to replace disappearing activities. An economy is never purely stagnant: some people start and create, for example, when they build new houses, and others destroy assets or let them deteriorate. So, there are always pockets of growth, while capital is limited in quantity. For these transactions, a moderate interest rate is justified, as we have seen.

REAL LESSONS FOR THE FUTURE
The true message of the doctrine: money and its destination

But at the same time, it would be a grave mistake to confine ourselves to the foregoing considerations, for the principal lesson of this doctrinal experience would be lost. In the first place, economic analysis must be distinguished from moral appraisal. Fundamentally, *the first essential message in the condemnation of usury is that money, on its own, is sterile.* Now, morally and socially, this message is just. Money produces nothing by itself, and he who relies on money alone to make profits makes an error that is in general also a grave sin; it amounts to considering that one can withdraw from the community to rely solely on a material factor, committing besides the sin of pride. This mistake and defect is widespread in the present day, it goes without saying. In the second place, in the foregoing reasoning, we have taken for granted the modern hypothesis of the total *fungibility* of money. But then we get out of the mental framework of our authors, medieval and classical, and we lose the lesson they can bring to us. For to them in a certain way, *every use of money pertains to a certain type of human relationship*, and there is no reason to separate these uses and these relationships. And this idea keeps all its value. In other words, *each holder of wealth has a set of social roles to play, which includes a financial dimension, but is not limited to it.* There is no reason to consider money in the same way in all these configurations. On the contrary, a person who engages in financial transactions such as an equity investment has no reason to act with the same criteria if he then lends some money to a neighbor or someone in his family. And especially from a Christian perspective, he has every reason *not* to act with the same criteria.

However, this does not take away anything from the previous arguments about the legitimacy of an interest as a possible reference in the various acceptable cases of consumer or production credit. Nor even does it call into question the legality of the financial market as a whole. Indeed, we saw in a previous chapter *the utility of the market as a social instrument to try to arrive at the best possible approximation of a fair price*, provided, of course, that it works correctly and that it is managed by reasonably well-intentioned people. We saw that this was recognized by our scholastics. If it is true of each of these market sectors, it will be even more true of the relations between them: indeed, it is both inevitable and beneficial that the participants compare the possible solutions. If, for example, there is very little money going to consumer credit, and therefore interest rates are high, it is good for investors to put the money used elsewhere into that consumer lending. But *this leads us, and the point is again very important, to emphasize the significance of the purposes that holders of capital recognize.* Remember that the anathema against usury struck those who hoard, speculate in the wrong sense, leave money inactive or misused, or seek to make a disordered use of it. This reprobation keeps its full value. *The taboo was fundamentally against a misuse of money: it was right in that. The misuse of money remains bad. And besides, it was intended to promote another, more generous, use of money.*

This leads us to qualify the appreciation of this extraordinary historical adventure. Fr Hugues Puel,[22] analyzing what he calls the doctrinal fury of the Church against interest, believes that this is "due to the importance of their representation of the economy as a 'natural' economy. It is striking," so he says, "that the problems of investment and financial economy have never been fully dealt with in the great official texts of the Social Doctrine of the Catholic Church, as if there remained a basic refusal of the reality of a modern economy as a monetary economy of production and exchange." We can only partially adhere to this assessment. That there has been a one-off error is indisputable; it resides in the insufficient analysis of the money market and its function. Besides, of course, many ecclesiastical officials do not understand economic and financial realities. *But the basic intuitions of this thinking were correct, considered at the level that is the only one in which the Church claims itself competent: faith and morals; in this*

---

22   Hugues Puel in Dembinski, ed., *Pratiques financière*, p. 184.

case it is social morality. Paolo Prodi[23] is closer to the truth when he places usury within the more general problem of the relationship between business practices and societal values, stressing that the word *fides*, whose connotations refer to faith, trust, and fidelity, has a triple value to be considered together: theological, economic, and political. They cannot be separated, and we must constantly go from one to the other. In short, the sacred cannot deny the market where it has a meaning, and vice versa. But the existence of the financial market does not necessarily justify any use that is made of it, or any use one makes of money in general: sometimes it is investment in companies sharing their risks; sometimes it is solidarity and gift. Medieval people understood that, even though their analysis had its limitations from a purely financial point of view.

Donation or credit, direct relations or neutral market: the debate

But are we not embellishing this historical experience, which valued or encouraged gifts and relations between people, at least for certain uses of money? Drawing lessons from her study of pre-industrial practices, Laurence Fontaine concludes in a more critical way.[24] She notes that poverty was then constantly present, even though it was partly subjective, as now. To get out of poverty or even just to subsist, a minimum of capital was required, but also a market access in the broad sense, because at that time everyone was more or less marketable. Social, particularly familial, ties helped a great deal, but if there were no other means, they would resort to usury. The current need of microcredit therefore had its equivalent in pre-industrial Europe. The mounts of piety played their part well, but with the limitation of the ambiguity of their relationship to gift, which Fontaine says persists today. In fact, she says, for the weakest, market access is a powerful tool to get out of poverty:[25] the market must therefore be rehabilitated for the benefit of the poor. She notes that alternative thinkers insist on networks and donation, but the old regimes just functioned on this basis; as their example shows, this creates interpersonal dependencies

---

23   Paolo Prodi in Quaglioni, Todeschini, and Varanini, eds., *Credito e usura*, pp. 291 sqq.

24   Fontaine, *L'économie morale*, pp. 309 sqq.

25   She notes that today with eBay or garage sales, we see a re-appropriation of the market. She rightly adds that access to the market today, as in the past, requires, in addition to capital, know-how and training.

and therefore effects of domination. According to her, the market existing throughout pre-industrial Europe was already more a carrier of democracy (and individualism) than gift: thus "from the sixteenth century, Montaigne preferred the market to gift because with the market, he said, 'I only give money,' whereas with gift 'I give myself.'"[26] In addition, informal finance is expensive; as soon as the networks exceed a small number of people, fraud appears. Fontaine concludes[27] that it would be better not to "embellish gift with virtues it never had as such," especially since it has never ceased to exist in our financialized economy. And she agrees with Amartya Sen: give everyone the opportunity to take part in the market.

We cannot follow her on this ground. Her remarks are largely well founded. But as she notes herself, the personalized credit practiced by these societies, coupled with an ethics of gift and solidarity, and with control of usury, played a major role in the survival of the poorest strata, then a large part of the population. And if gift, or a flexible and not very demanding form of credit, can accompany or imply a generally pre-existing form of social dependency and power relationships, better a creditor animated by such principles than a usurer! Better this kind of relationship than subprime credits that prove to be collectively ruinous! Or, as in France, the difficulty in access to credit for the poorest strata. Above all, she neglects the role of gift as the only creator of social ties.[28] *In fact, the question remains open: What is the proper use of credit? The answer certainly implies the existence of a recognized and objective money market. But this is not enough; it requires the prudence of borrowers and the flexibility of lenders, especially if the borrower is poor. And a sufficient level of solidarity and responsibility.*

Conclusion

To sum up, based on a foundation of moral and social conceptions consistent with Christian teaching, the condemnation of interest-bearing loans was also based on a specific perception of economic reality and notably the role of money. According to that condemnation, money is only an unproductive means of exchange, which cannot claim remuneration outside particular contexts like

26 Fontaine, *L'économie morale*, p. 325. You could answer that's the question!
27 Ibid., p. 334.
28 See again here Godbout and Caillé, *L'esprit du don*, op. cit.

productive investment or compensation. In a society without a clear notion of growth, where profitability was linked to specific operations, and which also had no unified money market, this appreciation was understandable. Interpersonal ties dominated very widely. As a result, they did not perceive that, being potentially fungible in its use, money used financially is potentially representative of an investment and that therefore lenders, whatever their motive, use a resource that can bring a remuneration. And on the borrower's side, he gets a service, for which it is normal to pay. On the other hand, *the moral idea remains true: fungible in its possible application, money is in a certain way morally and socially not fungible, if we place ourselves on the side of the one who holds it and uses it in an operation that is inserted in a human society in which the role of everybody is variable, be it lending, consumption, or a pure investment.* Now such actions are never morally and socially neutral: the one who engages in them is responsible for what he does and cannot therefore claim that these operations are equivalent, especially morally. Without going back to a society of pure interpersonal ties, we must do with money what Christianity understood: *combine the two references — on the one hand, the money market which objectivizes the selection criteria by matching needs and availability at the level of society, provided of course that the market functions properly, and on the other hand, the mobilization of the multiple interplay of human and social relations in which any economic act involves us, with the corresponding responsibility.* From this point of view, Simmel's classical analysis[29] of the neutrality of money, which is supposed to free us from "too restrictive" human relations, presents a substantial risk of moral mutilation (we shall come back to this).

Specifically, as a technique, interest-bearing loans are not only economically justified, but also morally grounded. Christianity, which rejects no tools, has no reason to reject this one more than any other. Of course, this does not justify high rates or an excessive expansion of credit: because of the relative rigidity of the commitment, credit remains a potentially dangerous tool for both the creditor and the debtor. And, in the case of the poorest borrowers, in the absence of donation, it requires a specific practice, which today is embodied by microcredit. As far as normal economic activity is concerned, credit

29 Georg Simmel, *Philosophie de l'argent* (Paris: Quadrige/Presses PUF, 1987/1999).

is appropriate if taken in measured doses, for relatively low risks, and for them only. The mental attitude that should govern lending, on both sides, is caution and restraint: the recognition of a responsibility in the decision to resort to it. And in the case of lending to people, we must consider human realities, in the line of ancient gentleness. *Credit is not the royal instrument of economic life in the literal sense of the word, the one that makes it live: this role is destined for equity.* The recent financial crisis confirms these considerations, as we shall see again. But above all, let us remember the central medieval lesson, which retains all its value: we must distinguish between the operations and their intentionality. *Lending, because we think this loan is useful, equitable, based on a flow of wealth that it allows or mobilizes, and inserted in a network of exchanges that contribute to weave the social bond, is a good thing. On the other hand, lending because one thinks that money is productive without reference to its social integration and one seeks to accumulate as much as possible is bad and naive.* There are no pure financial transactions, disconnected from the social fabric and moral requirements. It is an essential point of the teaching of the Church, as we shall see again.

SECOND PART

Economy and Finance:
Christian Teaching and Debates

CHAPTER 6

The Social Doctrine of the Church and Market Economy

CHANGE OF SCENERY. AFTER THIS BRILLIANT PERIOD, the creative thinking of the Church in economic and social matters experienced a long eclipse, say between the beginning of the seventeenth century and the middle of the nineteenth, when the first Social Christians appeared. What is now called the Social Doctrine of the Church or Catholic Social Teaching developed from a number of papal encyclicals, most famously from *Rerum novarum* in 1891. The context was then radically updated, not only because of the industrial revolution, but above all because of the secularization of society in its dominant and official strata, which resulted in the emergence of new doctrines, liberalism and socialism, and, more recently, the questioning of objective moral references that were consensual in the earlier period. This profoundly changed priorities in the reflection and communication of the Church: the affirmation of such a morality became a central priority. In this context, our subject, finance, was only rarely an object of specific development in the Social Doctrine. But the general context of that Doctrine is quite illuminating for finance, as we shall see.

PROPERTY, PEOPLE'S INITIATIVE, AND THE MARKET

As is well known, the Social Doctrine[1] is in favor of a decentralized, free-initiative economy based on ownership and the autonomy of individual persons. In this, it presents important connections with current liberalism,[2] with respect to which it had to define itself as a priority. But the differences are significant. First, in the discourse of the Church, it is about free initiative and the autonomy of persons, rather than about market mechanisms and competition. Secondly, the notion of the common good becomes central: the Social Doctrine insists that the functioning of the community, including the

---

1 Quotations below are from the translations on the Vatican site: http://w2.vatican.va/content/vatican/en.html.
2 Liberalism is understood here in the classical meaning of the word, focusing on freedom (free markets, etc.).

economy, must provide benefits to all its members, and that this common good, resulting from the community as such, inherently exceeds personal goods. Certainly, the free play of people's initiatives contributes strongly to this shared good. But the Church considers that this good is not automatically obtained in that way, including through the market, and that at least regulatory bodies are necessary. Above all, the common good cannot be achieved through competition, arbitrating between selfish objectives. For the Church, it is incumbent on people to act in the direction of goodness and *the Church does not believe that strictly selfish behavior leads to real good. The conscious search for the good therefore matters morally more than the "invisible hand" of the market.* That is a major divergence.

Right to private property and the universal destination of goods

Other discrepancies arise from this, particularly about property rights, which are important for finance. For the Social Doctrine, they must be exercised in the direction of the common good, especially with a view to the use of that property by labor. Not that owners must always be the ones who work on it. But they must always have in view that their asset is there so that it can be used in an optimal way from a collective point of view, especially through work. In addition, the wealthiest have a responsibility toward the poorest, and especially by way of sharing. This does not imply that the State or another entity should decide in their place, let alone dispossess them, except in special cases. But this implies that the use of these assets should be sound, and that this concern should be constantly present in the intentions and action of the owner. The right of property must therefore be clarified by what is called *the principle of the universal destination of goods*, the idea that the earth is given to the whole human race. As Leo XIII said in 1891: the earth, even though apportioned among private owners, ceases not thereby to minister to the needs of all. Such a principle also leads to the search for the widest possible dissemination of private property — but not to a massive intervention by the State, or a more or less confiscatory tax mechanism. The first priority is to ensure that the minimum that is "due" to all is accessible to all; secondly, there must be an active use of wealth by those to whom it is entrusted, in the direction of the common good. On one hand, they have to share out from their excess wealth; on the other hand, they must actively invest in what is socially useful, for example, the creation of enterprises that are sources of employment. If this use is abundant and generous, then one may speak of the virtue of "magnificence."

These principles go a long way. The conclusion is that "private property, in fact, is under a 'social mortgage,'" as Pope St John Paul II said (*Sollicitudo rei socialis*, no. 42). This does not mean that it must be managed exclusively for the benefit of the community, in the political sense of the word. But it cannot be used at will, subject to a solidarity levy: a redistribution tax does not dispense with one's duties on the remaining assets. *What is criticized is the liberal notion of an alleged right to use one's property as one wishes* (assuming it has been acquired legitimately), *the free interplay of egoisms being supposed to lead to the optimum*. Also, where there is "mortgage" there is a debt, and therefore if this debt is not honored, the property may have to be withdrawn.

The role of the market

Personal property means a matching of people's decisions, which constitutes a market. The right role and the correct use of the market, according to the Doctrine, are deduced from the preceding considerations; this is an important point for finance. The *Compendium* of the Social Doctrine of the Church describes the free market in no. 347[3] thus:

> The free market is an institution of social importance because of its capacity to guarantee effective results in the production of goods and services. Historically, it has shown itself able to initiate and sustain economic development over long periods. There are good reasons to hold that, in many circumstances, "*the free market* is the most efficient instrument for utilizing resources and effectively responding to needs" (CA). The Church's social doctrine appreciates the secure advantages that the mechanisms of the free market offer, making it possible as they do to utilize resources better and facilitating the exchange of products. These mechanisms "above all . . . give central place to the person's desires and preferences, which, in a contract, meet the desires and preferences of another person" (CA).

---

3   Following John Paul II in the encyclical *Centesimus annus*, in particular nos. 34 to 48. Hereafter "CA."

But the same text reminds us in no. 348 that:

The free market cannot be judged apart from the ends that it seeks to accomplish and from the values that it transmits on a societal level. Indeed, *the market cannot find in itself the principles for its legitimization*; it belongs to the consciences of individuals and to public responsibility to establish a just relationship between means and ends (CA). *The individual profit of an economic enterprise, although legitimate, must never become the sole objective. Together with this objective there is another, equally fundamental but of a higher order: social usefulness, which must be brought about not in contrast to but in keeping with the logic of the market.* When the free market carries out the important functions mentioned above it becomes a service to the common good and to integral human development. The inversion of the relationship between means and ends, however, can make it degenerate into an inhuman and alienating institution, with uncontrollable repercussions.

More specifically (350),

Market operators must be effectively free to compare, evaluate and choose from among various options. Freedom in the economic sector, however, must be regulated by appropriate legal norms so that it will be placed at the service of integral human freedom. "Economic freedom is only one element of human freedom. When it becomes autonomous, when man is seen more as a producer or consumer of goods than as a subject who produces and consumes in order to live, then economic freedom loses its necessary relationship to the human person and ends up by alienating and oppressing him" (CA 40).

Thus (349):

The Church's social doctrine, while recognizing the market as an irreplaceable instrument for regulating the inner workings of the economic system, points out the need for it to be firmly rooted in its ethical objectives, which ensure and at the same time suitably circumscribe the space within which it can operate autonomously [Paul VI, *Octogesima adveniens*]. The idea that the market alone can be entrusted with the task of supplying every category of goods cannot be shared, because such an idea is based on a reductionist vision of the person and society (CA). Faced with the concrete risk of an "idolatry" of the market, the Church's social doctrine underlines its limits, which are easily seen in its proven inability to satisfy important human needs, which require goods that "by their nature are not and cannot be mere commodities" (CA), goods that cannot be bought and sold according to the rule of the "exchange of equivalents" and the logic of contracts, which are typical of the market.

Limits of the market

Benedict XVI[4] clarified this point:

> 35. In a climate of mutual trust, the market is the economic institution that permits encounter between persons, inasmuch as they are economic subjects who make use of contracts to regulate their relations as they exchange goods and services of equivalent value between them, in order to satisfy their needs and desires. The market is subject to the principles of so-called *commutative justice*, which regulates the relations of giving and receiving between parties to a transaction. But the social doctrine of the Church has unceasingly highlighted the importance of *distributive justice* and *social justice* for the market economy, not only because it belongs within a broader social and political context, but also because of the wider network of relations within which it operates. In fact, if the market is governed solely by the principle of the equivalence in value of exchanged goods, it cannot produce the social cohesion that it requires in order to function well. *Without internal forms of solidarity and mutual trust, the market cannot completely fulfill its proper economic function.* And today it is this trust that has ceased to exist, and the loss of trust is a grave loss.

The market is not self-sufficient: it needs other realities to exist, and not just the State. This is essential. It follows that:

> 36. Economic activity cannot solve all social problems through the simple application of *commercial logic*. This needs to be

---

4 Benedict XVI, *Caritas in veritate*, June 29, 2009, nos. 35 and 36.

directed toward the pursuit of the common good, for which the political community in particular must also take responsibility. Therefore, it must be borne in mind that grave imbalances are produced when economic action, conceived merely as an engine for wealth creation, is detached from political action, conceived as a means for pursuing justice through redistribution. The Church has always held that economic action is not to be regarded as something opposed to society.

And here the pope comes to another point, which is essential:

In and of itself, the market is not, and must not become, the place where the strong subdue the weak. Society does not have to protect itself from the market, as if the development of the latter were *ipso facto* to entail the death of authentically human relations. Admittedly, the market can be a negative force, not because it is so by nature, but because a certain ideology can make it so. *It must be remembered that the market does not exist in the pure state. It is shaped by the cultural configurations that define it and give it direction. Economy and finance, as instruments, can be used badly when those at the helm are motivated by purely selfish ends.* Instruments that are good in themselves can thereby *be transformed into harmful ones*. But it is man's darkened reason that produces these consequences, not the instrument *per se*. Therefore, *it is not the instrument that must be called to account, but individuals, their moral conscience and their personal and social responsibility.*

We find here a leitmotiv: the Doctrine does not criticize the tool (with proper regulation) so much as the motivations of those who use it, which can completely change its effect. This point is essential — especially today.

Gratuitousness

This goes a long way because for Benedict XVI, it is within the very heart of economic activity that these concerns must intervene, including gratuitousness. Pope Benedict continues:

The Church's social doctrine holds that authentically human social relationships of friendship, solidarity, and reciprocity can also be conducted within economic activity, and not only outside it or "after" it. *The economic sphere is neither ethically neutral, nor inherently inhuman and opposed to society.* It is part and parcel of human activity and precisely because it is human, it must be structured and governed in an ethical manner. The great challenge before us, accentuated by the problems of development in this global era and made even more urgent by the economic and financial crisis, is to demonstrate, in thinking and behavior, not only that traditional principles of social ethics like transparency, honesty, and responsibility cannot be ignored or attenuated, but also that *in commercial relationships the principle of gratuitousness and the logic of gift* as an expression of fraternity *can and must find their place within normal economic activity.* This is a human demand at the present time, but it is also demanded by economic logic. It is a demand both of charity and of truth.

This point is essential: *besides the phase of calculation, or even before it, there is necessarily the phase of gift.* Nothing is complete or even possible without gift. In a certain way, it amounts to asserting the insufficiency of any mastery and any narrow calculation. This is directly relevant to finance, since it seems to be, by definition, the very opposite of gratuitousness, because pursuing a monetary result and measuring has a central role there. That said, it is not relevant to dream of absolute gratuitousness. What is at stake here is, first, not to look systematically for a return from everything we do. And then to put our personal objectives in a broader framework of reference. The pope links this to three terms: solidarity, justice, and the common good. And in the final analysis, to the *creation of the social bond.*[5]

Action by the State

All this makes it possible to clarify what is expected from the State. Its role is to provide more structuring action than in the liberal (free market) approach; it is to establish rules aiming at harmonization and orientation, in particular for purposes of solidarity. It only goes further in exceptional cases, such as when the market (people's initiative) does not produce the results that are expected of it. The *Compendium* notes in no. 351 that:

---

5   Thus, in a certain way, we find some convergence with the theses of Jacques Godbout and others on the role of gift—but placed in the more fundamental context of Christian charity. Godbout and Caillé, *L'esprit du don,* op. cit.

the action of the State and of other public authorities must be consistent with the principle of subsidiarity and create situations favorable to the free exercise of economic activity. It must also be inspired by the principle of solidarity and establish limits for the autonomy of the parties in order to defend those who are weaker.... In order to respect both of these fundamental principles, the State's intervention in the economic environment must be neither invasive nor absent, but commensurate with society's real needs. "The State has a duty to sustain business activities by creating conditions that will ensure job opportunities, by stimulating those activities where they are lacking or by supporting them in moments of crisis. The State has the further right to intervene when particular monopolies create delays or obstacles to development. In addition to the tasks of harmonizing and guiding development, in exceptional circumstances the State can also exercise a substitute function" (CA 48).

Because (no. 352):

The fundamental task of the State in economic matters is that of determining an appropriate juridical framework for regulating economic affairs, in order to safeguard "the prerequisites of a free economy, which presumes a certain equality between the parties, such that one party would not be so powerful as practically to reduce the other to subservience" (CA 15). Economic activity, above all in a free market context, cannot be conducted in an institutional, juridical, or political vacuum. "On the contrary, it presupposes sure guarantees of individual freedom and private property, as well as a stable currency and efficient public services" (CA 48).

Ultimately (no. 353):

It is necessary for the market and the State to act in concert, one with the other, and to complement each other mutually. In fact, the free market can have a beneficial influence on the general public only when the State is organized in such a manner that it defines and gives direction to economic development, promoting the observation of fair and transparent rules, and making direct interventions — only for the length of time strictly necessary (CA 48) — when the market is not able to obtain the desired efficiency and when it is a question of putting the principle of redistribution into effect. There exist certain sectors in which the market, making use of the mechanisms at its disposal, is not able to guarantee an equitable distribution of the goods and services that are essential for the human growth of citizens. In such cases the complementarities of State and market are needed more than ever.

Therefore (no. 354):

> With a view to the common good, it is necessary to pursue always and with untiring determination the goal of a proper equilibrium between private freedom and public action, understood both as direct intervention in economic matters and as activity supportive of economic development. In any case, public intervention must be carried out with equity, rationality and effectiveness, and without replacing the action of individuals, which would be contrary to their right to the free exercise of economic initiative. In such cases, the State becomes detrimental to society: a direct intervention that is too extensive ends up depriving citizens of responsibility and creates excessive growth in public agencies guided more by bureaucratic logic than by the goal of satisfying the needs of the person (CA 48).

Capitalism: a "balanced response"

But "decentralized," or "market economy" does not necessarily mean capitalism, even if this is the case in our societies. What the Social Doctrine tells us about the present economic system is consistent with the points just mentioned. Thus, *Centesimus annus* at no. 35:

> In this sense, it is right to speak of a struggle against an economic system, if the latter is understood as a method of upholding the absolute predominance of capital, the possession of the means of production and of the land, in contrast to the free and personal nature of human work. In the struggle against such a system, what is being proposed as an alternative is not the socialist system, which in fact turns out to be State capitalism, but rather *a society of free work, of enterprise, and of participation*. Such a society is not directed against the market but demands that the market be appropriately controlled by the forces of society and by the State, so as to guarantee that the basic needs of the whole of society are satisfied.

And even more so in no. 42:

> Can it perhaps be said that, after the failure of Communism, capitalism is the victorious social system, and that capitalism should be the goal of the countries now making efforts to rebuild their economy and society?... The answer is obviously complex. If by "capitalism" is meant an economic system which recognizes the fundamental and positive role of business, the market, private property and the resulting responsibility for the means of production, as well as free human creativity in the economic sector, then the answer is certainly in the affirmative, even though it would perhaps be more appropriate to speak of a "business economy," "market economy," or simply "free economy." But if by "capitalism" is meant a system in which freedom in the economic sector is not circumscribed within a strong juridical framework which places it at the service of human freedom in its totality, and which sees it as a particular aspect of that freedom, the core of which is ethical and religious, then the reply is certainly negative.

THE COMPANY AND ITS PURPOSE

Private ownership and the market today take a particular form: the enterprise. The connection between capital and labor is an essential question, especially for our exploration of finance.

Capital and labor: What are we talking about?

In *Laborem exercens*, the priority of work is clearly affirmed by John Paul II, no. 12:

> We must first of all recall a principle that has always been taught by the Church: the principle of the priority of labor over capital. This principle directly concerns the process of production: in this process labor is always a primary efficient cause, while capital, the whole collection of means of production, remains a mere instrument or instrumental cause. This principle is an evident truth that emerges from the whole of man's historical experience.... Since the concept of capital includes not only the natural resources placed at man's disposal but also the whole collection of means by which man appropriates natural resources and transforms them in

accordance with his needs (and thus in a sense humanizes them), it must immediately be noted that all these means are the result of the historical heritage of human labor.... We must emphasize and give prominence to the primacy of man in the production process, the primacy of man over things. *Everything contained in the concept of capital in the strict sense is only a collection of things. Man, as the subject of work, and independently of the work that he does — man alone is a person.*

From this point of view, it can and must be said that production associates capital and labor and that they must not be opposed but complementary, but this cannot bring us to put them at the same level: the first is physical, the second is human. This implies in particular that the interest of capital cannot be the only criterion of decision.

The pope goes on to say in no. 13:

A labor system can be right, in the sense of being in conformity with the very essence of the issue, and in the sense of being intrinsically true and also morally legitimate, if in its very basis it overcomes the opposition between labor and capital *through an effort at being shaped in accordance with the principle put forward above: the principle of the substantial and real priority of labor, of the subjectivity of human labor and its effective participation in the whole production process, independently of the nature of the services provided by the worker.*

That, he says, is opposed to a fundamental error of thought, which "economism" can imply, namely, that the materialistic conviction "of the primacy and superiority of the material ... directly or indirectly places the spiritual and the personal (man's activity, moral values, and such matters) in a position of subordination to material reality." Incidentally, this pope's understanding of work is more complex than that of his predecessors: it appears to encompass all human activity, including that of the entrepreneur. When former popes spoke of "capital," they included under this category owners and bosses. Now it seems that pure, material capital, and possibly its proprietor as a pure owner of it, is opposed to the acting man, including entrepreneur-owners. Here we find an echo of current themes.

Business and work

The pope develops his idea in no. 15:

> The Church's teaching has always expressed the strong and deep conviction that man's work concerns not only the economy but also, and especially, personal values.... In the mind of Saint Thomas Aquinas, this is the principal reason in favor of private ownership of the means of production. While we accept that for certain well-founded reasons exceptions can be made to the principle of private ownership — in our own time we even see that the system of "socialized ownership" has been introduced — nevertheless the personalist argument still holds good both on the level of principles and on the practical level. If it is to be rational and fruitful, any socialization of the means of production must take this argument into consideration. Every effort must be made to ensure that in this kind of system also the human person can preserve his awareness of working "for himself." If this is not done, incalculable damage is inevitably done throughout the economic process, not only economic damage but first and foremost damage to man.

For it is necessary to dispel an illusion (no. 14):

> Merely converting the means of production into State property in the collectivist system is by no means equivalent to "socializing" that property. *We can speak of socializing only when the subject character of society is ensured, that is to say, when on the basis of his work each person is fully entitled to consider himself a part-owner of the great workbench at which he is working with everyone else.*[6]

It follows (CA no. 43) that:

---

6 As the pope continues, he recommends exploring the following path: "a way toward that goal could be found by associating labor with the ownership of capital, as far as possible, and by producing a wide range of intermediate bodies with economic, social, and cultural purposes; they would be bodies enjoying real autonomy with regard to the public powers, pursuing their specific aims in honest collaboration with each other and in subordination to the demands of the common good, and they would be living communities both in form and in substance, in the sense that the members of each body would be looked upon and treated as persons and encouraged to take an active part in the life of the body."

A business cannot be considered only as a "society of capital goods"; it is also a "society of persons" in which people participate in different ways and with specific responsibilities, whether they supply the necessary capital for the company's activities or take part in such activities through their labor. To achieve these goals there is still need for a broad associated workers' movement, directed toward the liberation and promotion of the whole person. [...] Ownership of the means of production, whether in industry or agriculture, is just and legitimate if it serves useful work. It becomes illegitimate, however, when it is not utilized or when it serves to impede the work of others, in an effort to gain a profit that is not the result of the overall expansion of work and the wealth of society, but rather is the result of curbing them or of illicit exploitation, speculation, or the breaking of solidarity among working people. *Ownership of this kind has no justification and represents an abuse in the sight of God and man.* The obligation to earn one's bread by the sweat of one's brow also presumes the right to do so. A society in which this right is systematically denied, in which economic policies do not allow workers to reach satisfactory levels of employment, cannot be justified from an ethical point of view, nor can that society attain social peace. Just as the person fully realizes himself in the free gift of self, so too ownership morally justifies itself in the creation, at the proper time and in the proper way, of opportunities for work and human growth for all.

In practice, this view leads to considering the complete separation of labor and property as a real problem, a regression from earlier forms of organization of the economy, where the artisan and the peasant were (or could be) owners of their work tools: the ideal would be in a sense to link work, property, and management to the greatest extent possible. Practical implementation of this is not simple; participation and employee ownership are recommended but not sufficient. In any case, shareholder ownership is not condemned, but it involves duties on the part of shareholders, in particular in relation to the persons they directly or indirectly employ, including, among other things, the search for participatory forms of operation for the company, as a community of people. Or new types of companies.

Value and profit in the company

That said, the responsibility of the company, and therefore of its owners, does not stop at work. Another point concerns the use of the goods produced, and therefore their value, expressed in intrinsic terms and not solely on the basis of their market potential. This implies that this production is directed toward socially beneficial goods or services. More precisely, what gives meaning to products is that they serve the development of the human person in accordance with the divine plan, which includes the production of goods and services for the common good of mankind. This essential point would need to be developed but is outside our scope here; indeed, in our time the question of what to produce becomes crucial, to a degree never reached before.

The same considerations also lead to a balanced assessment of the notions of *profit and financial management* of the company. As we have seen, if the company is valued as a place of free initiative, it is encouraged to be primarily a community of people and therefore cannot operate solely on the basis of profit. Lust for power or greed cannot be the driving forces, because they are in contradiction with the notion of human community. Profitability, productivity, competition, and more generally efficiency, measured financially, are therefore not primary principles; they are *tools* for other purposes. Pope John Paul II told us, for example (CA no. 35) that:

> The Church acknowledges the legitimate role of profit as an indication that a business is functioning well. When a firm makes a profit, this means that productive factors have been properly employed and corresponding human needs have been duly satisfied. But profitability is not the only indicator of a firm's condition. It is possible for the financial accounts to be in order, and yet for the people — who make up the firm's most valuable asset — to be humiliated and their dignity offended. Besides being morally inadmissible, this will eventually have negative repercussions on the firm's economic efficiency. In fact, the purpose of a business firm is not simply to make a profit, but is to be found in its very existence as a community of persons who in various ways are endeavoring to satisfy their basic needs, and who form a particular group at the service of the whole of society. Profit is a regulator of the life of a business, but it is not the only one; other human

and moral factors must also be considered which, in the long term, are at least equally important for the life of a business.

Or, as Benedict XVI[7] says, "Profit is useful if it serves as a means toward an end that provides a sense both of how to produce it and how to make good use of it. Once profit becomes the exclusive goal, if it is produced by improper means and without the common good as its ultimate end, it risks destroying wealth and creating poverty."

The company and its multiple responsibility

Benedict XVI[8] addresses even more directly the question of the owner of capital and that of the multiple responsibilities of the enterprise:

> Today's international economic scene, marked by grave deviations and failures, requires a profoundly new way of understanding business enterprise. Old models are disappearing, but promising new ones are taking shape on the horizon. Without doubt, one of the greatest risks for businesses is that they are almost exclusively answerable to their investors, thereby limiting their social value. Owing to their growth in scale and the need for more and more capital, it is becoming increasingly rare for business enterprises to be in the hands of a stable director who feels responsible in the long term, not just the short term, for the life and the results of his company, and it is becoming increasingly rare for businesses to depend on a single territory. Moreover, the so-called outsourcing of production can weaken the company's sense of responsibility toward the stakeholders — namely the workers, the suppliers, the consumers, the natural environment, and broader society — in favor of the shareholders, who are not tied to a specific geographical area and who therefore enjoy extraordinary mobility. Today's international capital market offers great freedom of action.

Let us note the reasoning: at the center of that evolution is the leader, who can now more easily disengage from his or her multiple responsibilities, to favor only the shareholders, themselves favored by their own mobility.

---

7 Benedict XVI, *Caritas in veritate*, no. 21.
8 Ibid., no. 40.

The pope insists on the distinction between the criteria that should govern the company and the sole interest of the shareholders:

> Yet there is also increasing awareness of the need for greater social responsibility on the part of business. Even if the ethical considerations that currently inform debate on the social responsibility of the corporate world are not all acceptable from the perspective of the Church's social doctrine, there is nevertheless a growing conviction that business management cannot concern itself only with the interests of the proprietors, but must also assume responsibility for all the other stakeholders who contribute to the life of the business: the workers, the clients, the suppliers of various elements of production, the community of reference. In recent years a new cosmopolitan class of managers has emerged, who are often answerable only to the shareholders generally consisting of anonymous funds which *de facto* determine their remuneration. By contrast, though, many far-sighted managers today are becoming increasingly aware of the profound links between their enterprise and the territory or territories in which it operates.

He then stresses the link between the company and its country of origin, without calling into question the possibility that globalization provides benefits:

> Paul VI invited people to give serious attention to the damage that can be caused to one's home country by the transfer abroad of capital purely for personal advantage.[9] John Paul II taught that investment always has moral, as well as economic significance.[10] All this — it should be stressed — is still valid today, despite the fact that the capital market has been significantly liberalized, and modern technological thinking can suggest that investment is merely a technical act, not a human and ethical one. There is no reason to deny that a certain amount of capital can do good, if invested abroad rather than at home. Yet the requirements of justice must be safeguarded, with due consideration for the way in which the capital was generated and the harm to individuals that will result if it is not used where it was produced.

---

9   Cf. ibid., n. 24; *DC* 64 (1967), col. 682–83.
10 John Paul II, *Centesimus annus*, n. 36.

Moreover,

> What should be avoided is a speculative use of financial resources that yields to the temptation of seeking only short-term profit, without regard for the long-term sustainability of the enterprise, its benefit to the real economy, and attention to the advancement, in suitable and appropriate ways, of further economic initiatives in countries in need of development.[11]

Furthermore,

> What should be avoided is a speculative *use of financial resources* that yields to the temptation of seeking only short-term profit, without regard for the long-term sustainability of the enterprise, its benefit to the real economy and attention to the advancement, in suitable and appropriate ways, of further economic initiatives in countries in need of development.[12]

With regard to the responsibilities of the various parties, the distinction between the entrepreneur and the shareholder, between the interests of the shareholders and the aims of the company is noteworthy. They must take into account the responsibility of the company toward all stakeholders, including the regions, in particular the region of origin. Compliance with these responsibilities is primarily the responsibility of the chief executive officer (CEO). But note the passage condemning speculative profit and short-term mentalities: logically it is addressed not only to the director, but also to the holders of capital, to the shareholders. *For, once again, if the text does not condemn the structure of the joint-stock company, it ambitiously gives it a framework by requiring shareholders not to use their power so that the managers of the company serve only financial profit, but so that they care about all the purposes for which the company is made.*

---

11   Cf. Paul VI, *Populorum progressio* (March 26, 1967), n. 24.

12   Coming back to globalization, Benedict went on to say: "It is true that the export of investments and skills can benefit the populations of the receiving country. Labor and technical knowledge are a universal good. Yet it is not right to export these things merely for the sake of obtaining advantageous conditions, or worse, for purposes of exploitation, without making a real contribution to local society by helping to bring about a robust productive and social system, an essential factor for stable development."

Which ethics should a company adopt?

If the aims of the enterprise are much broader than just the share-holder's profit, and must respect moral principles, we must understand better what morality we are talking about. Let us recall first that the intimate connection between economy and moral justice is a central point in the Social Doctrine.[13] Benedict XVI[14] goes on to state:

> The Church's social doctrine has always maintained that *justice must be applied to every phase of economic activity,* because this is always concerned with man and his needs. Locating resources, financing, production, consumption and all the other phases in the economic cycle inevitably have moral implications. *Thus, every economic decision has a moral consequence.* The social sciences and the direction taken by the contemporary economy point to the same conclusion. Perhaps at one time it was conceivable that first the creation of wealth could be entrusted to the economy, and then the task of distributing it could be assigned to politics. Today that would be more difficult, given that economic activity is no longer circumscribed within territorial limits, while the authority of governments continues to be principally local. Hence *the canons of justice must be respected from the outset, as the economic process unfolds, and not just afterward or incidentally. Space also needs to be created within the market for economic activity carried out by subjects who freely choose to act according to principles other than those of pure profit, without sacrificing the production of economic value in the process.* The many economic entities that draw their origin from religious and lay initiatives demonstrate that this is concretely possible.

The pope goes on in no. 45:

> Striving to meet the deepest moral needs of the person also has important and beneficial repercussions at the level of economics. *The economy needs ethics in order to function*

---

13 Conversely, we know that in the dominant paradigm the *a priori* idea often prevails that capitalism is amoral, that it is useless to appeal to the morality of participants and that any regulation must be done by law (that is, using external coercion). This prejudice is unrealistic and if it were implemented literally, it would be impracticable. I have elaborated this point in a previous book *L'Economie et le christianisme,* op. cit.

14 Benedict XVI, *Caritas in veritate,* no. 37.

correctly—not any ethics whatsoever, but an ethics which is people-centered. Today we hear much talk of ethics in the world of economy, finance, and business. Research centers and seminars in business ethics are on the rise; the system of ethical certification is spreading throughout the developed world as part of the movement of ideas associated with the responsibilities of business toward society. Banks are proposing "ethical" accounts and investment funds. "Ethical financing" is being developed, especially through microcredit and, more generally, microfinance. These processes are praiseworthy and deserve much support.... It would be advisable, however, to develop a sound criterion of discernment, since the adjective "ethical" can be abused. When the word is used generically, it can lend itself to any number of interpretations, even to the point where it includes decisions and choices contrary to justice and authentic human welfare. *Much in fact depends on the underlying system of morality.* On this subject, the Church's social doctrine can make a specific contribution, since it is based on man's creation "in the image of God" (Gen 1:27), a datum which gives rise to *the inviolable dignity of the human person and the transcendent value of natural moral norms.* When business ethics prescinds from these two pillars, it inevitably risks losing its distinctive nature and it falls prey to forms of exploitation; more specifically, it risks becoming subservient to existing economic and financial systems rather than correcting their dysfunctional aspects. Among other things, it risks being used to justify the financing of projects that are in reality unethical. The word "ethical," then, should not be used to make ideological distinctions, as if to suggest that initiatives not formally so designated would not be ethical. Efforts are needed—and it is essential to say this—not only to create "ethical" sectors or segments of the economy or the world of finance, but to ensure that the whole economy—the whole of finance—is ethical, not merely by virtue of an external label, but by its respect for requirements intrinsic to its very nature.

One must also bear in mind that the temptation exists to base ethics on the sole evidence of a long-term superiority of the organization in question in achieving material success. It then quickly reaches its limits.

APPLICATION: CAPITAL AND ITS OWNERS

This of course has important consequences for the entire financial dimension of the economy. We will discuss finance itself in more detail; it is the subject of our study. But beforehand, we must raise the question of capital, its ownership and its use. As we have seen, no magisterial text condemns "capitalism" in itself; we can also refer to the texts of John Paul II for a definition of an "acceptable" capitalism: it would be a capitalism balanced on one hand by moral requirements, individual or associative, and on the other by action from the State. But that does not, of course, exhaust the subject.

Collective capitalism and entrepreneurs

The first question concerns the identity of these collective owners, the shareholders. Let us first put aside the question of inequality of fortunes, which is very important from other points of view, but not relevant to our purpose. The ultimate economic ownership of capital is rather dispersed in our economies and often detached from decision-making power, since institutional investors work for millions of savers: pension funds, insurance companies, and collective management. *The question of the ownership of capital and of its role is therefore distinct from that of inequalities.* An economy in which all companies (at least of a certain size) would be in the hands of such collective investors could have a relative equality of fortunes, and yet, with regard to the ownership and management of large firms, it would be no different from ours. And therefore, *one could have an excessive or abnormal influence of capital on the rest of society, of a type that will be called capitalist, even though there would be no more pure capitalists.*

On the other hand, of course, entrepreneurs, individual capitalists, have often built fortunes and thereby control large amounts of capital. But besides the fact that most of the capital in the economy does not belong to them, they are entrepreneurs, and as such are in general beneficial to society (subject to a precise examination of their concrete action). Let us be clear: in their case, inequality of wealth is fair and *a priori* useful. Removing them would have a negative collective effect. Let us add once more that if, according to the Social Doctrine, capital is accumulated historical labor, this term of "labor" must incorporate the entrepreneurial element; the initiative shown by the builder of a business is at the origin of the fortune in question, which fully legitimates that he holds it. *We can therefore have significant inequalities in wealth alongside a useful and even indispensable role of the holders of important resources.* Beyond these builders, the concentration of resources in private hands may be indispensable for certain achievements, which require important means that the State is unable to provide. These considerations do not justify any inequality whatsoever, nor do they call into question the Church's call for a widespread dissemination of property: but having as many owners as possible does not mean maximum equality, which the Church never demanded. But this makes it possible to better understand the questions: considerations of social equality can lead to some redistribution of fortunes and incomes, within certain limits, but it is not an absolute imperative and *aiming for relative equality will not necessarily give the desired results in terms of a socially and morally beneficial use of capital.*

Capital and labor

Ignorance of the Catholic principle of the priority of labor on capital is on the other hand a true distortion. This principle represents a major difference between the Social Doctrine and most economic theories. The Catholic conception links property rights to work: ownership is seen as accumulated labor and must be used in particular to create work and, if possible, work that is rewarding to the worker. The term "work" must once again include the activity of the entrepreneur. On the other hand, traditional political economy reasons on the basis of two factors of production, capital and labor, both necessary and of comparable weight. But it often seems to consider labor as a mere instrument, reduced to its pure economic component, and measurable on the corresponding market. Moreover, it individualizes capital as an autonomous reality, as if by itself it was creator of wealth. In the Catholic vision, labor (activity) is basically the sole creator: in the past, it was work that created the present capital; and it is work that uses capital to bring about production. This is the problem posed by John Paul II (*Laborem exercens*, no. 14): means of production "cannot be possessed against labor, they cannot even be possessed for possession's sake, because the only legitimate title to their possession — whether in the form of private ownership or in the form of public or collective ownership — is that they should serve labor, and thus, by serving labor, that they should make possible the achievement of the first principle of this order, namely, the universal destination of goods and the right to common use of them."

The question is how to achieve this goal in our society. In principle, the right (and duty) of those who work today is to be able to develop themselves personally through their work, through the mobilization of existing capital, in order to create goods and services, and to be paid and to be able to acquire a reasonable share of social wealth, including a certain amount of property. If they are to be able to do so, they must have an adequate share of capital, and in particular a share in their working tools. In other words, they are entitled to the proper use of capital. But not to an exclusive ownership of that capital, of which they would not necessarily make better use than the present owners, according to the same criteria. What is important to them as workers is the possibility of using work tools and therefore the part of capital that interests them directly — which does not necessarily imply ownership by them, although of course a certain stake in capital is quite advisable.

The priority of work does not imply that we do not recognize conceptually and juridically capital as such. Indeed, the fact that capital arises from previous work does not preclude it from existing. While it has taken the form of machines, installations, organizations, or collective resources such as roads, it constitutes a set of tools that should be used to the best advantage of all; capital in the form of savings represents a monetary right on goods available on the market. Consequently, there is no sense in pretending to eliminate the role of "owners," regardless of their identity: they are the ones who decide and are responsible for the use of these assets. In a decentralized economy, which is the only viable one, they are multiple and autonomous. The question is to find the optimal use of capital, which implies among other things to calculate it: this is precisely the object of finance. It involves matching all possible uses of this wealth with their optimal allocation — provided that, as far as possible, this is done in view of the end purpose resulting from the notions of common good, human development, and universal destination of goods, especially the priority given to work.

The necessary ethics of the owner and therefore of the shareholder

In our present structure, a partial owner of a firm (at least of a commercial company) is what we call a shareholder (we shall then examine the question of the modes of ownership). Who else is in charge of this responsibility, which is exercised first by defining the articles of incorporation, including the company's purpose, then through the appointment of managers, and includes the ability to sell the business? Not directly the managers, who have their own different responsibility, or if they undertake part of that responsibility, it is only so as managers appointed by the shareholders and by delegation.[15] Nor the State, except in case of nationalization, because it merely gives a legal framework to the decisions of shareholders and managers. The Church's discourse on the responsibilities of the owners, and in particular the universal destination of goods and the primacy of labor, applies to shareholders. It is therefore essential that they are aware of their duties and able to carry them out. This has consequences for the functioning of the financial markets — we will come to that. But before that, giving the main orientations to the company is the shareholders' responsibility.

In the case of institutional investors, there are two levels to consider. First, that of investors: beneficiaries and ultimate owners, holders of pension funds, of life insurance, or of mutual funds, and other funds. Second, that of the professional managers, to whom the money has been entrusted. As a minimum, investors must determine an investment strategy that, in addition to the financial dimension, includes a definition of the priorities to be promoted in the management of the companies in which they choose to invest. *Hence the absolute need for rules of responsible investment, which should not be the exception but the norm,*[16] *including monitoring companies' compliance with these rules.* Moreover, this must involve active participation in decisions, particularly through general meetings, especially if the investor or the manager is in charge of significant amounts. All this is not feasible without a significant intellectual and moral investment in the company in question, which means that it will not be easy or even possible without an important dimension of *long-term relationship*. We must not make an absolute precondition of that either: it is more important to see good guidelines adopted than to maintain a relationship if

15 Excluding special cases such as sponsorships, partnerships, etc.
16 We will not elaborate on this essential point: significant and complex work is needed, and partly under way, on this issue of Socially Responsible Investment. It includes an examination of the social, environmental, cultural, political, and other dimensions of a company's behavior, and the establishment of appropriate selection criteria. In both quantitative and conceptual terms, we are only at the beginning of this process. The same is true of the complex issue of the possible legal accountability of shareholders.

it is not really fruitful. Better sometimes that shareholders vote with their feet (as they say) by selling, if it is for a good reason.

Anyway, it is also clear in this respect that the role of the stock exchange and of financial intermediation in general should by nature be subordinate: it is an auxiliary in the formation of prices, the principal decision-maker being the owner, the investor. Even then, the role of finance in the broad sense remains important, as financiers are generally more competent and active than actual investors and can guide the functioning of the system. This is all the more true since this role is not limited to the allocation of resources, but also extends to that of power in the firms. And if the ultimate responsibility rests with the owners, in many cases they exercise it through finance. From this point of view, the role and responsibility of finance are essential.

Let us note incidentally an immediate consequence of the points just raised: *the unique and central importance of shares* among current financial instruments. Not only are they the only instruments that naturally cause an association with the risks and successes of the company, but they are the only ones that in principle give real power: the power of the owner of a company,[17] at least collectively. Other financial instruments are claims in one way or another, mainly debt securities: they give a certain right on the company, more precisely the right to a specific sum that can be claimed before courts. But this does not build a form of solidarity with the successes and failures of the company. *It is therefore essential that the tax and legal systems help and encourage shareholders to assume their responsibilities as mentioned above and recognize their unique role.* It should be noted that the reality is generally the opposite: most tax systems penalize shareholders in favor of creditors, improperly encouraging indebtedness, leverage, and diminished liability.

Other ways of holding capital?

We have reasoned on the basis of the existing system. What remains is to examine the hypothesis of different ways of distributing the power

---

17   It is sometimes said (for example the authors of the Bernardins group cited below) that the shareholder is not a real owner because his liability is limited. But in legal terms the concept of ownership does not generally imply unlimited liability on all decisions made about the asset. When, for example, an owner is completely responsible for the property (as in the case of certain partnerships), he is certainly more responsible, but you cannot say he is more of an owner.

and therefore the ownership in the firm. This point is regularly raised by some Christians. Thus Puel[18] engages in radically calling into question the public limited liability company. In his view, there is no law governing business activities, but only a commercial company law. But, he says, the business activity, or enterprise, should be an institution, because it is a community, and the entrepreneur should represent the whole company. But, he says, this does not interest capitalists; their only aim is to put labor at the service of capital. There is, moreover, no shareholder democracy: it is a "machine for the conquest of savings," "it only serves to guarantee the anonymity of management." In short, "the limited liability company is based on two legal fictions: the shareholders are the owners of the enterprise, and the company's managers are the proxies of the shareholders." It is therefore necessary to distinguish between a company and an enterprise. In a more subtle and elaborate form, we can see in a similar sense the interesting collective research work carried out at the Bernardins in Paris in 2010 and 2011[19] by Fr Baudouin Roger and Oliver Favereau.

We can only briefly mention this very broad question. First of all, I continue to consider that the shareholders of a commercial corporation *do* have the function of collective owners of that company: the law is very clear on that. We should then remember that while a public limited company must abide by its corporate purpose, there is no requirement to define and implement it in a strictly financial way, as is too often done, forgetting the community that the enterprise comprises, as well as the common good and any similar consideration. And shareholder accountability includes this. The recent trend (exclusive cult of shareholder value) is not intrinsic to the status of a trading company. Moreover, if we follow the line of thought we've just mentioned, we'll want an answer to a complex question: How do we define an enterprise as distinct from a company? It is an intuitive concept, but it does not currently have an overall expression, outside of the company in the legal sense, of which the owner is, as we have seen, a group of shareholders.

However, there remains another legitimate question: Should shareholders always be given the power to decide on the future of

---

18   Hugues Puel, *Une éthique pour l'économie: Ethos, crises, choix* (Paris: Cerf, 2010), pp. 210 sqq.
19   That resulted in a symposium in April 2011. See http://www.collegedes-bernardins.fr/index.php/pole-de-recherche/economie-homme-societe/economie-homme-societe-seminaire.html.

"enterprises," that is to say, legally making decisions about companies?[20] This brings us to distinguish in the ownership function, at least partially, the relation to the investment at risk (the role of equity investors), from the power to decide the broad lines and essential decisions for the company. Among the different but conceivable distributions of power and property, three cases can be distinguished, which may all be combined. The first two refer to the inside of the company: managers and staff. The manager class gives a special role to the management of the company, then associated with shareholding and enjoying special rights: it is a very old situation, even more so than the public limited company; it is the case, for example, of limited partnerships. There are many arguments in its favor. At the same time, one must recognize its relative decline. This may be due to the fact that these examples of division of power between capital-providers and entrepreneurs easily lead to blockages, which would explain why investors prefer situations that are simpler and safer for them. They are the owners of the funds, so they are free to invest them or not. Hence their tendency to assume full ownership of the company, once they have decided to invest in it. But there are cases where these association structures would be better adapted, and they should be encouraged, in particular because they allow a better accountability of managers in return for their autonomy (in the sponsorships they are responsible to the limit of *all their possessions*).

The second class of organizations, the staff class, is one that aims at achieving some form of collective ownership for another category of people within the company, usually the staff, or part of it, but sometimes also the clients, in the case of cooperatives. We are not concerned here with the ownership by employees of the capital of the company, which is a development of the shareholder function among the staff; it is quite beneficial in itself but has its limits, first of all financially, but above all if you want to avoid overly concentrated risk-taking on the part of that staff in their company.[21] This

---

20 We will not elaborate here on the question of the other major form of financial decision: public decision — government decision or similar. While it is often useful or even necessary, it can hardly be recommended to give it a central role in financing the economy. Since it has then no external benchmarking or control such as the market, and is almost never questioned efficiently, it is often very inefficient and concentrates on the very short term.

21 In the event of bankruptcy, they lose on all levels, as employees and as savers.

also includes mutualist organizations in a broad sense. The idea is attractive. But although legally possible in many places, they are relatively uncommon in practice and rather on the downturn, with the exception of the financial sector, and even then, only in some countries. And they involve little or no possibility of recourse to external capital, which may be an important limit to their development. It is also necessary to distinguish between situations varying according to the values that animate them, the mechanisms of power that prevail in them, or the organization of responsibility of each party.[22] A very important point here is that *the fact that "ownership" is collective does not automatically imply a different hierarchy of priorities*. In addition, there is the concrete and difficult question of the entry and exit of individuals into the ownership structure and its financial arrangements.

The recommendations of the Church go yet further, evoking a third possible class of ownership. It may be recalled here that our current understanding of ownership has not always existed. In the feudal system, for example, it did not have the same meaning as today: the disposition of assets was divided between the lord and his vassals, and the notion of ownership as an absolute and exclusive right did not exist so clearly: it was divided into several hands, with different roles. We can therefore imagine other conceptions of ownership and thus of the "company" that constitutes the enterprise. According to John Paul II, as we have seen, a certain form of collective control of companies can be envisaged, provided that it ensures what the pope called "the subjectivity of society," that is to say that people are fully co-owners of the large "worksite" on which they are all engaged. We can imagine different ways to do that: this pope suggested for example a form of association between capital and labor in "a wide range of intermediate bodies with economic, social, and cultural purposes" functioning as living communities respectful of people and subject to the requirements of the common good (*Laborem exercens*).

These are apparently associative forms, which are not necessarily limited to internal stakeholders and to pure investors. This would undoubtedly entail an organization of power that would involve

---

It should be noted that this risk may also arise in the case of a mutual company.
22 In the Catholic context, the *Focolari* in Italy and the *Mondragon* cooperatives in Spain are often cited as examples of a search for a different set of rules, with a more explicit altruistic aim ("economy of communion"). This confirms the primary importance of the values that animate the participants.

stakeholders, especially workers, in a different way, giving them some right of control, and a part of the ownership rights in their enterprise or more generally. But, if one understands correctly, the principal decision-making role that is the role of any owner would be held by an associative structure with broad objectives. It would then embody the enterprise[23] by bringing together long-term partners, investors, managers, and employees; this would bring us closer to the mutual institution mentioned above, but in a more complex way. Or it could be something else: Perhaps a foundation? Or some form of a fund in the broad sense, managed with objectives of the common good? Participants (entrepreneurs, miscellaneous workers) would associate with investors, who would not be full shareholders. Such a program is ambitious and there are few examples in this sense, except mutual companies; we will leave the question open. In all these cases, the question of power and responsibility is one of the most difficult to deal with: in this kind of structure, they can be diluted or blocked to a degree unknown to the commercial society, and it can be collectively damaging. In any case, the issue cannot be treated purely *a priori*: it is on the spot, through concrete experiments, that such formulas must be tested if they are to be proven viable.

That said, even in such a case the reality of what we call ownership would remain, namely the legal right to decide the allocation and use of goods, in this case production goods. Now, except to eliminate any fungibility between these goods, by preventing any "owner" from selling or buying, investing or lending, the expression of this right of ownership is at least partly monetary: the possibility of selling, or purchasing for that matter, a certain right. Similarly, the assignment of proceeds, profit or remuneration, will be at least partly monetary. It means that even then, the problem of the legal and monetary measure of this right and the corresponding decision-making process would remain. This brings us back to our main subject, the function of finance and its basic questions: how to arbitrate the allocation of this rare resource, capital, and how to assume the duties related to ownership. From this point of view, *whatever the ownership regime, the essential is the state of mind and the priorities of those who manage the assets and make decisions*, even though other dimensions are very important.

---

23 This is, for example, evoked in the work carried out within the college of Bernardins and quoted above.

CHAPTER 7

The Social Doctrine of
the Church and Finance

A SPECIFIC CHRISTIAN TEACHING ON FINANCE?
Finance and morality

As we see, finance needs a strong moral foundation, like any economic activity. When we speak of morality, we must distinguish two levels. The first is less original, it is personal or corporate deontology; it aims to regulate the behavior of participants. In principle, this goes without saying, but the recent crisis confirms, if need be, that in practice it is not self-evident, however important it is. As will be seen, a large part of the errors that were committed then can be considered as professional wrongdoing under a fairly basic code of ethics, starting with subprime credits. But this is not our main subject here, especially since in principle the current system does not necessarily refuse this idea.

The second level is less often put forward; it concerns the preferences of participants and their collective organization. This is of much interest to the Christian. Even with the same deontology, participants can prioritize their actions in very different ways, according to their moral values. What Christians seek is to direct economic activity toward the full development of man, and the common good, according to a certain conception of man and in relation to God. This is much less clear in the dominant mentality. And too often Christians themselves, and more broadly, ethically-minded people, reason as if the economy had a technical function, independent of the priorities and hierarchies of the players. In doing so, they take up the idea received in the teaching of political economics textbooks. On the contrary, it is clear, and this point is essential to us, that *the matching of market preferences*, and consequently the functioning of the whole economy, *will produce different results if these preferences are different*. Markets that are driven by actors seeking a certain good or objectives other than pure profit will produce different results and different prices from markets that are driven by actors seeking only their profit in the immediate material sense, or even just for enjoyment. It's not just a short-term/long-term difference, or a question of respecting the rules, or of cheating: it's a matter of priorities. In the case of finance, this has a major consequence: it means that *even if the players respect a professional code of ethics in the ordinary sense, and the market is reasonably regulated, this is still not enough, and we cannot assume that we have completely fulfilled our moral responsibility, and may now concentrate on profits.*

This statement is true for all economic agents, and *a fortiori* for financiers whose task is the confrontation of all economic projects in view of their financing, since finance is the true hub of the whole economy. *That is why the already mentioned issue of ethical funds, and more broadly the idea that ultimately financial investors must be concerned with rules and references other than immediate results, are very important issues.* And in this sense, we are (almost) all financiers, because almost all of us have savings, and their orientation sends a strong message to the economic system — even if the responsibility of financial professionals is the primary one. And so, if the question is: Does finance require a specific moral teaching? The answer is: yes.

A specifically Christian teaching?

Another question, however, is whether it should be a specifically Christian teaching. We have seen that, despite the denials and ambiguities that continue here or there, most of the technical structures of a market economy are validated or considered neutral by the Church. It starts with private property and the principle of *subsidiarity*, which confers on the person a responsibility for his actions and contemplates intervention by a higher authority only when it is demonstrated that such intervention is necessary and will not create more inconvenience than advantages. But this is only part of the picture, because this validation is made with two essential reservations. One is that the effectiveness of these mechanisms is not judged to be automatically reliable — even less, spontaneously in line with the common good. Nowhere is the functioning of the market, and more generally the free interplay of actors, considered as optimal. There must therefore be sound legal principles, not as a substitute for the morality of participants, but as a framework and a means to encourage it, and to prevent the intrinsic limits of these mechanisms from causing serious harm to the common good and especially the poorest. Those rules may come from participants, or when necessary be enacted by public authorities.

The second reservation is the major divergence between the Social Doctrine and the gospel, on the one hand, and on the other hand, current ideas, precisely on the role of morality, values, the common good or ultimate purposes. The obvious example is the universal destination of goods, which underlies the otherwise recognized right of property. But this also applies to the subordination of finance to the service of the economy and of development. In the Christian conception, contrary to the social democratic tradition, you should not have players who do what they want provided it is within the law, and then a State which corrects the markets by laws and taxation that redistributes wealth. Christianity recognizes a moral requirement concerning aims and purposes that is the responsibility of all participants, at all stages. This applies not only to professional decisions and investment choices, but also to the use that each person makes of their money, even if legitimately earned.

You can then understand the possible meaning of a Christian teaching on finance. But even so, the Social Doctrine is expressed in terms that are acceptable and relevant to every person of goodwill, even an unbeliever. In other words, the specificity and the urgency of the position taken here concern the fact that Christians can and must act on these grounds, but not that the requirements of their faith would *by nature* be different from what would be recognized under natural morality. The pontifical texts speak of the dignity of the human person, and of natural morality. Even though they have biblical foundations (man made in the image of God for the first, a divine foundation for the second), these values are of course accessible to the non-Christian.

But on the other hand, it must be admitted that the views of people are often divergent, and that in practice the lure of gain and other passions dominate. Therefore, constantly upholding demanding moral ideals requires clear ideas and a particular inner strength, especially if you go against the ideas and practices accepted in the surrounding society. It is *a priori* uncommon that this commitment comes from something else than a religion. Among these, it is also uncommon for this commitment to come from a religion other than Christianity—for it is the only one to have developed a consistent body of reflection on this issue—and especially the Catholic Church, while respecting the relative autonomy of earthly realities. It thus appears that in practice, even in the name of the dignity of man and of natural morality, the role of the Christian is (or rather, should be) deeply different at least in intensity from that of most non-Christians. An example of this may be given by the attitude one should maintain as a participant in a market: *the true asceticism that the rightly-understood Christian tradition imposes on the merchant or virtuous operator is theoretically conceivable in the context of natural morality, but it is in practice so far removed from general or spontaneous behavior that it seems unlikely without a solid and mature faith*, except in specific cases.

But we must go even further. The limitation of our aspirations to natural morality would imply that we fall short of charity, in the full sense of the term: theological love, love taken in the superlative sense of the term, the love of God. Obviously, it is difficult to imagine a society built on a general requirement such as charity (outside of profound and widespread conversion!). But this does not mean that the role of Christians, under their personal or collective responsibility, is not so important in this respect also. This is especially true when we speak of gift, which is an essential Christian theme. Certainly, gift is not the Christian's monopoly either. But conceiving the economy as saturated by gift and the service of other people (as well as their full human development) is hardly practicable for someone who does not believe in a God of love. Here again, investment offers a good example: the Christian faith, if taken seriously, pushes one to go beyond the simple considerations of natural morality. If, for example, we put pressure on companies, and invest only in those that have some respect for social, environmental, and other standards, and which are in useful or at least non-harmful sectors, we are still at the level of "normal" natural morality, even where this is very good. On the other hand, if it is a matter of promoting a dimension of genuine gift, or even of engaging in large risky operations, undertaken in the name of a higher interest, all this from an evangelical perspective, we change the perspective, even if financial techniques can help those who thus want to give generously and intelligently — and effectively practice the corresponding virtue of "magnificence." This can be reflected notably in new types of enterprises, as the pope recommends them, but also in more classical activities, thereby engaging in behavior that contrasts sharply with current rationality.

But that does not mean that in practice there will be a sharp gap between the two levels. Certainly, the act of conversion is a major break, which is reflected in the gospel message when it introduces the consideration of eternal life into economic calculation, as we have seen. But one's behavior does not change at a stroke, and the concrete actions envisaged will still be economic acts. We therefore progress only gradually, at the rate of the development of moral and spiritual exigencies, from merely well-intentioned and simple acts, to acts increasingly animated by higher spiritual demands. The responsible attitude toward the markets, for example, ranges from simple concern for respecting minimum ethical rules, to a genuine struggle for in-depth reforms of this market, or to generous acts in response to a given situation or because of the culture of the company we run. On the other hand, gift will go from the occasional gift to a poor client, what any compassionate baker could do, to the creation in a company of a mentality that integrates internal and external relationships such that profit is just the ultimate verification, and not a rule of conduct. This progression can ultimately arrive at radical generosity and voluntary poverty, in the case of achieving holiness. We then recall our friend Homobonus of Cremona, the holy merchant.

FINANCE IN THE TEXTS OF THE SOCIAL DOCTRINE

All this provides us with a series of references that allow us to see finance from a different angle. That said, in the Social Doctrine of the Church few texts deal directly with finance.[1] The most developed is *Caritas in veritate* (2013). It is the first to address, on an anthropological basis, the question of finance and its role in a context of globalization. Yet its central point is development, understood as integral development of the person, from a moral and spiritual perspective.

---

1 Among the oldest, the most significant is *Quadragesimo anno* of Pius XI (May 15, 1931): this remarkable text retains its value, especially in view of the recent crisis. Two texts are to be quoted before considering those of Benedict XVI: a speech by John Paul II (Speech to the participants of the meeting organized by the foundation *"Centesimus Annus-Pro Pontifice"* on September 11, 1999, which dealt more deeply with the theme "Ethics and Finance"), and especially the *Compendium of the Social Doctrine of the Church* of 2004 (published under the auspices of the Pontifical Council for Justice and Peace). Benedict XVI responded after the beginning of the 2007–2008 crisis with three documents (*Letter to Gordon Brown on the work of the G20, Meeting with the clergy of the diocese of Rome* on February 26, 2009, and the message *"Fighting poverty, building peace"* of January 1, 2009) which were followed by the encyclical *Caritas in veritate* (June 29, 2009). All are available on the Vatican site.

Neutral or good tools, oriented in the right direction

The general idea of Social Doctrine is that financial activity and its tools are not bad in themselves but must be properly oriented. Pius XI pointed out in *Quadragesimo anno* (no. 136) that

> Nor is it to be thought that gainful occupations are thereby belittled or judged less consonant with human dignity; on the contrary, we are taught to recognize in them with reverence the manifest will of the Divine Creator Who placed man upon the earth to work it and use it in a multitude of ways for his needs. Those who are engaged in producing goods, therefore, are not forbidden to increase their fortune in a just and lawful manner; for it is only fair that he who renders service to the community and makes it richer should also, through the increased wealth of the community, be made richer himself according to his position, provided that all these things be sought with due respect for the laws of God and without impairing the rights of others and that they be employed in accordance with faith and right reason.

The *Compendium* of the Social Doctrine of the Church begins with a positive assessment (no. 368):

> Financial markets are certainly not an innovation of our day: for a long time now, in different forms, they have been seeking to meet the financial needs of the productivity sector. The experience of history teaches that *without adequate financial systems, economic growth would not have taken place.* Large-scale investments typical of modern market economies would have been impossible without *the fundamental role of mediation played by financial markets,* which among other things brought about an appreciation of the positive functions of savings in the overall development of the economic and social system.... The creation of what is called the "global capital market" has brought benefits, thanks to the fact that the greater mobility of capital allows the productivity sector easier access to resources; on the other hand it has also increased the risk of financial crises.

As for financial globalization, John Paul II pointed out:[2]

---

2 John Paul II, speech of September 11, 1999, op. cit., no. 4. In *Caritas in veritate* (no. 42) his successor goes in the same direction.

It should also be added that *the processes which are globalizing markets and communications do not in themselves possess an ethically negative connotation,* and therefore a summary and *a priori* condemnation of them is not justified. However, those processes that, in principle, appear as factors of progress can have, and in fact already have had, ambivalent or decidedly negative consequences, especially to the detriment of the very poor.... Globalization will have many positive effects if it can be sustained by a strong sense of the absoluteness and dignity of all human persons and of the principle that earthly goods are meant for everyone. *There is room in this direction to operate in a fair and constructive way, even within a sector that is much subject to speculation.*

Limits of the financial system: short-termism, lucre, and loss of purpose

But there is the other side of the coin. What is at the center of attention is the preponderance of the short term and the fact that finance strays from its purpose, which is development in the broad sense.[3] Pius XI (no. 132) already noted that

> The easy gains that a market unrestricted by any law opens to everybody attracts large numbers to buying and selling goods, and they, their one aim being to make quick profits with the least expenditure of work, raise or lower prices by their uncontrolled business dealings so rapidly according to their own caprice and greed that they nullify the wisest forecasts of producers.

The *Compendium* emphasized more broadly (no. 368):

> The financial sector, which has seen the volume of financial transactions far surpass that of real transactions, runs the risk of developing according to a mentality that has only itself as a point of reference, without being connected to the real foundations of the economy.

Moreover (no. 369): "A financial economy that is an end unto itself is destined to contradict its goals, since it is no longer in touch

---

3 But they also note the technical risks. For example, immediately after its overall positive assessment of the financial system, of the "global capital market," and of its mobility the *Compendium* (no. 368) added that increased mobility "on the other hand has also increased the risk of financial crises."

with its roots and has lost sight of its constitutive purpose. In other words, it has abandoned its original and essential role of serving the real economy and, ultimately, of contributing to the development of people and the human community."

And

> the sudden acceleration of these processes, such as the enormous increase in the value of the administrative portfolios of financial institutions and the rapid proliferation of new and sophisticated financial instruments, makes it *more urgent than ever to find institutional solutions capable of effectively fostering the stability of the system without reducing its potential and efficiency*. It is therefore indispensable to introduce a normative and regulatory framework that will protect the stability of the system in all its intricate expressions, foster competition among intermediaries and ensure the greatest transparency to the benefit of investors.[4]

Benedict XVI[5] goes in the same direction. Referring to financial globalization, linked to the development of electronics and to policies of liberalization of money flows between countries, he pointed out:

> Objectively, the most important function of finance is to sustain the possibility of long-term investment and hence of development. Today this appears extremely fragile: it is experiencing the negative repercussions of a system of financial dealings—both national and global—*based upon very short-term thinking, which aims at increasing the value of financial operations and concentrates on the technical management of various forms of risk*. The recent crisis demonstrates *how financial activity can at times be completely turned in on itself, lacking any long-term consideration of the common good*. This lowering of the objectives of global finance to the very

---

4 "In light of the extreme imbalance that characterizes the international financial system, the overall picture appears more disconcerting still: the processes of deregulation of financial markets and innovation tend to be consolidated only in certain parts of the world. This is a source of serious ethical concern, since the countries excluded from these processes do not enjoy the benefits brought about but are still exposed to the eventual negative consequences that financial instability can cause for their real economic systems, above all if they are weak or suffering from delayed development."
5 Message of January 1, 2009 (no. 10).

short term *reduces its capacity to function as a bridge between the present and the future*, and as a stimulus to the creation of new opportunities for production and for work in the long term. *Finance limited in this way to the short and very short term becomes dangerous for everyone*, even for those who benefit when the markets perform well.

Let us note here the legitimate ambition that the pope has for finance: "to function as a bridge between the present and the future." This is an ambition that justifies the effort to promote a Christian approach to finance.

At the origin of these deviations we see the passion for gain, the thirst for profit (lucre). We recall, from *Quadragesimo anno*, no. 132, that "hence arises that unquenchable thirst for riches and temporal goods, which has at all times impelled men to break God's laws and trample upon the rights of their neighbors, but which, on account of the present system of economic life, is laying far more numerous snares for human frailty." Pius XI noted that it was the result of the crisis of 1929 that "some have become so hardened to the stings of conscience as to hold that they are allowed, in any manner whatsoever, to increase their profits and use means, fair or foul, to protect their hard-won wealth against sudden changes of fortune." Whether at the individual or collective level, as the pope continues:

> The laws passed to promote corporate business, while dividing and limiting the risk of business, have given occasion to the most sordid license. For *We observe that consciences are little affected by this reduced obligation of accountability*; that furthermore, by hiding under the shelter of a joint name, the worst of injustices and frauds are perpetrated; and that, too, *directors of business companies, forgetful of their trust, betray the rights of those whose savings they have undertaken to administer.*

Similarly, in connection with the crisis of 2007, Benedict XVI[6] stressed that behind this greed there was a degree of idolatry:

> On the other hand, it is also necessary to speak with great ethical awareness, created and awakened, so to speak, by a conscience formed by the gospel. Hence it is necessary to

---

6   In his meeting with the clergy of Rome on February 26, 2009.

expose the fundamental errors, the basic mistakes, now being shown up by the collapse of important American banks. In the end, it is a question of *human avarice in the form of sin* or as the Letter to the Colossians says, *avarice as idolatry*. We must condemn this idolatry which stands against the true God, as well as the falsification of the image of God with another God, "Mammon." We must do so courageously and concretely.

We find here what was at the heart of the great medieval debate on usury, and beyond: the evangelical concern about the power of Mammon, the "god" who believes that *by itself alone it can produce anything*, and, conversely, the evangelical insistence on the necessary reintegration of money into the multiple and varied fabric of projects for human development, the term being taken in its broadest sense.

THE DIRECTIONS OFFERED BY THE SOCIAL DOCTRINE FOR FINANCE
Moral orientation toward the full development of man

As we have seen, the question is not of banning finance or even riches, but of ordering them to a just moral and spiritual positioning. Besides charity, the moral demands concern justice, especially regarding the poor, and human dignity. As John Paul II said:[7]

> Christians who work in the economic sphere and, in particular, in the financial sector are called to identify viable ways to fulfill this duty of justice, which is clear to them because of their cultural background, but which can be shared by anyone who wishes to place the human person and the common good at the center of every social project. Yes, the objective of all your activity in the financial and administrative field must always be never to violate the dignity of man and, for this reason, to build structures and systems that will foster justice and solidarity for the good of all.

For his part, Benedict XVI recalls the link between crisis of confidence and moral crisis and stressed the decisive importance of ethics in the whole of economic life.[8] In *Caritas in veritate* (no. 65), he noted that

---

7 John Paul II, speech of September 11, 1999, op. cit., no. 3.
8 In his letter to Gordon Brown: "Financial crises are triggered when — partially due to the decline of correct ethical conduct — those working in the economic

Finance, therefore — through the renewed structures and operating methods that have to be designed after its misuse, which wreaked such havoc on the real economy — now needs to go back to being an instrument directed toward improved wealth creation and development. Insofar as they are instruments, the entire economy and finance, not just certain sectors, must be used in an ethical way so as to create suitable conditions for human development and for the development of peoples. It is certainly useful, and in some circumstances imperative, to launch financial initiatives in which the humanitarian dimension predominates. However, this must not obscure the fact that the entire financial system has to be aimed at sustaining true development. Above all, the intention to do good must not be considered incompatible with the effective capacity to produce goods. Financiers must rediscover the genuinely ethical foundation of their activity, so as not to abuse the sophisticated instruments which can serve to betray the interests of savers. Right intention, transparency, and the search for positive results are mutually compatible and must never be detached from one another. If love is wise, it can find ways of working in accordance with provident and just expediency, as is illustrated in a significant way by much of the experience of credit unions.

In addition (no. 68):

The development of peoples goes awry if humanity thinks it can re-create itself through the "wonders" of technology, just as economic development is exposed as a destructive sham if it relies on the "wonders" of finance in order to sustain unnatural and consumerist growth. In the face of such Promethean presumption, we must fortify our love

---

sector lose trust in its modes of operating and in its financial systems. Nevertheless, finance, commerce and production systems are contingent human creations which, if they become objects of blind faith, bear within themselves the roots of their own downfall. Their true and solid foundation is *faith in the human person*. For this reason all the measures proposed to rein in this crisis must seek, ultimately, to offer security to families and stability to workers and, through appropriate regulations and controls, to restore ethics to the financial world. . . . If a key element of the crisis is a deficit of ethics in economic structures, the same crisis teaches us that *ethics is not 'external' to the economy but 'internal' and that the economy cannot function if it does not bear within it an ethical component.*"

for a freedom that is not merely arbitrary but is rendered truly human by acknowledgment of the good that underlies it. To this end, man needs to look inside himself in order to recognize the fundamental norms of the natural moral law which God has written on our hearts.

Let us note incidentally an echo from a non-Catholic banker. For Stephen Green,[9] president of the HSBC banking giant[10] and an Anglican priest, morality is essential to economic life itself. "If we are to restore trust and confidence in the markets, we must therefore address what is at its root a moral question."[11] Regulation is not enough: we are responsible for our actions. And he notes this is what his employees want, including in the financial sector: the vast majority of people want to feel they are true contributors to society. He further notes that our task is to maximize lasting value.[12] Certainly, we must simultaneously be realistic, including on the remuneration of capital, and therefore we exclude nebulous projects. But also, we must be responsible to the community and the long term and maintain a constructive relationship with the communities in which a company works. All these elements are mutually reinforcing and are also a factor of personal achievement.

The means at the overall level

Beyond these preoccupations — which concern all of us — we must explore concrete solutions. Let us recall that Benedict XVI posed a prerequisite that was little mentioned before him: competence. He explained[13] that in economic matters "I see now how difficult it is to speak with competence on this subject. If we do not deal competently with the matter, it will not be credible." He added: "lofty moralizing does not help if it is not substantiated by knowledge of the facts, which also helps one understand what it is possible to do in practice to gradually change the situation." *One cannot speak of the morality of an activity without competent knowledge of the corresponding reality.*

---

9 Stephen Green, *Good Value: Reflections on Money, Morality, and an Uncertain World* (London: Penguin Books/Allen Lane, 2009).

10 Even if HSBC's behavior has been subject to criticism, especially as regards money laundering.

11 Ibid., p. 132.

12 Ibid., pp. 155 sqq.

13 In his meeting with the clergy of Rome, February 26, 2009.

Solutions are not equally developed by the popes. In particular, they develop very little on questions related to the organization of the financial profession, of markets or banks. What they particularly insist on is a well-ordered *regulation*, particularly international, and therefore based on a framework that comes mainly from without, but they do not specify it. But this does not exclude the accountability of participants; on the contrary. John Paul II noted:[14]

> When dealing with the question of the "globalization of the economy" in the Encyclical *Centesimus annus* (no. 58), I called attention to the need to promote *"international agencies which will oversee and direct the economy to the common good,"* while also remembering that economic freedom is only one of the elements of human freedom. Financial activity, in accordance with its own characteristics, must be directed to serving the common good of the human family. One does wonder, however, which value criteria should guide the decision of financial operators, even over and above the functional requirements of the markets, in a situation such as that of the present day where there is still no adequate international normative and juridical framework. And again: what are the appropriate authorities for preparing and providing such guidelines as well as for controlling their implementation?

The pope then calls agents to their collective professional responsibility: "A first step must be made *by financial operators themselves,* who could try to prepare *ethical or professional codes* that would be binding for the sector." He adds: "those responsible for the international community are called, then, to adopt appropriate *juridical instruments* for dealing with critical situations that, if not 'regulated,' could have disastrous consequences not only within the economic sphere, but also in social and political life. And certainly, the weakest would be the first to pay and would pay the most."

The *Compendium* was also in favor of regulation but stressed (no. 369): "it is therefore indispensable to introduce a *normative and regulatory framework* that will protect the stability of the system in all its intricate expressions, foster competition among intermediaries, and ensure the greatest transparency to the benefit of investors." Hence also the need for international regulation (no. 371):

---

14   John Paul II, speech of September 11, 1999, no. 2.

The more the worldwide economic-financial system reaches high levels of organizational and functional complexity, all the more priority must be given to the task of regulating these processes, directing them toward the goal of attaining the common good of the human family. There is the clear need not just for States but for the international community to take on this delicate chore with adequate and effective political and juridical instruments. It is therefore indispensable that international economic and financial institutions should be able to identify the most appropriate institutional solutions and formulate the most suitable plans of action aimed at bringing about a change that, if it were to be passively accepted and simply left to itself, would otherwise produce a dramatic situation detrimental above all to the weakest and defenseless classes of the world's population.

Finally, in *Caritas in veritate* (no. 65) Benedict XVI sets out two main avenues of approach: "both the regulation of the financial sector, so as to safeguard weaker parties and discourage scandalous speculation, and experimentation with *new forms of finance*, designed to support development projects, are positive experiences that should be further explored and encouraged, *highlighting the responsibility of the investor.*"

Private initiatives; Ethical funds and microfinance

As regards private actors, Benedict XVI noted (as mentioned earlier) in *Caritas in veritate* (no. 45) that "the economy needs ethics in order to function correctly," recalling that "banks are proposing 'ethical' accounts and investment funds." But he places the emphasis rather on specific initiatives, animated by concerns other than the material result. He notes that "'ethical financing' is being developed, especially through microcredit and, more generally, *microfinance,*" and states that "these processes are praiseworthy and deserve much support" while stressing that "it would be advisable, however, to develop a *sound* criterion of discernment, since the adjective 'ethical' can be abused. When the word is used generically, it can lend itself to any number of interpretations, even to the point where it includes decisions and choices contrary to justice and authentic human welfare." John Paul II[15] pointed out that, pending the implementation

---

15   John Paul II, speech of September 11, 1999, no. 4.

of a sense of global justice: "it is very opportune to support and encourage those *projects of 'ethical finance,' microcredit, and 'fair and equitable trade'* which are within everyone's reach and possess a positive and even pedagogical value for global co-responsibility." We have seen that in *Caritas in veritate* (no. 65) Benedict XVI gives as an example the cooperative credit.

Furthermore, the *experience of microfinance*, which has its roots in the thinking and activity of the civil humanists — I am thinking especially of the birth of pawnbroking — should be strengthened and fine-tuned. This is all the more necessary in these days when financial difficulties can become severe for many of the more vulnerable sectors of the population, who should be protected from the risk of usury and from despair. The weakest members of society should be helped to defend themselves against usury, just as poor peoples should be helped to derive real benefit from microcredit, in order to discourage the exploitation that is possible in these two areas.

As one can see, these developments about possible solutions remain limited: we have regulation on the one hand, codes and ethical funds on the other, plus specific initiatives such as microfinance. But they are, of course, an invitation to lay Christians to assume their responsibilities more widely in this field.

CHAPTER 8

The Debate on the Role of Finance

THE COLLECTIVE FUNCTION OF FINANCE AND THE ROLE OF PROFIT

The role of finance is the subject of a widespread debate; it has been sharpened by the last crisis. What is or should be the use of finance? We know the answer in principle: to collect the available money—savings—and to invest it in economic projects that justify it. Unlike owners' direct use of their resources, intermediaries collect this money, analyze the projects and compare them, be it in the country concerned or in the world. It is thus a hub, enabling economic actors who do not themselves have financial means to get access to these projects and build their future. This also implies for finance a double relationship of trust: with the holders of resources (savers) who entrust their money to it, and with the users, to whom it entrusts that money. And since it directs resources on projects, waiting for future results, it bridges the present and the future, as Benedict XVI said, according to priority criteria tempered by the probability of success or failure and therefore the risk. As can be seen, it is a considerable responsibility, and at the same time a risky one: by definition the future is neither known nor controllable, and the criteria of choices are complex and multiple. But this is what gives meaning to the financial system, using it to implement the vision that society has of the future, its priorities, and its choices in an operational manner.

The criticism thus focuses on the role of finance in society. In general, finance would *send negative signals to the economy*, using and imposing improper criteria of choice, because the sole purpose of finance would be to maximize its own profit, the measurable monetary element, which is preponderant for finance. Moreover, the financial system is itself an economic agent, and it fulfills its function by seeking to satisfy its own objectives, which may not coincide with its social function. The main group of criticisms therefore deals with the role and nature of profit in its activity. This role is necessarily very important since, finally, it boils down to the inevitable demand that investment produces more than what has been invested, notably in monetary form, since the resources are monetary and the product also. But at the same time, the characteristics of profit in the financial sector lead to many questions. First, there are those related to its remuneration, which is considered excessive: we shall see this point in the third part. But the most serious accusation is that of distortion. Critics describe, for example, the financier as a destructor of companies, opposing the "good" industrialist to the "financial villain"; and they denounce the dictatorship of the quarterly result, which would lead to a preponderance of the short term over the long term. The so-called financial take-overs are criticized as oriented toward speculative profit without the creation of wealth, and so on. The general question is therefore the capacity of the financial system to finance the so-called real economy according to the appropriate criteria. For example, in the case of mergers and acquisitions, it has been argued that most of them have destroyed value (even measured by stock market prices). Similarly, the formation of bubbles and collective movements, which is not limited to markets (it is also found in the most traditional bank loans), can lead to considerable collective waste through misguidance of resources. These criticisms are multiple and based on real phenomena. Again, to a large extent, they boil down to a central point: *only one criterion ends up prevailing over all others, profit—and not just any profit, but that which is measured in the short term, and as perceived by a certain finance.*

Let us therefore examine the content of these accusations: finance is guilty, because of its excessive role and its deviations. It is a widespread theme. The main point is what is called financialization of the economy and thus of society, which makes it an issue for civilization. Paul Dembinski[1] has brilliantly expressed this point of view.

IS FINANCE GUILTY AS SUCH?
Remuneration of capital and the growing autonomy of finance
The first level he criticizes is the remuneration of capital as such. Let us recall that in previous societies it was not self-evident. Not that owners were not trying to derive financial results from their assets. But as we have seen, their relationship with these assets was different: it was part of a social position and inserted in a particular context of business and other relations. This was true of the feudal system, of course, but also of monasteries, or even of Florentine

---

1 Dembinski, ed., *Pratiques financières*, pp. 311 sqq.

merchants. They were in fact seeking to make money and the best of them tried to optimize the use of their resources, but without an autonomous notion of the remuneration of a capital, designated as such. According to Paul Dembinski, capitalism has assumed the conjunction of "the ethos of efficiency" with the justification of the remuneration of "capital, as an autonomous factor of production, which became the subject of calculation," this remuneration becoming distinct from personal profit. He adds: "the development of finance is perfectly in line with this trend, since it seeks to ensure that capital has the maximum economic efficiency and therefore the maximum remuneration, which is called 'return on capital' and is expressed as a percentage of the invested amount." And this feeds the collective references. "The understanding of the world from the point of view of capital and its 'right' to remuneration leads to the 'financialization of mentalities,' which is reflected in the perception of socio-economic realities in terms of capital, of which finance gives an elegant expression."[2] Consequently, "labor is then only a means of making capital grow and ensuring its profitability." Hence the appearance of what is called financial assets, which are "risk-bearing and return-bearing objects for their owners" and exist "by derivation from the reality that serves as a crucible to them."

In this context two phenomena appear. The first is "the appearance of an *autonomous mental space, specific to finance.*" He then recalls the emergence from the 1950s and 1960s of

> two dimensions that will henceforth structure the mental space of finance: the dimension of risk and that of yield. Using these two dimensions, any financial asset — and thus any part of reality transposed into the space of finance — can be described and parameterized. Thanks to this intellectual breakthrough, the space of finance becomes self-sufficient. The operator only has to manipulate the various elements present in this space by buying and selling them, or by assembling them, to orientate his future in terms of risk and return on his or her capital.

---

2 "Be it 'health,' 'human capital,' 'capital of competence,' 'intellectual capital,' or 'social capital,' the underlying image is everywhere the same: that of an autonomous stock of wealth, which has the function of generating a flow of 'remuneration.'"

In addition, "the assertion of the autonomous space of finance is linked to the extension of the role of the financial market that allows the possibility of transactions, without which finance could never have become a dynamic activity and, at least partially, an autonomous one toward the economy." For this autonomy leads to a relative disconnection from the "real" economy: "if economic calculation feeds and rationalizes the entrepreneurial behavior of the person who makes things happen ... financial calculation fuels the passive behavior of a speculator or of an annuitant, who juggles with positions within the financial space without ever leaving it."

Misleading promises?

Dembinski adds that a major fault compounds this artificial autonomy: *finance does not keep its own promises*, because "the control of risk — therefore both of the future and of the fear of the future — is at the heart of the promise of modern finance. Indeed, finance is based on two complementary assumptions: on the one hand, the risk can be quantified; on the other hand, in the occurrence of an adverse event, monetary compensation is possible." But in his view this dual claim is unfair. For the first, "this claim to master the future rests on a profound confusion between uncertainty — which is present in all future — and risk, which is its very partial modeling. Indeed, the quantification of risk assumes that not only all the possibilities are inventoried, but also that probabilities can be assigned to them. But beyond the probable world there is uncertainty, and it is synonymous with unknown. Where there is uncertainty, the measurement of risk has no meaning and hence its rational coverage becomes impossible." Hence, *"in the face of real uncertainty, modern finance, despite all its technical apparatus, brings no solution and leaves man as defenseless as in the past."*[3] As for the claim to "possible compensation for adverse events, it is verified only in theory, and is based on an accounting equivalence between loss and compensation." But as he says, the

---

3 Hence the proliferation of constantly new products that must be constantly adjusted to the evolution of risks, which is a perishable product par excellence. And thus "great benefits for the coverage providers." "Also, with a touch of malice, one could say that 'risk,' or rather the coverage of risk, was one of the best sold products during the last quarter of a century. Thus, it is the basis of the prosperity and the business of those who operate the systems organized around financial markets."

attacks at the World Trade Center have shown sufficiently how much loss of life and compensation were mutually immeasurable.

The result is a lack of accountability.

The dissemination in society of the idea that finance offers real possibilities of risk-hedging has resulted in a change of mentality in this matter: the proactive attitude in which each person has to take the responsibility of the unknown, of the uncertainty at the best of his or her competence and responsibility, has given way to a more passive, disempowering attitude, in which it is simply a matter of choosing the appropriate hedging instrument and acting as if the risk did not exist. It is highly likely that the possibility of covering the risk through a set of insurance and material equivalents has had three effects: the disempowerment of certain actors who have given up risk control since they knew it was insured; the appearance of the illusion that a risk-free society could exist; and the individualization of personal destinies, since risk-taking was entrusted to institutionalized intermediaries. The management of uncertainty through preventive measures and informal solidarity had therefore lost its *raison d'être*.

Dispelling confusions

This severe criticism ultimately leads to the idea that there would be an intrinsic bias in finance, conducive to a mutilating and overly simplistic vision and treatment of reality.

What shall we think of that? Let us note first that two sets of ideas are here narrowly woven, but quite different in reality. The first one highlights the characteristics of financial logic: the economic calculation of what an owner can draw from his or her assets, taking into account not only the expected results but also coefficients of probability, particularly of risk, in addition to a comparison, made at the society level, of the various possibilities offered, notably on the financial market. The second set of ideas says that this leads to a virtual activity, disconnected from the real economy, which is also misleading in its conclusions.

On the first point, however, it seems difficult to reject the idea that the possibility of making more precise calculations of what is obtained by using material resources under a monetary form (capital), and of its risks, is *one of the basic tools* of an owner worthy of the name, that is to say, he who is responsible for the use that is made of his capital. Furthermore, being able to undertake a broad confrontation at the level of society on the financial markets is also an essential asset. But it is of course on condition that we do not absolutize these tools (which cannot give certainty), nor the control of the risk that a certain financial ideology claims to insure against,[4] and that we do not declare (ideologically) that the responsibility of each individual stops at this measure and at this dimension. Denouncing this ideological generalization is justified, as well as its reflection in behaviors. On the other hand, deducing from this that the instrument necessarily entails such consequences is inaccurate.

Indeed, from a Christian perspective, and one of natural morality, management decisions must incorporate many factors besides price. To take a simple example, it is one thing to manage real estate assets, to sell or buy them when needed, to measure the profitability of improvements on them, or to set a level of rent consistent with a real market. It is quite another to limit oneself to these considerations, without taking into account the situation of the people who live in these assets, or the alternative possible use of these funds, the social or urban needs, et cetera. Now, no market, by its very existence, has ever compelled anyone to buy or sell, or to consider financial aspects alone. It is therefore difficult to see how the existence of financial tools *automatically* leads to the deviations of the second series. We can imagine how the medieval Cistercian monasteries, attentive to the intelligent and active use of their resources, would have used the references and tools of financial analysis. But we do not see what would have led them to renounce their priorities of life (*ora et labora*), any more than the use of water mills or the introduction of the European wool trade had any such effect. On the other hand, of course *it is legitimate to denounce any social practice or accepted idea that leads owners to consider themselves released from any consideration other than a financial one in the narrow sense*, and *a fortiori* to denounce the modern economic ideology that justifies that.

Similarly, it is rational to engage in the calculation of potential risks and benefits. But it is erroneous or perverse to believe that in doing so we will have measured all the possible futures, that we will have gained some guarantee of security, let alone that we would get rid of our responsibilities, or that we can believe that financial compensation can replace human losses. This is not a promise made by finance

---

4 And who themselves have their ideological, even mythical content, like the theory of "efficient markets."

per se; any conscious stock market participant, who is constantly recording gains and losses, knows that perfectly. It is in fact *a certain current ideology and collective practice of finance*, which is of course a source of comfortable profits for some people. In all these cases, the instrument is not itself responsible for this deviation. The deviation results from a system of values, sometimes personal and more often collective, translated into structures and organizations, which in the end and according to a time-honored scheme, puts money before man and also betrays the market itself. This behavior is much more widespread in a relativistic period like ours, which professes that there is no objective moral value other than rules of the game that are then arbitrated, precisely, by the market.

INSTANT TRANSACTIONS AND LONG-TERM RELATIONSHIPS

Another objection to modern finance questions the role of *transactions* in our societies. According to this school of thought, the exaggerated importance of financial markets perverts relationships between persons. Critics emphasize then the benefit of long-term relationships, which are contrasted with supposedly fugitive and irresponsible transactions. We find this well-articulated and argued analysis again in Paul Dembinski.[5] He emphasizes "an inversion of purposes that would have occurred during the last quarter of a century...a shift in which the transaction increasingly uses relationships, which are understood as a mode of human social and economic interaction, as instruments. The transaction then means *a unilateral and abrupt exit from the relationship*." Let's take a closer look.

Transaction as the enemy

The main point for Dembinski is *a radical change in the connection between transaction and relationship*. For our author, the long-term relationship has been broken up by introducing the possibility for one of the two parties to sell to other players their place in the financial relationship they established. This possibility is asymmetrical and plays in favor of the investor: "the other party remains passive (and captive) during the transaction." Hence a distinction between banking (loans) and financial markets. The first is described as perennial and robust; its success rests on industry executives. The second, as a pure,

---

5   Paul H. Dembinski, *Finance servante ou finance trompeuse?* (Paris: Parole et Silence, 2008).

mobile intermediation, is supposed to penalize errors more quickly. But it is fragile, hypersensitive, easy to manipulate, and depends on the psychology of markets, which overrides economic foundations.[6] In addition to this, there is the cult of shareholder value: the only duty of managers is to work for shareholders, through rising prices or by returning capital. Hence the financialization[7] of companies: they no longer invest, they bet on the financial market to boost their bottom line, and they put pressure on the rest of society. This has nothing to do with the enterprise of the past: "in the greatest part of the period of the Industrial Revolution, the liquid assets that were saved were only means to achieve economically profitable achievements; they did not have financial result as their main objective." Finance would then have been solely a means; it was not competent in matters of purposes. That is what would have changed: "instead of being regarded as simple fuel, used for the material equipment and supply of a living organism that is the productive enterprise, money is now considered to be the living organism, and the company with its human activities becomes its fuel and instrument. In such a way, profits are no longer the normal fruit of the company fueled by money, but the normal fruit of money, fueled by the company."

But the system has its limits. Large-scale instrumental use of trading relationships directly affects stakeholder relationships and trust disappears, but an investment project assumes trust. "The sterilization of the relationship through a transaction perspective in fact deprives the economy and society of the flexibility that the duration of relationships offers." In a situation of widespread mistrust, cooperation is no longer possible, therefore no more creativity, no more innovation; economic sterility becomes a threat. Moreover, the complexity of the whole increases and so does the risk of chaos. Apart from the fact that tolerance of inequalities has its limits, other limitations

---

6 It is true, he says, that there are regulations, in order to guarantee the integrity of the market, in a "constant struggle between the lure of easy gain, and public confidence in a social institution." But the operators "know that, in the end, the King of the market is less well-dressed than the discourse of legitimation would like, that strategies can be deployed to change it (for a few seconds), that assessments are not as objective as the public thinks, and that business accounting is less objective than one might think."

7 Hence also the increase of the share of capital in the distribution of results, and the multiplication of leverage effects (debt that replaces equity, which increases the return on equity, but weakens the concerned entity).

are "the feeling of generalized meaninglessness, the erosion of ethical foundations and the feeling of ethical impotence and alienation." The transaction also calls into question the fundamental principle that the strong must take care of the weak.[8] All relations become depersonalized. For finance is "a place particularly conducive to the generalization of situations of ethical alienation." "The manipulator of symbols, enclosed in rigid procedures, can easily become indifferent to the meaning and implications of what he or she does. In many cases, ethical alienation becomes a habit, all the easier to acquire since compensation is high." In consequence: "today, economic and financial logic is not only free from the influence of metaphysical, social, and political considerations, but it also imposes its domination without encountering any established opposing powers."

What can be done? An idea that comes immediately to mind is to moralize finance. But, says Dembinski, this has a limited scope. The central point is the disappearance of the concern for the common good: to put it back in the center, we must give priority to relationship and duration. For example, we can increase transaction costs, create preferred shares for loyal investors, set up trust structures such as solidarity finance and microfinance. But above all, another behavior must be induced, favoring shorter distances, personal knowledge, and modified remunerations. This new approach must more radically accept frugality, as well as a certain amount of improvidence, of lack of concern for the future, "to abandon the artificial haven of market transactions, in favor of the continued wealth of relationships." The whole "conceals in reality a social dilemma: between a market society hinged on instantaneous and mechanically pure transactions, and a society of lasting relations, open to the other person, a society concerned with the common good that we have to develop."

Who is responsible? The market or the actors?

Here again, it seems to me that the diagnosis of the effects is fair enough, but their attribution exclusively to finance is excessive. Most of the problems he raises relate more to the overall logic of modern capitalism in its questionable dimension than to its financial component

---

8   He also explains that in many professions, there is a switch from an ethical approach to the strict contractualization of relationships — it is notably the case in professions based on knowledge and expertise, where the relationship is inherently dissymmetrical.

considered as a branch of activity. This is the case, for example, with profit conceived as an exclusive end, environmental materialism, the instrumental use of people, the impoverishment of relationships, and so on. Naturally, finance plays an active role in this, since it deals with capital and money. But we must not confuse them, and attribute to the financial function alone what is an overall feature of the system. The harmful role that money can play is not limited to the last twenty years. And what is said of large enterprises only presupposes an obsession with profit, which has been known since the beginning of capitalism: the idyllic vision of an ancient capitalism not preoccupied primarily by profit is unrealistic. In other words, *there is a tendency to confuse, on the one hand, finance as an institution, and, on the other hand, the general obsession with financial results, with money, which is dominant in a capitalist system without cultural, moral, or spiritual counterweights.*

What is still to be measured, however, in the radicalization of the system is what is actually due to finance itself. Hence the question of the balance between *relation and transaction*, the first judged proper and the second harmful. Dembinski, along with much of the public, identifies transactions with financial markets. We know that financial markets are not the only possible method of financing, even in a market economy: the same lending or placement operation could be carried out by a bank or a direct investor. In this case, there is no secondary market: the investor or the lender keeps the operation through to its term, via a loan, or indefinitely, through shares. Dembinski prefers this method. But in my opinion, his analysis mixes two ideas: on the one hand, there is the technical idea that market finance is inferior to an economy like the economy after World War II, in which bank financing was central, and which left industry managers a high degree of autonomy, and which was supposedly oriented toward long-term development. On the other hand, there is a more structure-oriented idea, which holds that through the market, long-term face-to-face relationships have generally been replaced by the search for instantaneous and impersonal transactions, thus degrading the whole of society. Let us look at these two points.

Bilateral relations or market financing

The first point is the most debatable: the post-war era appears in retrospect as a very peculiar and fugitive moment in the history of the capitalist system, where business leaders acted in a free and safe way in a world where growth was expected, and innovation focused on already tried and true products. There was no need for much capital since risks were low; loans could be repaid over time without major risks. But, in addition to the fact that retrospective views are easily too idyllic, this world disappeared in the 1970s crises. Historical capitalism that preceded it (until the war) was very different, and much closer to our world, but was in fact much less regulated.

More fundamentally, it is unrealistic to think economies such as ours can be financed without a broad appeal to financial markets.[9] What are we talking about? If there is no market, either primary or secondary,[10] the investor or the lender keeps the transaction to its term (loans) or indefinitely (shares). They say that the relationship can then be more direct and personal, leading to better accountability. But it soon runs up against its limits. Apart from the fact that the preceding effect is not self-evident,[11] the lack of market reference implies first of all that there is no external indication, in particular of price, or any way to confront the opinions of third parties on the transaction in question. Except in the case of loyal and competent partners, arbitrariness prevails. Then there is the lack of liquidity. In the case of an equity investment, you don't know how to get out of the commitment, and you can remain indefinitely "stuck," at the mercy of the owner of the company. Unless there is a particular reason for this, such as a personal relationship with an entity you know well or over which you have some power, you won't take such risks on a large scale. Therefore, the vast majority of investors has neither the desire nor the means to bind themselves in that way to a particular enterprise. This is why the provision of equity on a somewhat significant scale presupposes a financial market, at least since the nineteenth century.[12] On the other hand, the role of finance is not to bring money to managers without taking risks: it is the result of the evaluation of the right risk/results tandem, which takes then the form of an investment, of risk-taking in the long-term, a difficult

9   This does not imply that this market must be global. Globalization is a completely different issue from the use of the financial market as a tool.

10   The primary market is the initial offering of securities, the secondary market, subsequent purchases and sales of these securities.

11   Being linked does not mean that the "relationship" is responsible. Notably the recipient of the funds can then more easily afford to do anything.

12   And in a sense since the Middle Ages, knowing that they were then engaged mostly in successive punctual operations.

exercise in a rapidly changing world like ours. The right way to do this is through equity and not primarily through debt.[13]

In addition, the main objects of market finance are stocks, which represent money invested almost for forever, and bonds, which are loans over a relatively long time. Behind the short-term fluctuations, arising from the fact that they can be bought or sold at any time, *this is money entrusted to companies over the long or very long term.* No other system does the same. And given the limitations of public finances, no system in general can provide such financial resources over such lengthy periods. It is therefore not by chance that they are publicly traded securities, which the investor can sell if he has to: it limits the effect of such a commitment. Without this, nobody would invest, or not as much, over such periods, or only in a position of strength, as a majority shareholder. This in no way implies that we should not encourage a stable shareholder base, on the contrary. But encouraging it, through tax incentives or increased rights, does not mean indefinitely tying up the investments.

There is still the issue of bank financing, which Dembinski exalts nostalgically. Its contribution is obviously essential. But a bank, which lends with a significant leverage, cannot contribute share equity, because it is too risky. And bank credit is not a universal way of financing the economic system. It is a specialized method playing a particular role of distribution and allocation of credit where the nature of the debtors or of the transactions is such that the claims in question must be granted on a case-by-case basis and kept by the lender in his book. This happens because they are too small (in the case of individuals, Small and Medium-sized Enterprises, or SMEs, etc.), or because they are complex and very specific (large projects, complex assets, etc.). Moreover, in such cases the bank must be able to carry the asset in question throughout its duration. In so doing, it is exposed to the risk of failure on the part of the borrower, especially in the case of large or complex operations. But this also happens in the case of a collective error (real estate in particular is a regular source of banking crises). It is therefore inevitable that banks should be potentially high-risk companies; history shows that most of the major crises were bank credit crises. Anyone who believes they can solve the problems of finance by transferring all financing to loans on

---

13 Moreover, debt itself, if it is on a large scale, also takes the form of securities placed on the market (bonds), which are also subject to the financial market—with the advantage of a general matching and potential liquidity.

bank balance sheets forgets the innumerable crises that occurred in this context: the Latin American debt crisis in 1982, real estate bubbles throughout all periods and especially in the 1990s (2007 was also one), and so on. Banks must therefore be managed with great care and with a high level of regulation. The 2007 crisis in particular fully confirmed the risks of a debt economy (we will see that in more detail). Moreover, there is every indication that the future role of financial markets in financing the economy will not be reduced, but increased, for reasons that cannot be developed here.[14] This makes it all the more urgent to channel the markets and moralize them as much as possible.

Relationships or transactions: Is there really a dilemma?

The second point of Paul Dembinski, which transitions from relationships between people to supposedly impersonal transactions, is much more interesting: it is a real question. As Rowan Williams says:[15] "it is necessary to abandon an economic model that is simply a money-generating mechanism, and to try to recognize the role of trust, which needs time to develop; therefore, we must move away from a notion of wealth and profit in which we imagine that they can be obtained without risk." The basic principle is not to care only about one's own interests, but also about those of one's partners and of society as a whole. One cannot base everything on contracts where each party pursues selfish interests. *We must have as much as possible long-lasting and, above all, different relationships, based on common values, starting with the very valuation of the relationship itself.* And there Paul Dembinski is in the right.

In the financial field, however, we must recognize the limits of the romantic vision of supposedly optimal face-to-face relations. Anyone who has been stuck with an investment that he cannot get out of, knows the worth of liquidity. It is essential for most capital that a possibility of redeployment exists and that a matching of investments is possible, which is called a market. *Certainly, a long-term relationship, cultivating mutual trust, is an excellent thing in finance too,* and it is highly desirable to orient the system in this direction. But let's not mix levels: neither

---

14 Global extension of transactions, credit restrictions due to the strengthening of bank prudential ratios, demand from governments, banks, and companies for capital and long-term financing, etc.
15 Former (Anglican) Archbishop of Canterbury; Rowan Williams in Dembinski, ed., *Pratiques financières*, p. 106.

companies nor commercial relations are necessarily bound to last forever; they are neither families nor countries. And money relations are not idyllic relations in which you have to enter on a permanent or lasting basis; neither is such a fidelity always a moral duty.

Transaction does not exclude relationship. Our medieval merchants of Franciscan inspiration were oriented toward the formation of a Christian social fabric, therefore of long-lasting relations, but they operated essentially through transactions. *They even considered the market as an essential social bond. The desirable return to more complete, loyal, and responsible relations must not be based on the disappearance of the market but on a different use of that market.* It is not by preventing people from selling that one creates loyal and mutually beneficial relationships, based on a broader perspective than pure performance calculation, but by *cultivating the (right) idea of the benefit of these long-term relationships when they are possible, and this is very often the case.* But of course, regulatory measures can and should help, notably tax incentives granted to long and faithful relations and investments. Let us also note that *nothing in the teaching of the Church condemns the transaction as such, nor does it always recommend the alternative of a lasting relationship*, especially if it is based on indebtedness. And even in this case, there is no price reference to such an operation other than market prices, the risk lying in harming the counterparty or the partner. And thus, *in economic matters there is no reason to divide a community in the Christian sense of the word into networks of rigid relations, excluding non-participants.*

In other words, and beyond all the justly denounced excesses of a sometimes irresponsible or unbridled finance, there is no point in incriminating the market for questions of society that are actually essential, but which arise at a level that is much more fundamental. A market always has to be enclosed in rules, to be regulated: this is an indisputable point and the subprime crisis reminded us of that in a violent way. But, let us say it again, a market is mainly determined by the value system[16] of its participants: *what makes the market is the hierarchy of priorities of these participants.* And here we find again the fundamental values of the society in question. Beyond the regulations, or the ethics of intermediaries (they are both indispensable), the main path for further reflection is here. Criticizing market ideology as the

16   This term is understood here in a broad sense, including the collective functions induced by these values.

ultimate key to social relations in a relativistic context is justified. Seeking how to strengthen human communities is essential, including those more temporary communities that are companies and business relationships. But it *depends on acting at the appropriate level, the political level, and — even more — on the values of the considered society, and of its participants*. And without breaking those thermometers that are or can be the markets — if they work.

CHRISTIAN CRITICISM: SEARCH OF PROFIT AND STRUCTURES OF SIN
Reminder of the positions of the Magisterium

Part of the accusations made against finance, which we have noted here and there, are, as we have seen, taken up by the Church. We are not aiming here at the political left, whose references are often outside the Social Doctrine. Nor at that utopia[17] that is cultivated in many Christian circles: a world without big business or financial markets; it is neither realistic nor desirable. Certainly, an SME has the great advantage of being based on a direct relationship between people, and it immediately connects the manager to capital and to major decisions. The Social Doctrine has always been very favorable to that. But, apart from its limitations, it is difficult to develop an economy solely on this basis. Apart from the fact that it is not realistic to try to eliminate large companies, which have their own essential role in many activities, this is particularly meaningless in financial matters. This is confirmed by the fact that finance developed already in the thirteenth century, in a context that was considerably more local, but even at that time it quickly became apparent that, for certain larger or riskier operations, it was necessary to combine capital, and to go well beyond limited family property to do so.

The Social Doctrine does not take this route, but, as we have seen, it criticizes several important features of current financial activity — always as possible deviations, not as an intrinsic feature of their activity. And without surprise this accusation is ultimately aimed at the "exclusive desire of profit," listed by John Paul II (*Sollicitudo rei socialis*) as one of the characteristic "structures of sin" of our time. Benedict XVI described it as an idolatry, which gives it a metaphysical and religious dimension — that of a profound conceptual error on what is essential

---

17   Recall that Catholic Social Teaching is not a plan for a utopia, but a rule for collective behavior.

for us. Obviously, this does not concern only finance in the strict sense: the target of the Social Doctrine of the Church is exclusive profit, understood as a central law governing companies in general. But it has a special importance in the case of finance, because it works on money: it is much easier to ignore the other dimensions of a decision in favor of profit considerations. Of course, the teaching is aimed first at the desire for individual gain, at greed, which some people did not hesitate before the crisis to magnify as a paradoxical virtue. But, as we have seen, the criticism is more generally aimed at rapid gain, at "speculation" (always a negative word in the Doctrine), at the preponderance of the short-term, and ultimately at the risk that finance will lose sight of its collective justification, by following *"an ever more self-referential logic, unrelated to the real basis of the economy."* Even in the short-term, it reminds us that this disturbs the price formation system and makes it more difficult to forecast and manage companies, making the economy more unstable and less transparent. And it does not then deliver the service expected from it, this role of a bridge between the present and the future which is one of its essential functions.

Structures of sin and technological neutrality

In order to shed light on this question, it is necessary to recall here that there are two types of financial injustice to be considered, that of individuals (greed) and that of collective functioning. If the former is obvious to the public, which is scandalized by the glaring profits of some speculators or traders, the latter is more essential and more significant. Indeed, as we have seen, the pressure of the search for profit stems less and less from the personal behavior of traditional owners and more and more from professional managers operating in markets. Being responsible for this management on behalf of others, they are not free to do what they want. Moreover, the product of the pressure exerted by finance potentially benefits a large number of people, besides intermediaries: pensioners, policyholders, or insured persons. But, of course, the potential immorality of rapid profit or at least its disadvantages do not disappear. When management logic is based on monetary profit alone, it is unlikely that the common good will be completely satisfied. Furthermore, the "collectivization" of this ownership, in the form of fund managers supposedly defending the interests of millions of people of modest means, leads to viewing some of these profits as normal and even morally "just," while they would be recognized as questionable if they were put in a larger perspective. This leads us to identify here a possible *structure of sin*.[18]

It is necessary to consider more generally as structures of sin some of the features of the dominant ideology of the moment, insofar as it can strongly condition the priorities and the actual behaviors of operators. For example, *two theories, in vogue in recent years but economically and morally erroneous, can function as structures of sin*, or at least can be used as their origin or justification: *the idea that the company must act in the exclusive interest of the shareholder and the idea that markets are perfectly efficient*.[19] This notion may include whole classes of products or practices and the corresponding markets[20] (we will come back to this). But as Jacques Bichot tells us:

> it is not the financial market that is a structure of sin; it is institutions and customs that have been introduced into the market to distort its functioning, to introduce darkness where the market requires good quality information.... Christians should...clearly distinguish between bad practices and the financial market: institutions that ensure that the market works are—if they do their job—an excellent tool for dismantling structure of sins.[21]

Should the requirements of high profitability be classified in this category of structure of sin? Antoine de Salins[22] notes on this subject:

> there is a certain mythology of this famous ROE (return on equity)[23] of 15 percent put forward by many essayists. When we look at all the studies that have been done on this subject, we see that companies that do not reach this level of return are not penalized by the financial market and that the

---

18 A notion used by the Church to designate those cases where the organization of society pushes its members to sin, even though this does not remove the personal responsibility of the person who commits it.

19 We can also add here the erroneous idea that government bonds are the risk-free benchmark for the fixed income market.

20 Thus, in the last crisis subprime and more generally over the counter (OTC) securitizations, some predatory leveraged buy-outs (LBOs), and of course synthetic products like collateralized debt obligations (CDOs), can be given as examples of structures of sin.

21 Jacques Bichot in Dembinski, ed., *Pratiques financières*, p. 85.

22 Antoine de Salins, ibid., p. 248.

23 Ratio between profit and equity.

market is often more patient because investors believe there are prospects of return on investment in the very long term, for example in new technologies.

This is indisputable. Nevertheless, when, for a period of time, a reference is spreading on the market, it finally compels the actors, and proves harmful if it leads to erroneous decisions. This was probably to an important extent the case of this 15 percent.

Beyond natural morality

What has just been said could be applied to many of our contemporaries. But this question is of course more acute when one thinks, with the Social Doctrine, that *the role of finance is to finance the economy, itself understood as a tool of human development over time* (which can be put under the notion of the common good). This means that it should be directed toward this goal and organized for it; if it is not, it is no longer justified. *This gives an even broader and richer meaning to the idea that finance is or should be at the service of society.* As we have seen, the Church calls for a fundamentally ethical orientation of all economic activity. Benedict XVI said that the whole economy and all finance have an ethical dimension, not because of an external labeling, but because of compliance with requirements intrinsic to their very nature. We have seen the main points: justice, human dignity, concern for the poor and solidarity, respect for natural morality, and more broadly charity, in the full sense of the word.

The emerging question is therefore: Can the allocation of capital resulting from the functioning of the financial system be orientated through reforms toward better procedures of choice, integrating the dimensions that it must integrate? Toward something that aims to maximize its results for the population as a whole, but on the condition that this maximization is not judged simply in terms of yield or of consumption, but of personal and collective development (the common good)? This is an ambitious program, very general in this form, which needs to be broken down in more detail. It should be noted, however, that it is no longer a question for economists or technicians alone, but a reflection on the society that has been created, and what it brings to each member. This goes far beyond the question of finance. But since finance allocates productive wealth or a substantial part of it, it is also legitimately at the center of the debate. Let's see how we can address these issues.

THIRD PART

New Perspectives for Finance

CHAPTER 9
Logic and Function of Finance

FORECASTING THE FUTURE?
Market efficiency and forecasting

The first issue is what is called market efficiency. Since finance is or should be a bridge between the present and the future, what is the forecasting capacity of finance in general and markets in particular? Let us understand well: we are talking of a good allocation of available resources at a given moment, in view of what is foreseeable or analyzable. It cannot be a clairvoyant capacity that would enable the markets literally to foresee the future — which would be magic. The evidence shows that the ability of financial markets to really predict the future is at best variable. Niall Ferguson[1] reminds us, for example, that just before the 1914 war, financiers were aware that the war would be a catastrophe, but they thought it impossible; the market was not very sensitive to bad news (and even, initially, to the assassination of the archduke). Yet the outbreak of war resulted in a major dislocation of these markets, which remained closed for months, and the financial system had to be saved through public intervention. As Ferguson says, years of financial globalization exploded in a few days and it took two generations to catch up with that. But just before the event, there was no indication of this on the market, either because of the abundance of liquidity, a false sense of security, or mere incompetence.

More widely it is clear that markets do not function scientifically and cannot be reduced to rigorous mathematical models. Ferguson[2] shows it in a luminous way by two opposing examples. A success: that of the speculator, George Soros, who based his actions precisely on the idea that markets are not scientific. In his books, Soros[3] criticizes the economics-textbook hypotheses on market efficiency and proposes his theory of reflexivity: it is the market movements that form the future, or at least the future of the market, and not the markets that

---

1 Niall Ferguson, *The Ascent of Money: A Financial History of the World* (London: Penguin Books, 2008), pp. 298 sqq.
2 We will return later to the role of models in the 2007 crisis.
3 See Ferguson, *The Ascent of Money*, pp. 317 sqq.

foresee the future. Hence the bubbles, reflections of trends and errors of perception that interact; they are self-fulfilling prophecies since a forecast that there will be price increases comes true if there are enough people to believe it and thus buy the stocks. Overall, basing his action on collective psychology Soros was a massive winner — even though he did not always guess the herd's tendency.

On the contrary, the mistaken temptation is to search for total control based on a supposedly rational calculation: Ferguson cites the Long-Term Capital Management (LTCM) fund, which was created by mathematicians and based on the efficient market hypothesis[4] (liquid, integrating all data, without friction, with a normal bell-shaped distribution of yields). This fund had been very successful for several years and had become enormous. But the Russian default in 1998 caused volatility to rise above previously reached levels; in addition, there was an unprecedented correlation between markets. The whole thing thwarted all the statistical series, and so the models, their hedging strategies, and their diversifications. As the fund situation became catastrophic, it had to be saved and closed. These models were based on only five years of data; they did not even integrate the crash of 1987. Yet Ferguson notes that there was afterward an explosive development of hedge funds, often based on "scientific" claims. Notwithstanding, it is true that they can provide very high returns to their managers. This testifies to the naiveté or incompetence of many investors, because if a small number of people, like Soros, actually have great talent, most of these managers merely found a clever way to become rich. It can be shown by simple examples that, within normal market behavior, reasonably lucky managers with the right timing can obtain high returns for the funds they manage and thus become rich; they just have to take advantage of the good times, when the market is going in the direction of their models. Ferguson also recalls the emotional and herd character of the behavior of most participants in a market, which goes from enthusiasm to despair. Behavioral experiments show in addition the many irrational biases into which most investors fall.[5] All this is indisputable, and we shall

---

4 Ibid., pp. 327 sqq.

5 We rely on the data we already have in mind, without researching the relevant ones; we give more weight to what we have seen in the past or to what has an affective value; we generalize on the basis of inadequate information; we try to confirm the starting hypotheses rather than following the facts which may

return to it. But it should be noted at the same time that these are fundamental human facts: it is not easy to do better.

Managing the uncertain future

The role of finance as a bridge between the present and the future it forecasts and arbitrates poses major questions. They are almost philosophical. The central point is that by definition the future is not known. At most, we can put forward probabilities, but these are reliable only if the events in question are "knowable," that is to say similar to those of the past, and if they are numerous enough for errors to be corrected statistically. In these cases, the function becomes an intelligent treatment of what may be called the "least original part of the future." One can make the operation more rational, on one hand by improving the quality of the analysis or through technical knowledge, and on the other hand by playing on a sufficient quantity of operations in relation to overall activity. But of course, the process is still tainted with risk, and more general risks cannot be eliminated on the basis of these factors: economic activity, general credit demand, interest rate levels, and the future appetite of the public for a product, not to mention the limits of mathematical models.[6] In most cases, the uncertainty is given by nature and is important, whether it is related to a particular operation, such as the chances of success of a project or a company, ability to repay, et cetera, or to the overall economic and political activity.

FINANCIAL MARKETS: BUILDING THE FUTURE?
Markets: a general matching place that opens up opportunities for action

This brings us back to the more general question of the financial market as the ultimate place where operators meet and operate. The central point is to admit that its logic is not that of the ideological theory of efficient markets, which describes it as the best possible integration of all available data about the future. Rather, it is *the matching*

---

contradict them; we overestimate or underestimate the probabilities according to the way they are presented to us; we overestimate the validity intervals of our favorite hypotheses; we follow the crowd, etc. Ferguson, *The Ascent of Money*, p. 346.

6   See here, for example, the criticism of mathematical models made by the authors in the book edited by Christian Walter, *Nouvelles normes financières: S'organiser face à la crise* (Berlin: Springer, 2010).

of all the positions taken by all participants at a given moment, with reference to the future. For example, market interest rates tend to increase if operators fear a tougher monetary policy, or doubt the solvency of the issuing State, or anticipate a risk of inflation, et cetera. When investors apprehend such events, even in the long term, they change their policy. This face-off of opinions is not theoretical, since it translates into real operations, resulting in gains or losses. But *it has no reason to be fully rational,* nor coherent with the available data. On the other hand, *it makes it possible to find solutions*: for example, people who want to borrow know that they can find money at a given price which is recognized by all; a lender knows that he will be able to sell at that price with full liquidity: the market effectively allows participants to operate.

Again, it might be argued that an alternative method exists, financing on bank balance sheets, loans. It is not directly exposed to the general opposition of risks and remunerations, hence its limits, and also its advantages. But the question is a little more complex, as we have seen. First, it does not work with shareholders' equity. Then, if a bank is to manage its portfolios as well as possible, it must resort to the market, because the market provides the resources for that: own funds, hedging, and financing. The bank must therefore give a positive image of its overall management to the market, and in particular of its loans. This means that bank lending amounts to summarizing in an overall picture the accumulated individual financing decisions the bank makes. In contrast, when pricing bonds, the market examines different instruments separately, in the form of debts of particular borrowers. The two management modes are therefore different. In principle, the market works in the case of fairly large operations. The preferred area of bank financing is small loans — because they are relatively divided, statistically appreciable, and too small for the market — or, on the contrary, large, complex, and specific operations, which the market cannot easily analyze. But bank lending cannot fulfill the entire function of finance; it needs the financial market not only to find its resources or give them a price, but to be itself controlled from outside.

One might then be tempted to question the very idea of a general matching of resources within the framework of a financial market, and to look for other methods. However, the limits of possible alternatives immediately appear. If one were in a free economy that had no market, we would have a whole set of individual transactions without reference to this type of overall matching procedure. Due to the opacity and the risks that it would bring about, this would lead to many disadvantages and to immobility. In other words, only the market provides a general facing-off of opinions, at least those of active operators; if it did not exist, each investor or applicant for financing should judge alone all the relevant factors without broad external reference, which is quite difficult. Moreover, they could not cover themselves via some form of insurance against the various risks they may fear — using the fact that other operators might have a different perception of those risks and take positions accordingly.[7] They would therefore follow the operation through to its end, unless they meet by chance someone who wanted to buy it.[8] This would therefore greatly increase both the risks taken, and the difficulty of getting out of that agreement if things go wrong. And if, on the other hand, one relies on governmental decisions, in a democratic context or not, the rationality of these decisions is in general significantly lower than with the market.[9]

In other words, the primary role of markets is to offer opportunities to combine opinions with a possible action. They offer prices and references, which not only provide information, but provide an arena in which to operate if desired, one on a broad basis since it potentially integrates all operators. In addition to its concrete role of providing resources for some and opportunities for others, which has no equivalent elsewhere, the market makes it possible to match up a multiplicity of opinions and to offer price references, which, if limited to a specific role, are irreplaceable. This is why it continues to attract buyers and sellers, who could otherwise deal directly with

7   For example, to protect themselves against a subsequent fluctuation of the price of a foreign currency, or of interest rates. Even without a global market, the relative value of things, as it results from the multitude of particular operations, has no reason to remain fixed, except in a fully administered economy.
8   This would be *a fortiori* the case in a society without a separate financial function: each actor would be forced to play two roles simultaneously, his own economic function, and the financial function, the latter without a reference criterion such as is available in the market. In widespread practice, such a situation would be very inefficient and opaque.
9   The electoral hazard and the action of pressure groups distort decisions, hence they tend to be even more short-term, opaque, and irrational. Not to mention the Soviet model!

each other. But publicly bringing together opinions has never given a guarantee of truth! Again, fetishizing the market is a major mistake; one worse still is its corresponding ideology. Let us recall the intuition of medieval people regarding their markets: it is important, in seeking the right price, to seek outward objective references beyond the good will of the parties, and in particular the current state of possibilities existing in society, which means in practice the state of supply and demand in general. We need this matching of supply and demand, and the margin of freedom it gives, not only for efficiency's sake, but for the sake of commutative justice. At the same time, of course, it must never create an obligation to act: it must always be possible to decline to deal on the other's terms, or to deal at all. If this is the case, the existence of markets has mainly advantages: one can resort to them when one wants and abstain when one wants. One must never be obliged to deal at this or that price, let alone take it as the sole factor of a decision: it is a mere reference. It is a moral necessity to check constantly the risks and effects of products and activities, without relying solely on prices incorporated in the markets. We remain completely responsible for each of our transactions. But the market is an indispensable tool, if it works.

Limitations intrinsic to the indications given by the market

Having considered the benefits, it is also essential to see the limits. We must distinguish two very different roles of a market. The first and most immediate role is what has just been described: it is a place where transactions are made possible. This role is essentially pragmatic. From this point of view, the price observed at a given moment has only one meaning: it says what a purchase can cost, or what a sale can provide at that time, within the limits of the observed volumes. It is in this sense that Roman law said that a thing is worth what someone is willing to pay for it. This simply indicates, tautologically, that *on a market, a thing is worth what someone agrees to pay. This does not mean that it is worth that price "in itself," or all the time.*

A second, quite different role of the market is, by extension, to be an indicator used by participants in the wider functioning of the economy, at least by participants with a particular need at a specific time. The two meanings coincide if most of the products in question are actually for sale on the market: for example, this is the case for fresh fruit and vegetables. But not if the products have permanent and reserve value, and if as a result most of their owners do not constantly buy or sell them. This is the case for most financial products, which are assets, intended to retain value over their life. For then the market concerns only those who at some point wish to buy or sell. It is therefore *intrinsic to a financial market to suffer from partial representativeness, possibly very partial*. We can see this in an exaggerated way in market panics: there are too few buyers, so the price collapses, or too few sellers, so the price soars. In the first case, does this mean that all the holders of this asset consider that it is actually worth almost nothing? Of course not: most of them respond to the collapse of prices by keeping the asset. *The price is therefore different from what it would be if all the holders had to sell everything or buy everything permanently*. Therefore, in this case, which is the usual case, *it is absurd to consider that the market price gives a reliable indication of intrinsic value, even if the market works reasonably well*. It is therefore also absurd to want to operate the whole economy on the basis of these indications. *This does not mean that the market has no role, but rather that its role is limited; it serves for those who buy or sell, not for others*, except as an indication, without commitment. Of course, the situation becomes very different when the totality of the considered securities is at stake, as in the case of takeovers: that is why the price then becomes very different. Similarly, infrequently, and for some specific products, the market may be wide enough to be considered representative. But in practice, even for actively processed products such as government bonds, *the quantity exchanged and the motivation for these exchanges are not necessarily representative of the preferences of most of the holders or users of these products*. The majority of Govies are bought and held to maturity.

A first consequence of this observation is radically to challenge the ideology that is the basis of our current accounting system, the International Accounting Standards Board's International Financial Reporting Standards. This system is built on "full fair value," and in principle considers only the market price of each balance sheet item at any time (with exceptions, such as bank loans). But this only makes sense for trading portfolios, in the case of the institutions that are active in trading. And it is in contradiction with the principle we have stated that no one should be obliged to intervene in a market. As all market fluctuations are translated instantly into profit and loss, any investor who has to use such standards is transformed into a short-term-oriented trader. The existence of a market makes sense only if social practice does not lead to making a universal reference of it, either directly or indirectly through accounting rules.[10]

A second consequence is that the result of the market will not be improved by restricting participation — for example, as some think, by limiting it to long-term investors. Indeed, those of them who buy or sell at a given time, by the very fact that they have made such a decision that others have not made, are not representative of all investors. In addition, excluding intermediaries from the market would lead to a collapse of liquidity, and would make the market hypersensitive and therefore easier to manipulate.

A third consequence, more radical, relates to the proper use of market indications. If the management of an enterprise or of economic assets is or would be based exclusively on market prices, it would be irrational, even if the markets were functioning well, even if they were reliable in view of their object. For this object is limited; it is not intended to allow its product (the market price) to be used as a general reference. In other words, one of the problems of what is called financialization, perhaps the first, is the fact that *even when the financial market is functioning properly, it is not in a position to provide the indications that would justify giving a truly central reference role to finance.* Notably, the price of a share is only an indication of momentary appreciation, and is in no case a direct measure of the value of a company. Consequently, *managing a business primarily on the basis of its stock market price is not only questionable from a social, moral, and economic standpoint, but also from a financial one.*

Philosophy of our relationship to the future

Let us now return to the philosophy of our relationship to the future. In a world where there is a high degree of decision-making autonomy for economic actors, those decisions concern the future. These actors must then imagine possible futures, with a strong social or societal dimension, since they depend largely on other people. Tomorrow's situation, which we try to anticipate today, will result

10 Widespread marking to market (adjusting the value of an asset according to market conditions) is from this point of view a moral aberration, even more than a technical one. But let's be fair: a lax under-provisioning that takes advantage of too flexible rules is also a moral fault.

from today's decisions (and the intermediate changes occurring between the two dates), and it will be the result of multiple decisions by participants. In a sense, therefore, *today's market is a summary at present of what is anticipated from future interaction*, albeit partially; this distillation obviously depends on the views of the participants at the present time. In other words, *the market is a way of anticipating the economic interaction of society as active operators believe it will occur tomorrow*. Conversely, today's decisions are the consequence of what these operators think will be the situation of tomorrow: the result is that *to build society today is also to anticipate the society of tomorrow*.

This sheds light on the way in which the role of markets should be considered, and in particular how participants act or should act on it. *The primary criterion for approaching a market from the point of view of active participants is (or should be) the building of future society*, and the nature of that future society. It cannot be a matter of judging exclusively from the financial return to be had, even though it is in itself excellent that there is some.[11] But *this final result must reside within a moral vision of the implied contribution to the society of tomorrow*, naturally within the limits of the current situation. This question arises, moreover, outside any consideration about progress, whether social or technical progress: it is the simple fact that what we do today determines what the world will be like tomorrow and for some time to come, a time for which we are responsible. This principle is true of every human act, and *a fortiori* in the case of finance, since its role is to allocate resources to the construction of the world of tomorrow.

A global market?

If we speak of society, then the question arises as to which society we are talking about, domestic[12] or global. Economic logic seems to recommend the widest possible space, since the matching of opinions and opportunities will then be the widest. We have also seen that the Social Doctrine recognizes as both inevitable and rather beneficial the relatively free and comparative rapprochement and interaction that is called globalization. All this would push us to position the financial

---

11   It is intrinsically good that we end up with resources superior to those we've used, everything being equal.

12   Anything said here about the national level may have to be transposed where necessary to the European level.

market at a global level, and, as the market must be regulated to function well, to aim for a form of global regulation. But while this may remain the horizon for reasoning, there are many reasons for a more cautious approach. In the first place, there is very little global regulation of finance, and it is developing only slowly: consultation between national authorities can provide many services but remains imperfect. Secondly and above all, one can doubt the rationality of the choices made on such a large scale by people who are not very aware of the diversity of local situations. Finally, and more essentially, *the question arises concerning the framework on which society is built: for a large part, it is at the national level.* Hence, all that belongs to public or private intervention, any form of rule, is largely national. Thus, even if the horizon is in some respect global, and if it is logical that financial flows accompany trade intensification at this level, it may be necessary in some cases to provide for national restrictions on certain movements of capital or market mechanisms, or at least to favor those participants who respect some rules of solidarity, which is mainly by proximity and at the national level.

FINANCE AND PRIORITIZATION OF VALUES
Finance, a reflection of dominant values

All this leads us to place these reflections in the context of the society that these mechanisms must serve. In a decentralized and monetary economy, and therefore a market economy, decisions have by nature an important financial dimension, even outside the financial system. It is therefore always tempting to give a preponderant role to financial preoccupations, and to the search for monetary profit. It will even be the most logical choice if other considerations do not get the upper hand. From this point of view, finance makes explicit a basic feature of such an economy, in a pure and exclusive form. Its exaggerations are exaggerations of the system and vice versa. If, for example, the search for profit is the central criterion for the allocation of resources, it is because it is also at the heart of the current liberal economy, for it is its universal measure. If finance directs the management of firms, their purchase or their sale solely on the basis of pecuniary considerations, the fact is that any decision-maker can always do so in a free economy and, above all, in the absence of other criteria, he will almost necessarily do so. Similarly, it is shocking to see disproportionate profits. But there has always been some in decentralized economies:[13] market mechanisms cannot guarantee the full relevance of all the remunerations that each participant gets from them. And if the criticism made of finance relates to its tendency to become carried away and then to go in the wrong direction without cultural, moral, or spiritual counterweights,[14] it is obviously not the only social phenomenon to do so.

All this leads us to stress the central importance of the motivations and values of the society in question, of the collective structures that bear them, and therefore, also of the responsibilities we have to assume. *If deficiencies can be partly corrected by rules, it is basically the participants who have to assume their responsibilities.* This may be accomplished by individuals alone, or within the framework of *collective structures* that direct, determine, and elicit these choices, which are fundamentally ethical, but which, like all ethics, rely on collective behavior. If the actors want to think only of gain (lucre), they can always do so. Regulations can at best limit some of the excesses, but not reorient all priorities. We look to our medieval scholastics again, and their concern to create *a morally good trade mentality* (we would say of the economic operators), *which recognizes a social function and social responsibility.* Our questioning brings us back to the central problem of integrating a personal and collective moral norm into everyday behavior. In the end, once again, every market is a place of exchange between people, where prices result from the meeting up of personal appraisals, which are themselves dependent on values. It is inevitable that in our societies, characterized as they are by the absence of an explicit collective morality, situations develop where the particular wills that collide are arbitrated only by the market, expressed in monetary terms, and especially the financial market. The relativistic logic of our societies (liberal in the philosophical sense of

---

13   In fact, in any economy, except in the historically rare case of overall state control.

14   Of course, other factors are at work, and they can reinforce this trend. In particular, globalization mechanically increases the role of finance, since State regulation has no longer the same weight as in a compartmentalized world. But while this increases the relative role of finance, it does not give it a precise direction, except that it reduces the pressure of the surrounding atmosphere and facilitates the autonomy of the monetary criterion. This also undoubtedly increases the fluctuations and irrationalities of the market, because it puts us in a rapidly changing economy, which undertakes the progressive integration of extremely dissimilar economic systems.

the term) exalts the individual freedom of implementing one's choices as one thinks fit, subject to the equivalent right of the neighbor: this places money and then finance at the center of social life and gives them their central role in it, and their freedom to orientate it. *For the matching of decisions then has only one arbiter, which is seemingly neutral: money.* So, there is something fundamentally unhealthy in our economy, but *before considering the role of the financial tool itself, which is real, it must be remembered that today finance is at the heart of an economy that is the fruit of a society that has no other common criterion of choice than profit, because it does not recognize a higher standard, a moral or social reference other than the rules of the game.*[15]

Of course, this does not in any way alter the responsibilities of finance in this process, not only in terms of concrete decisions, but also in the dissemination of a dominant ideology that plays a strategic role by proposing a model of the economy that claims to be abstracted from all moral or social and ultimately human considerations.[16] This is obviously the case in specific ideological artifacts, such as the agency theory (the idea that the role of the managers of a company is exclusively to maximize the financial value for the shareholder), or the theory of efficient markets (which is contrary to experience, but apparently provides a universal criterion of choice, avoiding all other considerations). Understood in that way, Paul Dembinski's central analysis takes on an indisputable and essential meaning.

The role of money

We see this better by inserting this problematic into that of money in general. Let us take the theory proposed by Georg Simmel in a work that has become a classic.[17] For him, the strength of money is its capacity to be a universally, formally neutral representation of any economic value, which is stable in the face of the flow that carries all things away, and analogous to a universal concept, or a law. In

---

15 Possibly corrected by State intervention, fiscal redistribution, etc. But these devices do not intervene at the level of motivation. An entrepreneur or a finan-cier who is judged on his profits will act in this respect with the same logic, whether he operates under a free-market regime with weak taxation, or in a social-democratic system with very strong taxation.

16 See on this point, for example, Domènec Melé in Dembinski, ed., *Pratiques financières*, pp. 251 sqq.

17 Simmel, *Philosophie de l'argent*, op. cit.

order not to be chaotic, the universal relativity that characterizes our world presupposes this common measure. Detached from any relation to objects and their "intrinsic" value as from any mediation, money is a pure means, which does not predetermine its subsequent use unlike any other asset. In addition, money can be said to be the means of a liberation by the *objectification* it gives; in particular it may be the means of the so-called negative freedom, which results from the absence of determination.

But it can naturally then be a factor of dehumanization and enslavement, precisely because it does not take into account the present or possible relational factors and eliminates any specificity other than economic market value.[18] It reduces all qualitative differences to a common material measure. It is even more so when it is absolutized in the name of this form of universality; it ends up becoming the absolute finality. Simmel even points out that "money, which is the absolute means and therefore the meeting place of innumerable teleological series, has psychologically significant relationships with the idea of God." Like God, Simmel says, money is the link or the common center of all the opposites.[19] Indeed, if one thinks that the only absolute is the relativity of things, money is the strongest and most direct symbol of that. But it is also a factor in the rupture of society; it reduces all links, and is the source of negatively perceived inequalities, because they have no foundation in social links or in objective values. We find here, in a schematic form, the evangelical statement about the tempting power of Mammon, and at the same time its role: this shared, objective measure is useful for evaluating the material, economic dimension of any choice, but only this dimension, which is not the only one or even the main one.

Finance and the common good: the domination of money

We noted that this disproportionate role of money was not specific to the financial system but structured our entire society. But it might be argued that, more than the rest of the economy, the

---

18 Hence the example of prostitution, a major example of degradation of the person who is reduced to the role of a simple resource.
19 Simmel, *Philosophie de l'argent,* pp. 281 sqq. He explains in that way the prohibition of interest by religious authorities: it is about suppressing the competition with money at its root. A somewhat limited view of course but rooted in a fair degree of intuition: God or Mammon.

financial system intrinsically possesses this peculiarity of considering only the financial dimension of things, the monetary result of the activity of an enterprise, and no other considerations—of human beings, for example—which are of vital importance, especially to the Christian. In other words, if we were in a society that recognized common moral, social, and even aesthetic values, an intelligent and well-intentioned financial system might not restrict itself to the short term, but would rather prioritize the satisfaction of employees, their attachment to the company, and the company's positive contribution to the community if this improved image better ensures its future. But even in this ideal case, the system would not be interested in financing a project without financial return—at least in the long run. A first response to that argument is that it depends on the collective values: tautologically, if a society valorizes a certain kind of action, it will pay to implement it. But it is not necessarily relevant here: it is doubtful that investors will buy the shares of a company at the announcement of a spending decision that they do not believe will lead to future profits—at least, if stocks are worth the cumulative flow of money that one can expect in the future from the company concerned. In fact, unless there is specific enthusiasm, a company that makes impressive profits will tend to rate higher than another, more altruistic, company that is less profitable. But once again, this does not mean that we will automatically rush to the first one: *a price on a market has never forced anyone to purchase.* Of course, a cultural context in which people would preferentially buy the shares of an altruistic enterprise would imply a profound transformation of mentalities. But it is not in itself unthinkable and Benedict XVI calls us to do it.

Issues to explore

In any case, it is obvious that the recurrent mistakes of finance raise serious questions, and the main one concerns precisely *the hierarchy of effective priorities.* This is not to say that there is no need to think about the functioning of markets, their orientation, or intelligent regulation. On the contrary, we must (we will come to that again). But the question is deeper; it is the hierarchy of values and the decision criteria. We have seen how much the Social Doctrine of the Church may differ from the current systems of value (liberalism, socialism, or social democracy, which are not so far removed from each other).

It is here that a whole criticism of political economy should be made, starting with the academic textbooks: their basic presuppositions are marked by materialistic or relativist *a priori* views, in particular by Anglo-Saxon utilitarianism, and/or libertarian conceptions. Even when they are criticized, it is in the name of egalitarian or collectivist values that, besides their own danger for entrepreneurial, associative, or personal autonomy and initiative, are based on the same materialism, as the popes have shown.

In fact, it is the conception of man and society that is different. Certainly, this cannot be changed in a flash. But changing everything is not a prerequisite; the Church emphasizes this by calling for the multiplication of initiatives from within and without the system. In concrete terms, we have seen, for example, that the expected price of a share cannot be the only criterion for assessing whether to buy it or not. If we think that the price should be appreciated because the company will yield more money, this is not a sufficient reason to buy. To translate this into practice and move toward a healthier society requires significant changes in personal and collective priorities. It is by nature a difficult change that will never be completed, far from it. And we know that we cannot rely on the moral internalization of these criteria alone; we also need rules or laws.

About owners, or the issue of Socially Responsible Investment

In this evolution, parallel to changes in the personal behavior of investors and financial decision-makers, at least two elements can play an important contributory role. On the one hand, and above all, collective pressure, if only from public opinion, to which a commercial society, which must sell its products, is always sensitive. Strong public opinion pressure on a company generally turns out to have a significant impact. But on the other hand, it is also necessary to play on the owner of the property, who has ultimate responsibility for it. This can of course involve a different distribution of wealth, more conducive to direct holding by people. But it can also be the more significant emergence of two important phenomena. On the one hand, it may be the creation or the development of types of companies with new and different priorities, as the popes point out. On the other hand, it can be new forms of holding or management, which would operate according to new and different criteria, which we have mentioned above: pension funds or any collective investment vehicle, but with a wider and more elaborate set of priorities. This is in a sense a systematization of Socially Responsible Investment.

This is probably a central point: the instructions given to fund managers by those who entrust money to them are at least as important collectively as the priorities that the intermediaries of finance give themselves, starting with banks. *It is therefore vital that Socially Responsible Investment (SRI) develops and becomes the normal form of investment.* But it is equally vital that *Christians develop ambitious analytical references in this field,* which they can either use for themselves or propose to the rest of society. For under this very general term, people understand very different things. For example, some confuse it with the sole concern for sustainable development. But this last term does not cover all legitimate demands that have to be made on business or the economy: a slave economy could be in a state of "sustainable development" if you take the expression literally. Broader and more precise considerations are necessary, in the name of morality (or its duplicate, ethics). The fact that SRI officials often tend to reject the term "morality" is somewhat disturbing. Morality is the search for what is good: this is what the normal program of any owner should be; it is his share of responsibility in the common good.

THE VARIOUS FUNCTIONS OF BANKS

Let us now turn to the implementation, as it arises in the practice of the financial profession and especially of banks. We will focus on financial markets and investment banking, because they are at the center of the debate. This goes against an accepted idea, especially in Continental Europe, according to which the business of banking is first of all lending. But in doing so, financing the economy is limited to one channel among others, and it means not seeing that even behind retail banking, there are financial markets that provide it with equity, long-term financing, and a way to cover its risks. Above all, they assume the central function of a market: the determination of prices. Besides, historically wholesale banks or merchant banks in the broad sense appeared well before retail banks. That said, the bank that is familiar to all, retail or network banking, plays a vital role in our economies and raises important ethical issues, even if they are less specific than in financial activity in the narrow sense of the term.

Retail Banking

We will not deal here in detail with questions that are very important for the relationship between banks and their customers, but not truly specific[20] to the financial function as such, since many other activities pose the same or very similar problems. We find among those points the pricing of bank services, or of credit: they are difficult to appreciate because of their complexity and the specificity of the relationship. Or their duty to advise clients: an important issue, in particular with regard to client investments. Or further, the question of complex products, of their usefulness and their price, which are often difficult for customers to evaluate. Let us simply emphasize that in general those transactions are not constrained, and that neither a bank nor any other supplier has fully to take charge of the situation of the other party, who is free and responsible. But there remain questions concerning the correctness of the prices set, as well as the quality of the client relationship: the asymmetries of information and competence can be such that a cynical approach would be a sin or a fault against justice. As always, one must invoice in accordance with the reality of the service, and not exploit a favorable balance of power in an abusive manner. As we have seen, these questions were already developed by the scholastics, because they are key factors in any economic transaction. For example, the scholastics believed that the fair price was the result of the local market situation and considered it their duty to refer to it, and that one should not abuse another's weakness, or ignorance of the reality or the defects of the product. Now whoever sells a product, be it financial or otherwise, to someone who does not know how it works or does not understand the risks involved is deceiving his customer on the merchandise, the same as selling inadequate shoes. All this clearly goes beyond the simple consideration of interest properly understood, for competition and profit are compatible with both cynical and over-prudent actions. But again, this point is not specific to finance, and we will not develop it beyond that.

In this context, credit deserves special attention because banks

---

20 Certainly, the legislation or jurisprudence on the duty to advise and on conflicts of interest are much more developed in the financial industry than in others, which includes more and more complex investment banking products sold to customers. Ethical issues related to sales and consulting are particularly important here. But as such they are not truly specific to finance.

are the main providers of loans.[21] We have first the loan granted by a financial institution to an individual or an SME: in this case, the lender charges for estimated risk, in addition to the cost of money and processing costs, in the margin, and normally keeps the loan and therefore the risk throughout its term.[22] From the point of view of risk management, retail banking poses or should pose fewer problems of principle than wholesale banking: these loans are divided and, subject to a reasonable lending policy, they are statistically controllable.[23] That said, credit (loans) also raise moral questions. In the first place, the lender must reflect on the very possibility of the operation; it depends on the capacity of the borrower to repay (his solvency): in the logic of that business, one should not lend if this risk is excessive. But the moral preoccupation goes further, because sometimes the client can pay back (and in general they do, especially individuals, who are more rarely in default), but they *ought* not borrow, because the cost of the operation is disproportionate or too risky for them. And even if you can then charge a higher margin to cover the risk, it should not go to the point of playing roulette with the survival of the customer. Secondly, conversely, not lending enough means you refuse transactions that could have been accepted, that is, people who could have been financed: while this is rarely an economic fault, social responsibility requires bankers to do all that they prudently can and therefore to provide the necessary focus on transactions that are presented to them — without being content with a form of automatic scoring. There is therefore a need to develop a whole lending ethic, particularly in the case of risky borrowers.[24] Should we refuse to lend, in

---

21   The question of the status of deposits could also be raised, but they are now guaranteed in the majority of cases. This said, the old duty to care about deposits and their restitution remains valid. According to Luis de Molina, in the sixteenth century it was considered a mortal sin for a banker to put himself in a position of not being able to honor deposits because of the risks he had taken with that money. Grabill, ed., *Sourcebook in Late-scholastic Monetary Theory*, p. 210.

22   An exception to this is securitization (bunching of bank loans in the form of a marketable security that is then sold). It can be a very useful and acceptable tool if it is used well, which means in a limited way: it is viable only for some relatively standardized and transparent credits. Its extension beyond this field led to the disasters of 2007.

23   Even though the example of real estate shows that very serious crises can occur through this activity.

24   Moreover, in the event of a problem, there is the question of what behavior

order not to lock up people in unsustainable situations? Should we subsidize them, as some propose, in a Catholic context? But who will pay then? Should we not instead adopt in such cases another type of relationship, such as microcredit?[25]

Investment banking and financial markets

The same remarks apply *a fortiori* to investment and market banking. The recent example of the subprime crisis is at the confluence of the two fields,[26] and it recalls the importance of moral failures: lack of advice and vigilance, excess of greed, lack of accountability for what is produced, sold, or advised, et cetera. Products containing unhealthy credits and awarded under questionable terms were incorporated into overly complex and unreadable market instruments that were rated by rating agencies in a careless or sometimes irresponsible manner, and then sold to investors who themselves were blinded by the lure of profits. Beyond the sophisticated technology, even though the buyers in this case were for the most part supposedly competent professionals, don't we have here a sin against basic requirements such as fair selling and pricing, or advice? Of course, a central motivation was an immoderate appetite for profit. We must also be clear: as we have said, financiers do not have a monopoly on greed, which is an inherent temptation for any economic actor. But here again the fact is particularly evident in the case of the financial markets, for the economic movements there take on a particularly abstract character, whilst concentrating enormous masses of money conducive to considerable profits. The example of Jérôme Kerviel, the Société Générale trader, shows how this can end up being completely virtual to the operator: a financier is exposed to much stronger temptations than others. But this does not mean that financial markets are *per se* perverse, and that trading is immoral by nature: we will review that in more detail.

In conducting this review, it is important to recall at the outset two main principles we have already mentioned: on the one hand, the main function of any market is to carry out buying and selling

---

to expect from the borrower: in principle, what is due is due, but one cannot treat these cases in a purely legal way.

25　As we shall see, from a Christian point of view, this third model, which is essentially the choice of another type of relationship, is often the only acceptable one in the case of very small and fragile debtors.

26　These are retail banking products, packaged and sold by an investment bank.

transactions at optimal prices, keeping constantly in mind *the ideal model of a market that is driven by competent, responsible people, and oriented toward the search for a fair price*, based as much as possible on the current state of the economy and the perceptions or objectives of participants. This is the ideal reference we have seen in the reasoning of our medieval friends. To bring a responsible contribution to the proper functioning of the market, notably in the search for a fair price, which reflects the available data, is then a duty for participants. Far from any ideology of the invisible hand, *it is* (or rather, ought to be) *a conscious and responsible act*. On the other hand, it should be borne in mind *that the fact that a market works* even in a morally acceptable way *does not absolve the participants from their own responsibilities*: nothing obliges them to buy or sell even at a fair price, and their decision must take into account all the factors of choice that are present, including moral or social factors, for, as has been said, the financial dimension is not the only one to be taken into account.

Good use of financial markets

About financial markets, let us first recall some basic data. Finance arbitrates between possible investments, among the different projects in contention. Faced with this diversity, the question is choosing and financing those that produce the best results in the broad multi-criteria sense, in exchange for assuming a certain agreed-upon risk. There is no question of assuming zero risk, for this would result in paralysis and therefore a greater risk; but neither should one play roulette. The choices vary according to each person's specialty, i.e., the type of money he has the responsibility of managing for others. The financial market[27] is a tool, which informs these choices by the possibility it offers of finding a match from among the projects in competition, and of arbitrating between the different options. For those who participate, in principle the most attractive investment for a certain price collects the most money, and its price goes up. This is then basically a vote on the relative quality of projects, with the difference that there is ultimately a reward (or penalty) for each choice, since what is invested (or lent) will at the end of the day be

27 We group together under this somewhat general term a multitude of specific markets, which are more or less connected and can be organized quite differently, from the money market to the stock market, through forex, commodities, derivatives, or even complex financing, not to mention their impact on retail banking.

remunerated with success or failure as the case may be. And the market provides a form of measurement of that remuneration, proceeding as far as possible along the process, since the securities that are representative of the operation or of the lending are listed, and therefore permanently bought and sold. This is tantamount to determining at any time (or regularly) a possible value of each listed company or debt security: the stock price is an appraisal of the project it represents (but as it has been said, it is no guarantee of a fair value), with the advantage that it allows transactions on that basis.

Such a market is therefore not a market like others — not only because of its role in the economy, but because of its very substance, which is to deal with expectations about results in the broad sense of the term, which are not easy to assess. But it also deals with risks that are more central to the economy than others, and which by nature are difficult to predict; if they weren't, they would be avoided. Poor risk assessment is always possible because it can be accurately measured only after the fact. That complexity is multiplied by the exceptional role in finance of confidence and trust, and both are highly psychological and prone to cumulative effervescence. But as we have said, the market provides matching and benchmarking procedures; it does not dictate conduct and there is no reason for it to do so. On the one hand, opinions may vary in relation to the market: if I judge the price of a security too low, nothing forces me to sell it at that price. If I do not want this price, I keep the asset. On the other hand, as has been said, from a moral point of view and at least in an ideal world, criteria other that prices must be taken into consideration, depending on the position and responsibilities of each person, which can be decisive.[28]

It may be argued here that the foregoing reasoning applies only to the allocation of financial resources, but that, in the case of shares, one is buying and selling power over companies. We discussed the subject in a previous chapter in the case of an investor. The question is different if the business focuses on buying and selling stocks on a permanent basis, at least at short intervals, because one works for customers. It is clear that, *in itself, financial market intermediaries should not make decisions about the conduct of a business.* Even a

---

28 To take a simple example, tobacco companies are undervalued because many investors, particularly in the United States, do not buy them — and there is also a risk of tougher legislation on this product, or of liability lawsuits.

talented operator is not competent to judge them. But these persons also have a role to play, which is to *compare the assessments* of companies, managers, and their results, draw some conclusions, and take steps based on those conclusions. For an operator, those steps will usually not be taken by voting at a general meeting but, for example, by selling the securities of a company because he thinks that the market considers (or will consider) that it is not good: such behavior is moral if it is based on just criteria. The challenge then of course is to know what is actually happening in real life: we will examine that in more detail.

CHAPTER 10

The Functioning of Financial Markets

WE NOW EXAMINE ACTUAL PRACTICES: HOW THESE markets work and should work. We will look in turn at organization and practices, at the controversial issue of remuneration and finally at crises.

ORGANIZATION AND PRACTICES OF MARKETS
Speculation, anticipation, and risk measurement

The first issue raised by the functioning of the markets is, of course, that of *speculation*. The accusation is that the proliferation of such activities is at best parasitic, at worst downright harmful. That's what most people think; George Soros himself described by what means he brought the pound sterling to its knees. But we must make distinctions. Let's first put aside the use of non-public information, illegal market manipulation, rumors, corners, et cetera. In practice, such phenomena appear in every epoch. But the fact is that they are recognized by financiers as harmful distortions or cheating, which are *perverse from the point of view of the market itself, and contrary to the interest of almost all its players*, and they try to remedy it, including through criminal charges. Participants may be able to deal with that, individually or collectively; morally this brings us back to basic notions: do not cheat, do not steal, do not deceive, do not lie, et cetera. Otherwise, the phenomenon is such that it must be regulated by a text, law, or regulation, and then it must be done without hesitation, taking care that the regulation does not result in more drawbacks than advantages.

In contrast, we have the useful case of *arbitration*, which is the profit that can be made by bringing together several discordant market situations. If the price of a like or very similar asset is different in two markets, you buy it where its price is lower and you sell it on the other market; you make money when the low price goes up or when the high one drops. Such trade-offs are normally made at reasonable risk, since the market eventually corrects — if only in the long run, because of the arbitration itself, which corrects the distortion. These operations are useful for the functioning of markets and in principle have few side effects. They result in profits which, although they are not high in relation to the economy as a whole, can be significant in relation to the capital concerned and in absolute terms. But the opportunity normally disappears over time. There is no reason that these operations should be called into question.

A third case is an *opinion on prices*: an operator compares prices, risks, and outlook for profits, and finds that the price of one asset is too low compared to another, as regards their compared risks and expectations. Mergers and acquisitions can be considered in a similar way if they target useful restructurings. These cases are more interesting because they are at the heart of finance. The analysis of risks and of their remuneration, of anticipated profits and their probability of failure or success, is one of the main contributions of finance to the economy, as we have seen. Part of this role consists in taking over the management of risk, through appropriate instruments such as futures markets: the risks are then transferred from some person that is not in the business — and who has no desire or vocation to deal with them — to someone else, who is in a better position to handle them. But in the end, there are always operators to take on risk because they expect certain results, even where the knowledge of relative risks is imperfect, and uncertainty is often high and increased by globalization. Buying a stock then means that you think its price is too low compared to the "real" value. If you are right, the price goes up and you earn the difference. The money earned by the one who reasoned best is technically justified, and one cannot speak of "easy money" since the risk is real. This can also lead to selling a security that is considered too expensive, to buy another one offering a better ratio. This is in keeping with the role the market plays in price formation. It implies a capacity for real anticipation, because one really thinks the security is undervalued, or because one perceives there is or will be a *justified* market movement in favor of the security, et cetera. It is then a useful function, provided it remains within the pale of what is moderate and responsible: it allows prices to adjust faster in the right direction, while increasing liquidity.[1] In itself, this is not reprehensible. But it is naturally subject to the other criteria mentioned above, relating to the common good (we have seen that in order to decide to buy or sell, the quoted price is only one criterion among others).

---

1 This means that an investor who wants to sell can do so faster and better by dealing with such an intermediary than if he had to wait for a final buyer.

The agitation of markets and collective psychology

A fourth scenario is that of *market expectations*, the "bets" that traders make. Here we are no longer reasoning about value "in itself" or of equilibrium, but in assessing the probable evolution of short-term prices. In its noble version, it is similar to the above, which aims at the intrinsic value of the instrument, but takes into account the day to day or even minute by minute situation. The question is: given all that I know about the price of a given project or security or financial asset in such and such environment, is it too high or too low? As such, the function is theoretically useful; the intrinsic value at that time depends legitimately on the economic environment, which can cause price fluctuations in time. But in reality, it is not obvious that it should change as often as it actually does, and too much fluctuation can quickly become an evil in itself.

In fact, it is well known that in practice the intrinsic value is generally not at the origin of these movements. To a large extent, since the market is a collective phenomenon whose functioning resembles a crowd's, irrational collective movements prevail over objective consideration. *It then becomes more profitable for the trader to try to anticipate these collective movements than to look at the "intrinsic" value of the financial instrument in question.* What is considered here is pure trading: the "directional" positioning, the bet on the future evolution of the market by someone who has no intention of keeping securities and tries to profit from a market movement. Now, one can only recognize the tendency of markets to deviate in both directions, to exaggerate, and in particular to develop what are called bubbles: an irrational inflation of prices going far beyond any reasonable expectation. *The real problem posed by the functioning of the markets is here*, which is often further aggravated by the partial competence of those operators in judging the real value, obsessed as they are by the events taking place in the next minute. Especially if one takes into account the drug-effect of screens: power, money, fascination of the virtual, et cetera. In terms of results, two cases can be distinguished. Either people have no precise idea or method, and no reason to gain more than to lose (on average, the results for such people will be zero), or they deliberately play on collective actions even when these actions are irrational, following a movement and thereby amplifying it. And there it is harmful — but frequent.

What then? There are two levels here to consider. First, that of the operator: in my opinion, *to play on pure movements we judge irrational is not morally defensible — unless we contribute thereby to calming them down.* We are talking about morality, not necessarily about regulations. If, for example, a bubble appears on a security, or more precisely, if one believes that there will be a bubble, that is, an irrational and dangerous increase in price, the moral attitude is either not to do anything, or to sell the security, even short-selling it, unless the risk is excessive — even if that shocks some touchy minds. But the choice should not be to buy in order to go with the movement, calculating that one will be cleverer, or better placed, than the others and will be able to resell at the highest price before the bubble corrects, or bursts.[2] We can agree that this is not easy and supposes a certain asceticism, but that does not eliminate the rule.

Then there is the collective level, that of the market as a whole. Such phenomena, irrational and parasitic, are not easy to control — even though we know that the action of traders can lead to increased volatility, but rarely contributes to determining a real trend, since ultimate purchasers and sellers are investors. Apart from personal ethical solutions, the main role should be that of large investors, in particular the large pension funds; it should involve intervention in the markets to calm and correct them: this is what was formerly called in France the "gendarmes of the Bourse." From this point of view, the existence of at least one very large sovereign fund or pension fund, managed independently of the political power of the moment, may prove to be a necessity for each responsible country. Beyond that, it is up to the authorities to intervene if they can, first by acting on the organization and functioning of the market, even to the extent of restricting its movements, and then, by interrupting it when it races in one direction or another, even, if possible, by breaking the movement through appropriate interventions. And one should not consider *a priori*, as one widespread ideology claims, that the market is always right. Of course, such interventions themselves have significant disadvantages, especially for liquidity, and must be practiced with discernment.

---

2   Because in this hypothesis we know that current prices are not fair. In that case we must correct them or at least not encourage their drift. The issue is quite different from the perspective of somebody who takes existing prices on a market, which are justified in their context, but in another place or another time: our medieval people understood that.

Market organization: frequency of transactions, type of media, transparency

The modern markets also pose more technical but essential questions that are beyond our scope, but which we have to mention, albeit only briefly. Let us first recall *the major and essential fact that any significant market, especially if it is systemic, must be monitored and regulated by an authority*[3] who makes the rules of the game (or demands them from professionals, and endorses them), verifies the transparency of data, ensures access for all to both data and the market, verifies that operations are correct, and intervenes when they are not. Note that in our times, we tend rather to move away from this requirement than to move closer.[4] This is due in particular to the extremely low competence of political decision-makers in market knowledge, the lack of interest on the part of the public (except to condemn everything), and the fragmentation of decisions: the market is international, while decision-makers are national (or European). We have made some progress with the G20 and the organizations that prepare its work. But we are still far short of what is needed, and this is certainly one of the main points of concern today: we should move toward much more intense coordination, much closer to the realities of the market, yet we remain far behind, mired in disagreements between countries. Where there is disagreement or impossibility of accord on an essential point, unilateral measures can be envisaged, but they are often ineffective or counterproductive.

In this context, a number of specific questions arise, especially in recent days, which lead to a *growing and profound concern about the integrity of current markets.* Why primarily *continuous transactions,* if the issue is about determining the value of firms, which *a priori* does not change permanently? The main justification given is liquidity (ability to sell or buy when one wants). Two factors justify the need for liquidity: the need of some investors to get their money back, but this is not quantitatively the most important, and the requirements of active management, which involve buying or selling whenever it

---

3 But this presupposes that an authority is in a position to do so, which raises the problem of international markets, which should be regulated or co-regulated at that level.

4 The case of the stock market is the most obvious example of regression in this area but we have also seen the spectacular development of new markets, derivatives in particular, which are little or poorly understood by regulators.

appears advantageous, and which implies the need of frequent pricing to take account of new information, in particular because of changes in the macroeconomic, political, or sectoral environment. In itself, the argument is valid, and I see no reason to prevent frequent quotations, made at the rate relevant information comes in, if there is a market for it, and if it is deep enough. On the contrary, even if the point is debated among professionals, it seems difficult to justify transactions every millisecond (on the basis of computer programs, since no human can react at this speed) — what is called "high frequency trading." In my view, the spacing of transactions should be regulated in such a way that operators have a reasonable time to reflect on what they are doing. Therefore, at predetermined intervals one could consider which transactions to carry out, based on the ultimate purpose of a quotation, which is to best find the values and to integrate the relevant available data, which are those of the real economy. More generally, liquidity is not a value in itself: it is subordinated to the *raison d'être* of markets, which is the matching of positions between investors and entrepreneurs and the determination of a fair price.

Should there then be a plurality of competing trading platforms, exchanges, or the equivalent, as they have been set up in Europe and the United States for the last ten years? I believe that the ultimate principle should be the clarity, transparency, and universality of the market under consideration. This strongly argues for the uniqueness of the market, either on a single platform, in which case it has to be mutual or public, or by strict interconnection, leading to the same result. There may be several ways to achieve this uniqueness, but the goal is clear. This is one of the main ways to move toward fairer and more equitable prices.[5]

Should transactions be limited to investors? The idea can be tempting; it would mean reducing intermediaries to the role of pure brokers, possibly with some facilitation, such as buying or selling for a brief period, to bridge the gap if the market does not allow it, or,

---

5   So, there must be a strong reason for tolerating an exception. This can be the case for transactions on real blocks, these masses too large to be absorbed by the market. But even in this case the market may have to be "disinterested," that is to say, one should offer to small investors who have made bids or offers at the transaction price access to the transaction (i.e., one buys or sells their stock at that price). And no hidden swamps (the so-called dark pools).

less rigorously, to restrict it to duly registered market-makers with a well-defined role. It is not so much a question of fighting unhealthy "speculation," since it can happen without intermediaries, but of avoiding a possible risk of discrepancy between the price that would result from investors' decisions alone, and a price guided by intermediaries and thereby considered artificial. It should be noted, however, that in general there is no evidence of such an impact. Moreover, in the price formation process, there is no reason why only sustainable investors should have a founded opinion, especially since intermediaries offer a liquidity that not only is appreciated but can smooth out fluctuations. Whatever the case, the answer must be based on a concrete analysis of the functioning of the market.

However, we can more generally ask whether we can talk about the matching of the opinions of investors, when we see the market invaded as it is today by many practices that alter or distort its functioning. Some have already been mentioned; we could cite the development of toxic products that led to the 2008 crisis. We will also mention index-based fund management, which has become dominant: it means not having an opinion on prices but following an index reflecting the whole market or part of it. Commercially it is safer for a management vendor, who then explains to his clients that he is by definition acting within the average of the market. But this amounts to operating as a parasite on the real market, and results in the amplification of movements since the small number of operators that still act leads the others.

Another case is the "credit default swap" (CDS); it may be used to obtain compensation if an issuer goes bankrupt: it may be useful if it works as an insurance policy for someone who wants to hedge against an actual risk, but it is shocking when someone buys it without such a need. It is even the first time in economic history that one can buy instruments that prosper on the ruin of others. In fact, the CDS market, opaque and oligarchic, offers prices that are not always consistent with the rest of the market, or with common sense. Closer to a bookmaker's market, it should be regulated strictly, and considerably reduced. As can be seen, there are many areas where the current market, under the pretext of innovation, has diverged considerably from its initial logic and where active regulatory intervention, aware of what a market is, is more necessary than ever.

FINANCIAL MARKETS AND THE "REAL ECONOMY"
Short and long term

Several of the preceding questions can be linked with one of the major criticisms made against the market, which is that it loses touch with the real economy and fosters a dictatorship of the short term. This effect is possible even in the absence of the phenomena described above, because of the fluctuation of opinions and information. But first of all, let us note more broadly that any activity subject to some form of public debate runs the risk of focusing on the short term alone; this is, for example, even truer in the case of politics — even if voting takes place only every five years. The main point is information: in financial matters, if information is frequent, prices fluctuate, and using partial information, the market may give it too much importance, which alters its proper functioning. In addition, there is the temptation to structure the information given to the market according to the expected impact, and then to influence the management of a company to the detriment of other more essential considerations.

That said, let us remember again that the ultimate decision-maker in the markets is the investor. The existence of markets does not necessarily lead to short-term considerations only: equity markets have existed for a long time and have always been used to raise long-term money. Nothing has prevented long-term investors from making money. Only the market has been able to finance major long-term projects such as channels, tunnels, biotechnology research, or Internet companies. Similarly, financial analysis can be based on long horizons as well as on the short term: in addition to collective culture, what matters ultimately is market demand, and thus again investors. Besides, if a price does fall, someone else has bought the security from a seller; so, there is always an investor who has a different point of view from the seller; and the money originally invested always stays in the company. But the question remains: the pressure of the short term can be really strong, and unduly influence economic decisions. The market responds to the emotion sparked by quarterly results, and reacts in an exaggeratedly sensitive way to news, whether good or bad. In a sense, it does its job by constantly reviewing its own judgment, but in a too mobile and therefore less reliable way. It may be added that our epoch seems to be characterized by a generalized feeling of risk and uncertainty, which leads to shortened outlooks, in addition to the obsession with rapid profit and the agitation of markets.

Again, this involves two levels. The first level is the regulation of the market: we have seen that this is essential. But to act at this level is not enough, since it merely regulates the effects of purchasing or selling decisions that by their very nature are beyond the control of purely procedural rules. It is also possible to *promote long-term investments and commitments over time,* in particular by taxation, and to penalize short-term movements. This is quite feasible and even indispensable. But, as we have seen, it is not possible to freeze most positions without immobilizing activity: in a decentralized, free economy, there must remain an important space for free action. Then there remains the second level, that of the criteria or values that color the appreciation of the market. This brings us back to the essential question: What are or should be the dominant factors in the judgment of participants, and in particular investors? What are or should be the performance criteria and targets of these investors, particularly those working in institutions, managing money for others, actually managing the bulk of available capital but under pressure to achieve results? It is essential that the governance mode of these entities is such that the quarterly result is not emphasized, nor the random flow of isolated information. Here again, *at the level of each financial company and operator, there is a moral issue that should play an essential role beyond all regulations.* It is imperative that each link in the chain be made aware of its responsibility for the consequences of its decisions. Not that the long term is the only thing to consider. But *it is important at all times to remember that the logic of the exercise is the appreciation of the real potential of each project, of each company, of each asset, as it can be carried out at every moment, taking into account the time-frame of the project itself, with the search for its right price in view.* Anything that departs from this is suspect or reprehensible, apart from exceptional cases. And this applies to pension funds: the fact that they manage the assets of people who are often of modest means does not relieve them of their collective responsibility. In short, because regulation cannot do everything, it is essential that participants in an activity have a sense of responsibility and implement it appropriately. And they must know that their counterparts expect such behavior from them. This may involve a collective effort to reflect on the moral scope of certain situations or actions. Some will say: this is naive. Not so: it is lucid. For whatever the organization of economy and regulations, apart from a totalitarian system, one can always have such collective movements. And in the end, the last stop is conscience, based on common values and practices.

The question becomes even clearer if one takes a step back and inserts the investment decision within a broader framework, in terms of both horizon and abundance of criteria. The common tendency of politics and markets to favor the short term currently prevails, even though the importance of the long term is highlighted in public debate, particularly with regard to sustainable development. In addition to the obvious pressure of the situation, this tendency results from a deeper reality, namely that *reasoning on a long-term basis means to renounce immediate gain*. Managing in reference to pure monetary profit (or to popularity!) will in many cases lead to short-term action — except in the rare cases where it is clear that short-term behavior is so obviously risky that its negative consequences will prevail. *The best way to favor another consideration*, notably the long-term but not only that, is to *take into account something of a different order than pure profit, and therefore part of a moral order in the broad sense.*[6] In short, this implies an end purpose. We refer again to the intuition of our friends, the medieval Franciscans. *It should be valid for today's investors, which means, in concrete terms, that it should be included in their management charter.*

Stock market restructuring

A related accusation states that finance impels merger operations for purely financial purposes or puts pressure on companies to engage in "stock market" redundancies and avoid losing their independence; both are considered unjustifiably destructive of jobs. The same considerations apply here. If a merger creates stock market value, it is because investors believe that its implementation will produce more than the companies taken separately. Similarly, if redundancies improve the stock price, that's because people think it will improve results. Again, I don't want to shock anybody, but you cannot, *a priori*, say these are always irrational or unhealthy decisions. But of course, they can be so and too often they are. First, when perverse habits bring a spontaneously positive response to such decisions: it is then a case of market psychology in its most questionable form.

---

6 Even the desire to save a company over the long term is in a sense of this dimension, because it is based on the community that is this company, and not on a calculation of return.

Second, there is the question of the pressure exerted in favor of quick profits, possibly to the detriment of the capacity of the company over the longer term: it is the same question. What can we say, except that the issue here is not the mechanism of the market, but the socially accepted hierarchy of behavior and values? And generally, regulation will not provide an answer to this issue, although of course this may prove necessary in some cases. People have no right to further their own interests without any human or social consideration: it is as simple as that. At least in principle. And this may justify, if the investor's conscience does not produce the expected result, public intervention when such operations deviate from essential principles, or threaten collectively important achievements.

Finance and economic reality

More generally, the 2007–2008 crisis raised even more acutely the question of the purpose of finance: the fact is that, more than another activity, it can run exclusively for its own advantage, and that's what happened here, at least to a large extent, because of the confusion between creating monetary value and creating real value. The measure is monetary, and here more than in other fields, the ends that alone justify the means are easily forgotten. This raises the problem of the predominance of pure profit, apart from any other consideration. This is similar to the case of artificial and self-verified speculation on the market for psychological reasons, and it can *a fortiori* be the case when the market becomes *de facto* virtual. Of course, in the end, the market itself relentlessly brings you back to reality. But as this crisis has shown again, this return to reality can intervene only after years, and then in a destructive way. In other words, a key issue is how to moderate the market before it can self-correct, when its error is deep. During this whole period, when erroneous behavior dominates, the market expresses its temporary "truth," which is aggravated by the homogeneity and the small number of dominant participants in the markets, and the uniformity that it induces. This makes it dangerous for rational operators to go against such a trend. In Christian terms, one can identify this as a permanent or momentary structure of sin.

That said, it would be naive to assume that the answer is easy. Some say that as in other activities there is a simple criterion, that of the client and the satisfaction of his needs. But it is wrong to say that the customer's best interest validates any activity. Certainly, the

183

true financier, especially the Christian, considers his clients as persons and must provide real services; the relationship with the client must be a person-to-person relationship. But we can very well have real customers, give them what they ask for, and yet do things that are questionable. If we take the case of products that have now been classified as toxic since the crisis (CDOs with subprime), they were sold to investors who demanded high returns from the banks that provided them: satisfying them proved to be collectively damaging. Some also say that the financial institutions that were most resilient during the crisis were those that were serving real customers: there is no evidence of this. The delusive bubbles of finance make obvious that we are far from reality, but this may be consistent with the existence of actual activities and customers. More generally, from a Christian point of view, the end of finance as of the whole economy must be to serve the person and the common good, but there is no necessary correlation in the short term between profitable finance and human finance. If virtue were rewarded quickly, we would know it. In other words, once again, *we cannot let the immediate logic of an activity determine the way it works: we also need regulations and an objectively recognized morality.*

THE QUESTION OF REMUNERATION
First level of analysis: the market, its profits, and its players

At a concrete level, another big question posed by finance is the extent of the remunerations it gives and the justice of these remunerations. It should be noted at the outset that this question is different from questions of risk or market functioning: it is possible to conceive a sufficiently regulated financial system such that the allocation of resources it operates is acceptable without disproportionate risks, but where operators earn enormous sums. For it may be that the activity itself allows it, if only because of the quantity of money involved. And in this case, it is difficult to deprive operators of their benefits. The remuneration of traders should therefore not become an obsession: behind it, one has to be concerned first by the profits of the activity itself. A disproportionate gain is questionable in its very source, because it is disproportionate. The basis for much widespread criticism is that these gains seem disproportionate with the service provided and the social utility of the activity. They add that these very high wages result in "unfair" competition to other sectors, and draw away the best brains, especially in mathematics, and that this is a misallocation of resources; in human terms, it sends people in the wrong direction, for them and for society.

But there are opposing arguments. Apart from the fact that it is a high-risk activity, which commands a certain remuneration, we have seen how it can be useful, at least in the ideal case: it can ensure that the price formation mechanism works under the best possible conditions, and that it animates the market by permanently providing it with the liquidity it needs; thus it provides the basis for a better allocation of resources and at the same time it brings together projects (issuers of securities) and capital (investors). Of course, the real functioning of the market is not ideal in this respect, as we have seen. But the fact is that there is a real activity at the base, and thus the possibility of legitimate significant gains, even though they may be lower than they are at present. However, it is generally true (except in the case of cheaters) that the money earned on the market was *not* actually taken from someone else, assuming we put aside the question of possible predation by the financial system taken as a whole — to be discussed later. Take, for example, someone who takes an intelligent position by playing on the irregularities of the market and, by correcting these irregularities, makes a profit that, given the size of this market, can be enormous. It may be useful: otherwise the market would be more sporadic, less liquid, and less arbitrated, and therefore less reliable. Since traders earn this money (with the balance sheet and the image of their bank) they take their share, hence their remunerations, which can be considerable. At first sight, this is not abnormal in itself in consideration of the risks, and with the important proviso that operators adhere to their deontology. In an economy of autonomy and initiative (the argument continues) the morality of earnings is not to be confused with the equality of earnings.

Second level of analysis: the collective demands of justice in the case of persons

If we introduce a collective dimension, the issue of people with disproportionately high compensation raises specific problems because from the point of view of society this compensation has a meaning different from the meaning it has from the point of view of the company. But first, what does "disproportionate" mean? In general, many

Christians and others are shocked when bosses or simple traders are paid millions or tens of millions of euros or more, or when allowances to departing CEOs amount to tens and sometimes hundreds of millions, et cetera. That said, we have to look at the issue closely. On the one hand, contrary to an accepted idea, there is nothing in the Scriptures or the teaching of the Church that suggests a limit in itself: there is no absolute egalitarianism in principle. Many texts, even those whose scope is above all spiritual, lead to the justification of different outcomes. We have seen the extreme case of the parable of talents: it is distributed unevenly, and it is rewarded even more unequally. The fact may be surprising, but it can be explained. The emphasis is on responsibility, especially toward others, and on justice, which leads to rewarding each behavior according to its contribution. Scripture censures the rich not because they are rich, but for what they do: whether they forget their duties toward the poor (duties that are considerable and emphasized by the texts with extreme vigor) or when they make a god of their money, behaviors which are often linked. The use of goods counts more than their distribution. At the same time, *rejecting egalitarianism does not mean that it is justifiable to engage in any remuneration whatsoever*. For here comes justice again. The doctrine distinguishes between *commutative* and *distributive justice*. The first concerns exchanges: it implies that the two exchanged elements should have the same value; otherwise it is theft. Applied to remuneration, this means that it must correspond to the product or the service. It is not enough that there is a contract signed by free parties; the value of the service must actually correspond to its remuneration. Distributive justice comes next, out of appreciation of each person's place in society, and each person receiving what is "due" to him in this capacity, which varies according to each society. That is probably the question here.

Let's distinguish here managers, including those working outside of finance, from traders. In the case of managers and employers, their added value is measured economically by that of the company. In pure commutative justice, if the company's value has increased, provided, of course, we are not speaking only of the stock price, and if a fraction of this is attributable to the managers and employers, it is fair that they should receive a part of it, even where their share is very high. As for distributive justice, in my view it brings us to admit, with all the tradition of the Church, that a great boss who succeeds in developing an activity that is supposedly socially useful, has shown a high degree of social responsibility, and society can reward him accordingly, although to what extent is a subject for evaluation. Of course, two considerations must qualify this statement: one is that it is difficult to measure such an improvement and the actual contribution of this boss; in principle, it is the role of the owners of the company to make this assessment. The other is the consideration of the non-monetary dimension. If a company has acquired this value through offensive methods, for example by unnecessary layoffs, we should question this remuneration, at least from a moral point of view: it is impossible to believe that we owe them remuneration for what has been acquired by morally questionable methods. So much for the principle. It should be noted, however, that in practice, what actually occurs is discouraging. The examples — French, American, or others — show a weak correlation between the princely remuneration of many leaders,[7] and the running of the enterprise. This situation is shocking. The owners do not do their job. They must therefore be encouraged to do so, perhaps with vigor. And if the situation does not improve, public intervention is necessary — not for reasons of egalitarianism, but to restore justice.

Very different is the case of the high remuneration of certain job categories: traders, mergers and acquisitions specialists, et cetera. Their lot can be compared to that of specialists in other fields, and, of course, of singers, actors, or sportsmen. Let us take commutative justice first. Do they bring a "value" coherent with their emoluments? One may maintain as much, if we measure it only in money. Just as a famous singer attracts people, who pay for their seats or records, an efficient trader makes money, subject to the validity of the activity itself. And to hire them, you have to pay them dearly. This may be necessary if you care about the image of the company, of the music band, or of the film. Does this mean that all this is morally right? Nothing could be less sure. To determine this, you still have to judge the transaction itself. Certainly, the person has made a lot of money. Is it moral that such a benefit is so well paid? The problem is again upstream, in other words, in society's system of values, in the transactions that it

---

7   And clearly the main beneficiaries of changes occurring over the last twenty years, considerably more than shareholders. The "shareholder value," far from handcuffing leaders, has been an exceptional opportunity for them to become very rich.

allows or encourages. If, in a society, everyone pays to get access to noises produced by a vulgar singer, that singer will earn a great deal of money. But why do we pay so much for these stultifying noises? Before making laws on the emoluments of singers, we must again ask ourselves the question concerning collective values.

The same is true for traders. If what they do is useful in light of the legitimate collective role of the markets, the more talented of them will earn a lot of money, and at first glance, that is not aberrant. Naturally the question is more complex in this case. First, in the exercise of the trade. It is said that the financial market makes the people who work there irresponsible; indeed, the market is everyone and no one, and this is especially true for the agents who operate there; hence the feeling of a dilution of responsibilities that can also dilute the sense of risk and its social significance. In fact, working conditions in a trading room can promote anonymity and dehumanization, since operators often relate only to their screens and may have to react with abnormal speed; if they have interlocutors, these are other persons in similar jobs. Beyond that, there is the question of what these traders become in society, what their collective role is, and the question of the life they live: Is it healthy, are they not sacrificing their life, their family, et cetera? That said, the moral considerations do not end there. If you earn a lot, it increases your duties. Just as the origin of the gain may be reprehensible, so may its use. A part of the immorality of these (even lawful) gains lies therefore with the behavior of traders, for which their employers have some responsibility. Some critics, like Fr Samuel Rouvillois, propose to deal with this activity in a specific way, by trying to give operators a more proportionate vision of things, through more corporeal relationships in more tangible jobs, or by learning to combine creativity and justice, which he says is not possible in their current profession.[8]

Moreover, it would remain to question the collective effects[9] of

---

8 In addition, he suggests treating the benefits of this activity in a way different from that resulting from a "normal" job, through taxation or otherwise.

9 We can include here the impact in an area that is important although not widely perceived by the public, which is the common thinking of the profession or the authorities on these activities and their regulation. When questions are very technical, it is difficult to reflect on their advantages and disadvantages without calling on specialists. But when someone receives a bonus from an activity, if a regulation can challenge it or its profitability, it is strongly in the interest of that person to give a reassuring image of that activity. Naturally this

such remunerations: by their attractiveness, they can give these activities an unusual role or social prestige, which distorts the collective value system of society. For all these reasons, it is hard to see how in principle society should not care about remuneration that is systematically disproportionate to the role of the corresponding activity in that society. This raises a question of *distributive* justice. In cases where a distortion appears clearly, justice will tend to question such remuneration, well beyond the realm of finance. Again, public intervention may be necessary, because of the perversion of these collective values. Naturally this presupposes a precise analysis of the case in question and its effects and significance. And the remedy must not be worse than the evil: it is better, in general, not to intervene than to do so in a counterproductive way (public interventions are very often so). In addition, as we have seen, it is necessary, as far as possible, that such action should take place at the international level: otherwise the activity will relocate.

The question of the distribution of income, which leads to tax redistribution, is a different, more general question; it is independent of the source of income. *If it is thought useful to intervene in this or that particular income, it can only be on the basis of socially recognized values regarding these activities themselves.* Note that this is more natural in a society that recognizes such values than in a relativist society like ours. Ours has only one argument against money, egalitarianism: as a basis of appreciation of justice, it is too limited.

Third level of analysis: sector profits and predation

It remains to be seen whether, beyond remunerations, the profits of the sector are collectively justified. That is an essential point. If profits are high and justified, it is difficult to see how to prevent the remuneration of those who produced them from being proportionately high. A former CEO of major financial groups, Jean Peyrelevade,[10] carried out a vitriolic criticism of the issue. He said there is predation if there is a very high profit without service, which in particular relates to the existence of bets, as in a casino. We can argue here that if there were only bets, the algebraic balance of these activities would be zero and

---

is true of any complex activity: the employee of the firm will defend its profit. But much more if he or she has a direct interest in the proceeds.

10 Association d'économie financière, *Rapport moral sur l'argent dans le monde* (Paris: AEF, 2010), pp. 51 sqq.

all results completely random in time. But this is not what we are seeing: investment banks generally earn a lot of money. From this point of view the "casino" analogy is false.

What is more justified, he says, is to suspect the existence of a privileged position, allowing disproportionate profits, measured in the first place by an excessive return on capital (ROE) and an excessive remuneration of the actors. The point is also raised by Peter Boone and Simon Johnson.[11] The fact is that the graphs of comparisons between the profits of the financial sector and those of other areas of the economy show strange distortions: their relationship is stable from 1929 to 1987; there was then disproportionate growth in the financial sector, at least until the crisis of 2007–2008. The figures concerning the compensation of professionals show the same tendency to over-pay for finance compared to other sectors, over the same periods. Explaining this by dramatic growth in the relative productivity of the financial sector is not credible. The link with financial deregulation, on the other hand, is corroborated by the fact that the same gap existed in the years preceding 1929. It seems then that there has been an artificial creation of apparent wealth, but not of real added value. If so, we could then talk of predation.

Assuming that this analysis is confirmed, it remains to explain how this can happen. It seems that the explanatory factors can be grouped into two categories. First, there is everything relating to the organization of markets and activity. The use of dominant or privileged positions and a form of overbilling then seem likely. The remedy is an open and competitive market. If it is not so, predation is easier through the capture of income and dominant positions. Some of the possible ways of distorting markets can be mentioned briefly. One of them may be to create disproportionate volatility through market turbulence, hence profits on trading; this also leads investors to protect themselves by buying hedges and/or agreeing to pay for liquidity. Another may be the fetishism of liquidity, the cult of marking to market and other factors of short-termism and volatility. A third may be by agitating the mergers and acquisitions activity, which is not always creating value, even as understood in the stock market sense. A fourth may be through financial innovation, often linked to promises of better risk management: given the specific nature of

11   Adair Turner, Andrew Haldane, and Paul Woolley, *The Future of Finance: The LSE Report* (London: The London Publishing Partnership, 2010), p. 291.

the sector, it has never been obvious that any innovation in financial matters is in itself a source of progress (even if that very often is the case), especially if a customer pays dearly for a complex product that is unnecessary or, worse, incomprehensible to him. And naturally the competent insiders derive *a priori* more profit.[12]

A second major category is risk-taking. It probably plays a major role here. It may be first through models, according to probability-based strategies, whether conscious or not, which will allow considerable profit to be made during the period when statistical averages, which are taken as normal by extrapolation from the past, are respected. This applies in a sense to all models, which tend to ignore the less favorable case. The fact is that events that are considered improbable, like the tail of the Gauss curve, do occur, especially if in the end the market does not respect a distribution of this type.[13] But it can be rational for those involved to neglect this assumption, even if in the end it is collectively bad. The effect can then be intensified through credit. Among the dysfunctions, Jean Peyrelevade notes predation by excessive leverage, which is a form of misallocation of risks and remunerations. Either the risk taken by banks, which lend to the concerned entity, thereby allowing leverage, is excessive and/or under-paid, or society as a whole ends up covering the risk, especially via taxpayers. This does not in itself condemn leverage: as long as the borrower's own funds exceed the risks (measured with a margin of security), financing the rest of the needed funding by debt is justified. But this shows that in some circumstances the misperception of risk results in some people having too much or too cheap credit, which inflates immediate profits and personal remuneration.

We will not undertake an economic analysis of these charges and their significance. For our purpose, what matters is that they exist and that they can be significant. What can be done then? As always, there are two levels, that of regulation and that of personal conduct. For the former, it is clear that high profits or compensation over a long period of time should set off an alarm about whether the considered activity really provides an exceptional service, or if, more likely,

---

12 A factor that was prominent in this respect is the asymmetrical information between the financier and the client, in particular in the case of fund management: the high cost of very active management with high turnover of the portfolios was conspicuous, compared with the final result for the investor.

13 See in particular the already mentioned analyses of Christian Walter (op. cit.).

there is some market dysfunction. And if that proves true, regulators have to intervene if they can: public or professional rules may offer some elements of response, in particular the systematic organization of the market, like quotation on visible platforms, transaction rules, transparency of information, rules on compensation, et cetera,[14] as well as the monitoring of competition, and above all an increase of prudential requirements, as was done by the 2009 international regulatory accord, Basel III.[15] From the point of view of personal conduct, from a Christian point of view, remuneration cannot be considered justified simply because it is possible and legal. It is essential to verify in conscience that it is not based on an injustice toward someone else. This includes a possible over-charging for the service, exploitation of a situation that weighs on someone else, not to mention deceptive promises. This is not the case if one takes advantage of an objective price differential (we've seen already on this subject the reflections of the scholastics). But it is so if one exploits the naiveté of lenders, or their incompetence. It is also so if techniques are used to conceal abusively what is done in relation to the market, or to exploit a dominant position, et cetera. In these cases, morality opposes it, and regulation should also.

FINANCIAL RISKS AND DISAPPOINTMENTS
Lessons from the crisis

We have just mentioned risk: this is of course the third major issue posed by financial activity. The 2007–2008 crisis is again a case study. Without analyzing the crisis — and the possible technical solutions — in detail, we will attempt to draw some lessons from it. We have pointed out in the preceding chapters one of them, namely, moral failure, in the exercise of professional responsibilities (which also applies to public authorities), in the betrayal of trust between trade partners, and in the manifest irresponsibility of many actors. In particular, greed, combined with cynicism, led to disproportionate

---

14 Some recommend the introduction of a tax in order to slow down transactions. I do not believe that this means is effective, with its attendant viscosity which creates opportunities for excessive profit. But the point can be discussed. Moreover, it can be introduced only on a global basis and to cover a wide range of products.

15 Which could significantly reduce the profitability of the concerned activities in the future (written in 2013).

risks, especially as the gains were rapid and enormous. But it was the subject of a true collective mentality in too many circles throughout the period. It is obvious that this was a key factor in the collective downward spiral: if the players had been more competent and moral, the risk would have been much lower.

A second lesson, visible in most crises, is the risk resulting from over-confidence in tools and key participants, such as banks, rating agencies, and investors, followed, as is known, by the temporary disappearance of confidence, which was then also disproportionate but in the other direction, and which froze up the markets in the autumn of 2008. *It should be remembered that in financial history, the biggest crises have always been crises of false security*: we go too far because we feel confident — where we shouldn't have. In particular, in large crises there is often a sizeable element of real estate bubbles and/or sovereign debt: real estate is reassuring, as is the presence of the State. In this case, it was a credit crisis, disguised as a market crisis, since it was argued that a supposed market, with reliable agency ratings, would be the best arbitrator of the most complex financial needs — a market that in this case proved to be illusory because it had no depth and was based on a dramatic lack of analysis of realities. More broadly *the dominant vision in finance before 2007 was destroyed, which asserted that it was possible to distribute and better allocate risks by a securitization followed by repackaging, making it possible to sell to each investor the risk/return tandem they wanted.* This would have required an exhaustive analysis of these risks, which did not and cannot occur.

This enormous collective illusion, exposed during the crisis, in turn reveals an essential factor, which may be called the market ideology: not the recognition of the market role, which is very important, but the ideological claim that the market works always and everywhere to give the best mechanism of arbitration between economic realities, and that the less it is regulated the better it works. This proved to be false, not because the market could be unfair or manipulated, but because in many cases it does not work or even does not actually exist.[16] For it to work, there must be buyers and sellers who know what they are buying or selling, and criteria to determine a price — here we see our scholastics again. If one of these elements is

---

16 Many of the products that were found to be toxic were not subject to an active secondary market.

in doubt, the reality of the market disappears. That's what happened here. This also means that there are all kinds of markets, true and false, the safest and the least reliable. And they cannot be treated in the same way. Neither in risk management, in accounting, nor in the accountability of participants.

Market, trust, and collective rules

The third lesson is that this crisis reminds us of a central fact: it is in the general interest, and in the interest of the market itself, that the supervision of its functioning be taken in hand by an entity viewing it from without. This means someone who on one hand analyzes the situation to judge whether it is tenable or not, beneficent or not, and on the other hand, imposes rules on the game that channel perceptions and possibilities of action. *Without rules, there is no sustainable market; the financial market is naturally exposed to the risk of instability.* There is therefore a need for general supervision and regulation that cannot be limited to prudential rules, or capital ratios: it must also assess, on a market-by-market basis, what may go wrong, in particular on the basis of alternative assumptions or changeover scenarios. In other words, *the market knows better than any authority how to make prices in a given context over time, it can promote and reward innovation, but it does not know how to regulate and stabilize its own functioning.* Like arithmetic according to Gödel's theorem, it does not know how to self-reference; it cannot be built completely on its own postulates. This does not eliminate its central role but qualifies its functioning.

This role of an authority could be borne by the market players themselves: this would be in line with the ideal set by our medieval Doctors, as well as with the principle of subsidiarity dear to the Social Doctrine. But this presupposes on the part of these actors an ethic and an unprecedented force of will, difficult to conceive without faith, especially the Christian faith. Otherwise, public intervention remains essential. From this point of view, and contrary to popular belief in certain circles in our societies, *public authorities are essential for a market to function.* And not only in the mass rescue and the restoration of confidence. Even more since this activity is both profitable and dangerous. The role of public authorities is central to any risky activity, from chemistry, to oil extraction, to nuclear energy, or even to transport. *Regulators therefore need to intervene to curb the excessive risks faced by institutions, including systemic risks.* At the same time, of course, we must not give in to the illusion that regulators alone can ensure the safety and proper functioning of markets.[17]

Accountability of stakeholders

While in our societies we cannot rely on participants to exercise the supervisory role mentioned above, there could or should be a significant role for them in addition to public authorities. Public external intervention cannot do everything: what remains out of their reach are the rules that dictate the very behavior of the actors. We talked about moral failures. It cannot be repeated enough that *individual morality is a powerful factor in the quality of markets*. But at the same time, one cannot stop there, because one would not take into account the determining importance of collective movements. Whoever would be totally virtuous alone would pay dearly, for he would be excluded from the market. Being more virtuous does not change the market in which you work unless a majority of its participants think so. Unless there is general conversion, the action to be taken may be more modest: introducing social references, values that are commonly accepted in the society concerned. A relevant tool for this is a form of self-regulation,[18] the adoption of *professional standards or codes of conduct* (some go so far as to recommend financial professional orders or guilds). In addition to its role in conformity with the Catholic principle of subsidiarity, and recommended by the Social Doctrine, this is particularly important in a field such as finance where the technicality of the issues and the importance of case-by-case judgment make it difficult for officials or politicians to regulate it fully. This also has the advantage of encouraging these professionals to assume their responsibilities, since they have to respect norms they elaborated themselves (in addition, legal value must be given to these standards, including the possibility of enforcement in court). But of

---

17   Included in what Jacques Sapir calls the prudential illusion. In particular, any rule will often be ineffective in the face of a new event, which requires an ability to grasp this novelty quickly and well by other tools than existing ones. See Christian Walter, ed., *Nouvelles normes financières*, pp. 161 sqq.

18   Let us point out here the double meaning of the word self-regulation: seen as a spontaneous self-organization of markets, it is a myth. As professional explicit self-regulation it is potentially an essential contribution. I have developed the point in *L'économie et le christianisme* (Paris: Francois-Xavier de Guibert, 2010). Professional standards were recommended by Benedict XVI, as we have seen.

course, the propensity to assume this responsibility and the quality of the result obtained will be much improved if the collective demands integrate moral and, *a fortiori*, spiritual ambitions.

Financial markets and firms

In order to make the actors accountable, can we also act on the structure of financial sector companies? Here, we can mention proposals such as the separation between traditional retail banking activities and riskier investment banking activities, to include market and/ or unwieldy or complex financing. Taking it further than the former US Glass-Steagall Act, it is proposed here or there to isolate the activities in question in subsidiaries under a common holding entity and to provide for a specific control and accountability regime, so as to prevent the possible bankruptcy of an investment bank from affecting the sister retail bank.[19] On the contrary, the fact is that during the crisis this divided model did not prove its worth: the institutions that went bankrupt were homogeneous, and diversification is also a safety factor. The debate is therefore open. Let us simply note that it is probably more important to act on the risk of the activities themselves than to tolerate risky activities on the grounds that they have been separated from others.

On the other hand, we will discuss the question of the relationship between risk and remuneration, and beyond that, of accountability. There, besides the considerations of risk control, those of morality intervene. One principle should be clear: when profits are realized on repetitive and dangerous activities, it is necessary to be able to verify that over the long term the overall balance of risks and benefits is positive. *Those who take risky positions must therefore assume responsibility for the whole duration of their effects.* And if this moral requirement is not assumed sufficiently, rules must at least partially mitigate this drawback. The recent measures that require extending the remuneration of traders over time (three years) go in this direction.

---

19 Let us note that this concretely results in giving back to the markets the task of ensuring the functions that a conglomerate purports to provide, and in particular the synergies between activities. This, of course, presupposes that these markets are organized and regulated even better. And this shifts the function of the regulator, who must then be more market-oriented and less concentrated on the supervision of institutions. This can also provide the advantage of transparency.

The question is whether this should be taken further and establish a long-term relationship between remuneration and risk, at least in the case of institutions taking speculative positions which present significant risks. Let us recall the rule that prevailed in the United States until the 1970s: Wall Street firms were partnerships, which implied indefinite responsibility of the partners toward their firm, and liability of their personal property. This can be seen as a counterpart to the possibility open to them of making a fortune—while at the same time forcing them strictly to control risks over time.

But even that would still be external measures. At the same time, what is at stake is (again) an essential moral dimension: *a responsible human being admits that he must pay attention to his actions and assume their consequences*, and therefore the responsibility for the risks he causes to others—*a fortiori* if he assumes the considerable responsibilities involved in finance, even at the level of a simple trader. This is not given priority in their training, although many recognize this responsibility spontaneously. That would be indispensable. In fact, what is indefensible is the postulate of economic textbooks (and others): that all should be motivated only by the goals they set for themselves and by their advantages, subject only to the respect of laws. Property involves responsibility; it is ordained to the common good. *A fortiori* the management of funds, *finance in the broad sense, should be experienced as a serious moral personal responsibility toward all of society.*

CHAPTER 11

Finance and Society

BEYOND THE QUESTIONS RAISED BY ITS OPERATION, which we have just seen, finance affects the rest of society in several ways. We will discuss here two major issues that were already raised in medieval times; they are at the center of the problems encountered by finance in its mission in the service of society. The first is *debt*, and the last crisis has left us with a deep impression of its importance. A diametrically opposed issue is that of *exclusion*, which is equivalent to not dealing with needs that are considered insolvent. We shall then return to the global moral and spiritual perspectives.

A SERIOUS MORAL DILEMMA: THE DEBT DISEASE
Pathology of indebtedness: a supreme temptation

A great lesson of the recent crisis is that we have to resume the historical reflection on problems raised by indebtedness. The 2007–2008 crisis arose out of debt securities. They involve a very specific relationship: when you lend, you recover your money plus interest, and nothing more, but you have the right to claim these assets in courts. Whether the debtor succeeds or fails in his business does not change anything about this, except in the case of total bankruptcy: the lender's gain is capped but protected by law. On the other hand, if the debtor cannot repay, the lender may lose everything. When lenders lend, it is therefore because they believe that the risk of failure is very low, and as soon as there is serious doubt about the borrower's ability to repay, the value of debt collapses. In addition, creditors have often themselves borrowed the funds that they are lending, which is what banks do. If too many of their debtors cannot repay what they owe, they in turn cannot repay their own creditors[1] and go bankrupt. At best, they sell the assets for scrap, dropping prices, and unleashing a domino effect that can become catastrophic.

We have mentioned in previous chapters the question of confidence: it is obviously central to credit. Efforts are made to instill

---

1 In the case of banks, regulations impose a minimum level of own funds (equity), usually at least 7 percent of the weighted balance sheet and above 10 percent now, which is more than enough in normal times, but is quickly consumed if the bank has been reckless.

confidence, notably through agency ratings, prudential regulations, and so on. But, as has been said, there is a perverse effect here: if too much confidence is built, operators feel comfortable about developing operations which are supposedly almost riskless. This explains why the major dramas have all been debt crises and thus confidence crises (the 1982 Latin American crisis, the savings and loan crisis of 1986–95, the 1990s real estate crises, and even the 1929 crisis). *A good crook is one who looks honest and reliable; a really big crisis always occurs on supposedly safe, mom-and-pop AAA-rated values,* and on blind trust in collective mechanisms and know-how. Shares[2] are of a radically different nature and do not present the same problem. If a company finances financial or material assets by equity (shares), and its investment goes badly, it loses money and possibly its capital. But here the direct effect stops; this does not create a domino effect. In the 1987 stock market crash, no financial institution was at risk, after receiving some temporary cash support, and the same held true after the bursting of the "new economy" bubble in 2000. In summary, *holding debts gives the lender security, since it gives him a legal right over the sums in question,* which are owed and may be claimed before courts, *but it can be misleading if that indebtedness is not sustainable.* This also implies a distancing between the two parties, who are linked only by the lending operation: *a claim is not an association. It therefore contributes greatly to maintaining the illusion of the creative value of money outside of a human, social relationship.*

From the point of view of the debtor, debt also presents significant risks: since debtors are legally required to repay loans, indebtedness can easily lead to bankruptcy. Even if bankruptcy is avoided, the borrower must at least pay the interest, with no hope of release, whereas capital (equity financing) is never to be repaid and its remuneration (dividends) is not compulsory; it can be deferred in case of difficulties. For a company, therefore, it is the most suitable form of financing, all things being equal; indebtedness should occur as an additional means of raising money. *The only possible financing of risk is equity*: it is money the company owns; its loss can be envisaged, and the company alone is responsible for it. To forget that is devastating. Naturally, the risk for the investor is higher if it is equity, but its average remuneration is higher. We can therefore say that, *since the future is unpredictable, only the reasonably highly predictable part of*

---

2 Except of course if credit finances them, as before 1929.

this future can be financed by debt, and this part is limited; beyond that, debt is dangerous. And so, morality is first and foremost equity! Moreover, except where sums lent are moderate, recourse to debt, which may be deceptively reassuring to the lender since the claim is legally enforceable, also has dangerously seductive effects on the borrower's side: it provides the illusion that you can delay current obligations and choices to be made, the illusion also of being able to develop well beyond your real possibilities, and perhaps in the end, to break out of the limits of your condition. We see this also at work among policymakers, with the development of public debt, especially in the aging democracies of Western Europe, as was the case before with Third World countries' debt.

In general, what emerges is that debt (leverage [3]), while certainly very useful in reasonable doses, quickly becomes *a dangerous drug, inducing an illusory or perverse sense of security*. Because it can become a general phenomenon and because through its immediate facility it provides a form of apparent remedy for fears or conflicts in society, it may cause us to rush forward like lemmings to the abyss. Too often, *borrowing means not to confront a problem, but rather to postpone it*; we saw it again during the last crisis. [4] We find here an element of the essential truth of the Church's ancient preventative actions against interest-bearing loans: the security afforded by holding a legally enforceable debt can be a terrible temptation, if, from a status of mere complementary financing, based on the anticipation of a very probable future, it turns into an illusory way to control risks and, worse, to a kind of martingale strategy. Incidentally it should be noted that countries rarely take off economically by relying on high indebtedness (see China).

3　Leverage (borrowing to improve one's return on equity) should not be confused with "transformation," in which a bank borrows short and lends long. In part it is indispensable, since there are more short-term savings than long-term savings, but it is risky and must therefore be controlled with great care.

4　From some hedge funds, which boosted their earnings by leverage and had to sell their assets off in desperation because their refinancing lines were no longer available, to the American buyer of a house which he could not afford, and to the US government financing its power policy on credit (but is Europe better off?): everybody relishes it. It is the ease of the unilateral bet on the future that the perverse temptation of debt arouses, a cynical game of heads or tails (heads I win, tails it falls on others, and in particular the following generations). Debt is like alcohol: pleasant in small doses, lethal in strong doses. Even more painful is the fact we have to recognize: after 2008 Governments financed the rescue of the system by additional massive indebtedness.

Public debt is perverse debt

It is noteworthy that the biggest crises have all involved not only a large credit dimension, but almost always one of the two most apparently secure assets for investors: sovereign debt and real estate financing. Recall that both are elements of the terrible crisis the euro-zone has experienced since 2010. Real estate financing has its specific role, either to smooth the acquisition cycle of solvent people, or to finance useful new construction. But it should not be used to create leverage, let alone to accompany and nurture a real estate bubble (the most dangerous of all).

Similarly, apart from individualized and profitable economic projects, in principle a State should get into debt only in exceptional cases, and only for a limited period of time. If, as most developed countries have done for the last forty years, a State decides to let its budget deficit run out, and finances it by debt, it will sooner or later meet a ceiling because one cannot go into debt indefinitely. From that point on, it will be constrained to achieve a balanced budget because it will have to assume a rigid management of its debt burden, under the watchful eye of the markets. That State would then have lost all its room for maneuvering. In other words, *the facility of public debt only works for a time: it is the bonfire of one generation. But it weighs heavily on those that follow.* In concrete terms, if one thinks, for example, that the ceiling is 60 percent or more of the GNP (as foreseen in the European treaties), a country that arrives at that level must then not increase its debt faster than GNP, in order to stabilize this ratio. But since what is due mechanically increases the interest paid, at best of the same order of magnitude as the GNP growth, it can no longer borrow funds for any additional expenditure whatsoever. And this assumes that markets make no demands on a government and agree to renew debt maturities, finance the interest due, and do not increase spreads in the light of the increased risk. In other words, the generation that has borrowed has had the advantage of it, but that facility has been available only to that generation. Sometimes this can be acceptable: in times of war for example, because then the necessity of survival leaves no other choice. By extension, it could be justified in the case of an exceptional crisis, as in 2008, or perhaps after the 1973 oil shock. But surely not to finance current deficits and, as has been the case almost everywhere for the last forty years, to avoid having to make somewhat courageous and responsible political choices. Some may claim that debt can be justified if it finances investments, as companies do. But this is true only if this investment generates an increase in directly measurable financial results, which are used to repay the loan. Well-managed companies do it only with great care. This is obviously far from being the case with any government: it would require the clear isolation of that debt, then the allocation of it to truly profitable projects, and finally the evaluation of the real impact of investments, including the resulting tax revenue. Nobody does that.

Of course, there is a way out for borrowing countries, which has been used for a long time: the *de facto* reduction of debts, either by galloping inflation or by at least partial repudiation. This is of course neither very moral nor very responsible, except in distress situations where it can become justified, taking the form of reduction and rescheduling. However, this is not open to everyone. In general, indeed, the market reacts, and this type of strategy becomes expensive, except in specific situations like the United States, at least for the time being. And in any case, the inflation solution is not directly possible in a monetary zone like the euro,[5] which cannot give each member the freedom to draw on the common central bank. In short, therefore, after an initial phase of spending, which is usually only on consumption with no visible return, *a borrowing government only bequeaths unnecessary and dangerous burdens*[6] *to future generations, thereby alienating not only its political decision-making capacity, but also its debt capacity, which is vital in case of a real shock*. It is therefore deeply immoral.[7] From this point of view, the generalized debt accumulation in developed countries since about 1980 sheds a sinister light on the fragility of their socio-political equilibrium.[8] Hence

---

5 On the other hand, countries such as the United States as well as Japan, the United Kingdom, etc. offer the historically unprecedented case of countries that are indebted in their own currency, a currency that is no longer indexed to gold or to anything else. Hyperinflation is certainly immoral, but would save them, at least from their accumulated debt. But at a high cost...
6 Of course, claims are also transferred to the future, but they are not the property of the indebted government. For the community, it is a burden — except by dispossessing creditors through a default, or by overtaxing them, if they are in the country.
7 And it is contrary to democratic accountability, since those who approve the debts are not those who will repay them.
8 And also, on the errors of financial theory, which has been founded for forty years on the now obviously false idea that public debt can be identified

two conclusions. The first is that *the implementation of sophisticated borrowing techniques from the 1980s has been disastrous in proportion to its effectiveness*: it is like giving a toper free and immediate access to his preferred alcohol. The prior technique of large, highly visible public borrowings was politically much more honest. The conclusion is that *in the long run the only real solution is to organize the almost total disappearance of public debt.*

How to stop the accumulation of debt?

Let us go back to private agents. If debt is dangerous and cumulative, what can be done to curb it? The first thing, of course, at the level of the whole economy, would be to abstain from favoring debt over equity, as most fiscal systems do, oddly enough. Next would be to think about ways to deter this tendency. Let us recall that Mosaic law provided for a time limit to debt: every forty-nine years debts were extinguished, which obliged all parties to negotiate for terms over a finite period. To emerge from the current crisis, others are recommending various other debt cancellation processes. Preventatively, the issue is clear: one must be cautious and only take on debt when fully aware of its nature;[9] this means insisting on the borrower's information, on capping rates and so on. Naturally also, when borrowers cannot repay their loans, mechanisms exist everywhere to remediate this: over-indebtedness committees, or personal bankruptcy, or insolvency procedures for companies. Should we go beyond that? In any case, it does not seem wise to adopt cancelling any debt at regular or foreseeable intervals as a general rule. Lenders would take this into account, and it would paralyze economic activity at regular intervals, without justification if the concerned debt is reasonable. Such a generalization would be the result of a mistaken reading of the biblical measure. The texts on the jubilee must be understood in close relation to those on lending we mentioned at the beginning of this book: what was intended was a solidarity loan, without interest. The status of such loans must be significantly different from that of ordinary credit.

---

with risk-free investment, and which is used in that theory as an absolute and universal reference. This naturally encourages its cancerous increase: it is safe; therefore we can buy.

9   This is what justifies jurisprudence such as exists in France, which limits real estate borrowing by individuals by preventing instalments from exceeding a certain proportion of income.

In other words, and to recall what we have developed in the first part from the medieval experience, we must distinguish two types of credit. The first is a financing method for productive operations in the broad sense (economic activity or loan to a person who has a reliable remunerative activity[10]). We have gone over the possible conditions for introducing a method like that. But then there is a second type of credit, which must be analyzed as a special form of aid: it is not a gift, since it has to be repaid, and therefore there must also be a certain amount of productive activity by the borrower. It is a loan, but it would not be made under normal circumstances. If it is granted, it would follow a particular process that would be justified by the quality of the borrowers and their needs (clearly this means poor people, in the broad sense of the word). Hence three consequences: such a loan must be made under moderate terms; it must acknowledge the possibility of cancellation under certain circumstances. But since a loan is to be repaid, the relationship between lender and borrower must be made under conditions such that the borrower is actually committed to repay, especially morally, and he may have to be supported and advised in the process. Here we recognize the principle of *microfinance* or *microcredit* that Benedict XVI praised so strongly: in the end, it is an extension of the medieval mounts of piety. The origin of microcredit is well-known: loans made to people whom the traditional banking system would consider insufficiently solvent, but who can afford some borrowing given their real capacity to develop resources, like the lady who borrows money to buy a market stall. These borrowers' sense of honor combined with their commercial aptitude will result in them repaying. Besides let us not forget the social pressure and the possible financial solidarity that will bring other borrowers to help them. It is a tool to be developed more widely,[11] alongside solidarity in the form of gifts, which responds to immediate needs but does not relate to the activity of borrowers. More generally, if conventional loans have been granted in cases that would obviously have required systems of this type, or even donations,

---

10 Thus, an equipment loan to someone whose productive activity makes it possible for him to repay without excessive risk, enables him to purchase a useful asset (a car, etc.) sooner.

11 If, of course, it respects the previous principles and does not lead to concealed usury, or to excessive risks, as we can see here or there (in India in particular).

debts must be cancelled. This is what has been done, partly under significant pressure from the Church, for the debts of the poorest countries in 2000. We recognize the Jubilee here, and that is justice.

FINANCE AND EXCLUSION, OR THE NEED FOR ANOTHER KIND OF MONEY
Another logic

This leads us to the broader question of exclusion. Without going into the phenomenon of financialization, excessive concentration exclusively on immediate financial logic[12] is evidently a source of exclusion, although this serious evil of our societies has multiple causes. It is therefore interesting to examine how other logics can be inserted into the very mechanism of finance. These must be inspired by the conception developed by Benedict XVI in *Caritas in veritate*: adding to the economic and political logic a third form of logic, that of gift, including in the economic act itself. This is all the more important as financial decisions usually take the form of judgments based on calculation criteria as they are received and accepted at a given moment. Such calculations spontaneously create exclusion by the very selective processes they implement, and they do not take into account possible changes at the human level, such as the transformation of peoples' personalities or their introduction into new social relations. Yet these features are decisive when it comes to fighting exclusion.

To go beyond this, there is a general precondition: to place the calculation of profit only at the end of the process, in line with the concept of profit in *Centesimus annus*: a final criterion for judging whether one consumes fewer resources than what will be produced and sold. But it should not be a constant obsession, nor become a universal criterion. In this perspective, there is room for an alternative logic, intervening upstream of the final calculation of profitability. Even within pure banking and finance, this would already open up an appreciable space. As the role of finance is to orient resources according to the possible ratio between expected risk and benefits, the more reasoning takes place at a global and broad level, taking into account as many dimensions as possible without going too quickly to the final

---

12   Besides the fact that it induces a certain mentality, a certain order of priority that is similar to what our medievalists denounced as hoarding or the lure of lucre.

calculation, the more room is left for alternative forms of logic to intervene before the final judgment is made. We will briefly mention here areas where considerations of a different type can intervene in the field of financial calculation, and in particular more "gratuitous" considerations, which are not dependent on the prospect of rapid and measurable outcomes.[13]

Finance and exclusion

The Church teaches the principle of the preferential option for the poor. Who are the poor, in the social and human sense more than in the economic sense? First, whoever is left out, who lacks the capacity to act in the context of the society in which he lives and, therefore, who cannot bring and receive the contribution that every human being is called upon to share with society. In the area of material means that is our concern here, such a definition covers three quite different cases. The first is that of exclusion for lack of resources and of material access to the economic system. The existence of such cases means, among other things, that the logic of the financial system cannot provide the necessary resources to someone who nevertheless has a real personal capacity. It is then necessary to look for a way to do better, precisely by adapting to the situation of this person outside of currently accepted norms and by reacting quickly once the means are available. A well-known and obvious case is the already mentioned microcredit. This is obviously one of the most appropriate formulas if it is properly implemented. But one could conceive of other similar ways, like equity investment in very small companies. We can also mention initiatives such as fair trade: the creation of marketing channels with a different logic, which of course involves some financing.

A second, significantly different case of exclusion is what might be called "inability exclusion," when a person proves incapable of participating in social interchange and economic creation due to a lack of training, because he has no trade, et cetera, but more often by social or personal maladjustment. In such cases, a purely financial mechanism

---

13   This does not exclude the intervention of public authorities, in a field that the pope identifies as that of constraint, notably by regulation. The logic is different, but the distinctions between those fields are not rigid: a tax incentive, for example, is in a sense coercive, but it can be combined with a social initiative or with private aspirations, in order to enhance or direct the expected impacts.

is not enough: just giving or lending money leads nowhere. But there are still resources for action; a typical example is that of so-called insertion enterprises in the broad sense, which welcome people with a real potential but who cannot work in the "conventional" sector primarily for psychological or social reasons. The viability of insertion enterprises depends on entrepreneurs who have unwavering faith. But it also presupposes a specific kind of money, because they do not always succeed. It means money available to invest in these companies, mainly in equity. But this may also involve getting larger companies to help by trusting them as suppliers or subcontractors. Or, more upstream, institutions that are closer to charities, but inserted into the real life of the economy, or private initiatives in more institutional fields, such as independent schools experimenting with new methods in difficult slum areas. That has to be financed too!

A third case of exclusion is exclusion because of a fundamental deficiency, when there is no realistic prospect of inclusion in the conventional circuit, even in the long run. What is needed then is a logic based on gift, both financial and, in the case of promoters, personal. This was the case of hospitals in the Middle Ages: they dispensed massive collective generosity. It can be the role of foundations today as in that time.

What money is needed?

In most cases, such initiatives do not automatically portend that money will be spent and lost, at least for the first group of actions: such operations may ultimately be profitable, but the result will only appear in the end. For if one speaks of exclusion, it is because someone has been excluded, meaning that in normal operations somebody ended up falling through the cracks. But that does not mean that the excluded person is intrinsically unable to become integrated or to act. It follows that possible financing is not limited to pure gift: investment or loans can answer the question, but of course using non-conventional methods. For example, microcredit presupposes a specific environment: in France, in the case of banks, the charter signed for this purpose provides for the obligatory intervention of specialized associations supporting the borrower in his action. More precisely, the three forms of providing money, that is, equity participation, lending, and giving, can all play their part, but must take specific forms, each being based on a different human relationship. Each of them can and must contribute, but none can answer the question alone: capital invested in equity is scarce, especially for uncertain and high-risk projects; a loan implies repayment and this may therefore place an overly strong burden on the borrower. Even gift can be risky, for it can foster a dangerous addiction, as the example of public aid to poor countries shows.

What all this shows in any case is *the need for another kind of money*. As we have seen, money is fungible, but only as regards its use. On the side of its holder, it depends entirely on the ideas, values, and priority of that person; it is therefore not fungible in this sense, it depends on people. We are thus led to put Simmel in perspective, for whom money liberates by its very neutrality. *On the contrary, from the point of view of the universal destination of goods, which is an essential pillar of the Social Doctrine of the Church, money as well as any property is entrusted to the owner in order to make the best use of it, according to his position and vocation.* True liberation presupposes the transformation of our personality, which means a real conversion, to respond to our vocation. And then our money can make sense.

Another purpose for one's money

More broadly, the question is how the banking and financial system can work toward a more equitable society and economy. The answer is similar: beyond public regulations, it is possible if there is "well-intentioned" and "well-oriented" money. Here we find again the theme of Socially Responsible Investment, and more broadly the question of how far we trust the financial system to invest our money. This use must also be ordered to the universal destination of goods. If it is invested on the markets, its use is oriented toward companies that meet certain criteria. And ideally, we help to redirect these same companies toward types of behavior we consider better: this is the meaning of Socially Responsible Investment.

In the French context, the idea has not caught on, and people are more willing to appeal to the government with its dual power, taxation (authoritarian reorientation of resources) and regulation (channeling). It would be naive to deny the important role these tools can play, especially as an alternative if the initiatives of the other two levels — the economy and civil society — are failing. Or it can be in support, in particular fiscally. But this government power reaches its limits, especially in the face of two realities. The first is the very one we are talking about here: exclusion. The capacity of bureaucratic machines to fight exclusion is limited; it is indeed a question of inserting people into the real society, which in the end requires an action from that very society, a positive gesture of welcome and openness, which cannot be ordained, and which goes well beyond the mere monetary level. The second limitation is that the very modalities of State intervention, based ultimately on a logic of coercion, do not recreate social fabric and community behavior. We are faced here with a major theme of reflection and collective action for Christians. It can extend from the ambitious "What do you do with your money?" to initiatives in different fields that range from volunteer organizations to Socially Responsible Investment, which if they develop on a large enough scale can play a leading and structuring role in the rest of finance.

THE FINANCIAL SYSTEM AND MORALITY
Technique and morality

Let us return to the question of the financial system in general: markets and institutions. What emerges from all this analysis is a contrasting and complex picture. On the one hand, we cannot subscribe to a radical condemnation of finance or even financial markets, considered as techniques or tools, and the Social Doctrine of the Church confirms this. But we already discern how much they need to be regulated, because the reality is undeniably far from the ideal. On the other hand, this is obviously not an ordinary activity, if only because of its risks and temptations. The failures of those systems can have a considerable effect, material, psychological, or political. In proportion to its importance and utility, finance is therefore an activity that requires a specific effort; this obviously regards its standards and techniques, but also the values which must or should animate it. Not that it needs to redeem itself from some original sin, in comparison with a manufacturing industry that would be essentially good. In fact, any business must constantly reflect on its aims, purposes, and methods. First, because any business, including the ones with the best justification, can be carried out in a reductive or evil spirit; it can concentrate on individual profit, financial results, power, et cetera, and act without hesitation on the resources it uses. This may be true of any enterprise, large as well as small. But beyond that, the role of finance and the quantity of money involved is such that in a certain way it expresses the priorities of the whole economy and therefore of society.

An economy that does not regard morality as an essential dimension is necessarily more dangerous than one that does. In a society such as ours, which considers values and moral priorities as personal matters, subject only to compliance with the laws, where economic textbooks consider preferences to be a given, which takes as relevant criteria only results that are measured in quantitative terms and regardless of other purposes, you cannot expect that finance will do better. To a large extent, we have the finance we deserve: it reflects society and society reflects it. It should be noted that in the rare cases where other considerations are taking place in our society, such as sustainable development or discourse on ethics and governance, companies, including financial ones, must take this into account, at least in their communication, and the market adds its pressure in this direction. Is it really interiorized? We can doubt it, but it is already a pressure. This would be *a fortiori* the case if investors sharply changed their priorities, and if other collective values prevailed.

What to do in practice?

How can we go forward? We have briefly summarized six major topics that the financial system could pose: its criteria (and the ideologies that obscure its choices), the quality of price formation (and its temptations, volatility, and bubbles), how it takes the future into account (and the risk of short-termism), the reality of added value (and conversely the risk of undue capture of wealth), a control of collective risk (and, conversely, the danger of systemic slippage), and, finally, the level of indebtedness (and its danger if it exceeds its auxiliary function). We have previously discussed the question of Socially Responsible Investment and the need for money to be managed in the interest of the common good, of which the previous considerations on exclusion have also reminded us. In all these domains there are, at the same time, distinct and related issues: technical issues (starting with the organization of the markets and the models used), which we have touched on briefly, and questions of values, which are more distinctly the preoccupation of the Christian.

All this can take the form of binding rules, or principles of conduct. In such a dynamic and innovative field, regulations or laws must be used wisely. They should intervene when the targeted activities or methods are identified as harmful or dangerous, as in the case of cheating, lack of transparency, market abuse, or when the public cannot act on equal terms with professionals to protect their savings, and only when it is clear that the intervention will not produce a more harmful effect. The market is much like sport: it needs rules for the game, and it is not during a match that the rules are determined; they must be established beforehand and be consistent with the logic of the game. We have seen the insistence of the Social Doctrine on regulation, especially at the international level. This is not limited to the functioning of the financial market or its players, nor to rules fostering healthy competition and transparency. It is essential that the true objectives of the financial system are respected, and that excessive risks are avoided, especially for the weak. This will lead to a better delineation of the role of finance. Finance is essential in our system, but should not be looked to for moral guidance, given its tendency toward relativism. The collective work still to be done here is immense because *what is needed is a new foundation*.

It may be added here that the financial community, even more so than other professional circles, has a specific reluctance to consider collective actions and transparency. In fact, opaque market structures are by definition most easily profitable for those who play a central role in them, and in the short run they have no interest in creating more organized, open, and transparent markets. On the other hand, over time all intermediaries would benefit from such reform because volumes would be higher and security much greater. But because short-term reasoning prevails very often, in practice those who profit from the system oppose reforms going against them, except in case of emergency. Consequently, in the case of market structures, unfortunately professional self-regulation is not as frequent as it should be and is certainly only rarely spontaneous: public intervention is therefore indispensable. It has been said that the introduction of moral criteria and of notions of common good in the work of professionals is not easy, given the current hierarchy of priorities; it is *a fortiori* the case of initiatives trying to meet needs that are not profitable, or not immediately so. Here, one encounters the difficulty of using morally responsible references, especially in a society that does not acknowledge common moral values other than the rules of the game, and often fails to acknowledge even them. Without evoking a nostalgia for the Christian era, it must be remembered that it was then possible to invoke such values.

That said, within the inevitably broad regulatory framework, what matters first is the prudential and moral judgment of operators and investors; that is what determines the direction their action will go and where their responsibility will be. There is much debate about what matters most: laws or internal ethical regulation. Obviously, both are necessary. But personal (and collective) judgment is ultimately crucial, even if it is the only dimension that is not decided by law. It may be added that *very often, the more morality is assumed, the less you need collective rules* (even if you always need some): over time, morality allows greater freedom.

In contrast, in certain areas of finance, it is possible to hasten reform through private initiative, even on a minority basis: this is the case with Socially Responsible Investment. As a beginning, even small management companies can offer a model of fund management that obeys rules more in line with the concerns of the common good. The proliferation of such initiatives may eventually move the market, but there is no need to wait for that to start. And Christians can play an essential role there, both in recommending such propositions, and in developing the criteria to be used. I believe that this area should have a clear priority and that the Church should express it more forcefully.

The personal attitude: from morality to faith

Still, the personal attitude is central. Let us remember our Florentine merchants and their ideal, inspired by Franciscan poverty. The same attitude is possible in the present environment, possibly even to the point of sanctity. But which attitude? That of the seven founding merchants of the Order of Servites? But does that imply abandoning the world of commerce, or finance? Or rather Saint Homobonus, who kept working in his profession while selflessly sacrificing all? Rare cases, even at the time, but powerful through their meaningful example. This is the ideal. But most of us have to begin with basic principles: respect for elementary *morality*, which does not stop at the door of offices or trading rooms; the search for *justice*, which requires, among other things, a constant concern for the right price; *humility*, which implies constantly bearing in mind that economy and finance are incomplete and limited, and that they must be permanently placed in a wider human context. Every decision, every act must respect at least these three principles as a good starting point.

To this we may add a more essential concern, which brings us back to faith. And recent events also lead us there. In spite of the considerable and real effort that has been made, it must be recognized that the ongoing action of financial regulators and, beyond that, of the G20,[14] is not sufficient to prevent a major financial crisis in the foreseeable future. It is not merely a question of realistically recognizing that complete mastery of the future is not given to us, or that to seek it would result in an even more damaging sterilization, Soviet style. Neither is it limited to emphasizing the obviously serious imbalances of public finance or in the value of currencies. These facts are very real. But I am making a more prosaic reference to the fact that not all lessons have been learned from the 2007–2008 crisis, and that in particular those in charge have not crossed a significant threshold, accepting true international regulation of markets or restricting certain cross-border activity. One day, therefore, we must expect new major crises, although not necessarily in the immediate future. And this further justifies the role of faith: on the one hand, to try to put order and meaning where it is possible and desirable, while recognizing that the impact can only be limited, at least in the predictable future; and on the other hand, to stay focused on hope. For only faith allows us to consider with clarity such realities and threats, even when they are very disturbing, without denying them out of conformism, nor letting them paralyze us.[15]

14 Which nevertheless brings together every year the supreme leaders of the twenty major world economies [written in 2013].
15 For the economy in general I have discussed this point in more detail in my *L'économie et le christianisme*.

CONCLUSION

ANY FINANCIAL TRANSACTION IS A SOCIAL INTERAC-
tion. In a social interaction between human beings, there are always
two elements: firstly, the vocation and the unique role of each person,
translated into interacting individual priorities: it is already a form
of relationship. Secondly, the fabric of these relations, necessarily
multiple and specific, is the basis of society; fidelity and duration are
essential elements but must not become prisons. This brings us to
the collective result of all these decisions and operations, that is to
say, the existence of society itself, to which each person is responsible
and which each person must heed as an objective real reference and
as a possible alternative to each of the parties to any operation. In
the same way, money is non-fungible, if one looks at the priorities
and the mission of each person, which are specific, but it is fungible
in its actual use in society.

This can be summarized as follows. Every participant (customer,
investor, or company) must be able to commit themselves to relations
that appear to them in conformity with the common good, within
a perspective of fidelity and community. At the same time, every
participant must feel free to refrain from relations when the same
good demands it. In this context, everyone must be free to carry out
the operations that they consider objectively good, subject to their
commitments and duties. But at the same time, they must take into
account the socially available objective data, starting with the market
and the resulting prices, without being limited thereto, but cooperat-
ing in its proper functioning. The role of financial professionals is to
put their talent to use at the service of these missions. And it is the
business of all to make the best use of these collective tools. Lastly,
it is incumbent on the authorities to ensure by constant vigilance
and timely action that the collective organization of these decisions
is directed as far as possible toward the common good.

We see then that *finance is a complex, high-tech, high-risk job, involving heavy responsibilities*. It therefore demands a high level of reason
and virtue. A cool head turned in the right direction is a decisive
requirement, and this requires virtue. Yet too often, in practice, action
is not only self-serving but excessively emotive; too often one only
seeks to enrich oneself and loses sight of these virtues and the need

for them. How to work to reverse these trends, beyond enacting rules and laws? And this must be done without disrupting market techniques or the autonomy of participants, which would profoundly modify their outcome. No doubt here you will again resort to faith. In such an activity, the tension between temptation and duty can be very high. In practice and with few exceptions, only a robust level of *faith*, and therefore the help of God, can give the strength to overcome temptation. We have noted these facts in the chapters on Christianity. Again, on most points there is nothing specifically Christian in the moralization of finance, if you consider the rules that a non-Christian who believes in real moral values could adopt. But it is from the Christian that you will expect a defense and implementation of such ideas — forcefully and to their logical end.

A SHORT BIBLIOGRAPHY

Aquinas, Thomas. *Summa theologica*. Milan: Editiones Paulinae, 1988.

Association d'économie financière. *Rapport moral sur l'argent dans le monde*. Paris: AEF, 2010.

Bériou, Nicole and Jacques Chiffoleau, ed. *Economie et religion: l'expérience des ordres mendiants (XIIIe-XVe siècle)*. Lyon: Presses Universitaires de Lyon, 2009.

Calvez, Jean-Yves. *Changer le capitalisme*. Paris: Bayard, 2001.

Chafuen, Alejandro A. *Faith and Liberty: The Economic Thought of the Late Scholastics*. Lanham, MD: Lexington Books, 2003.

Clavero, Bartolomé. *La grâce du don*. Paris: Albin Michel, 1996.

de Lauzun, Pierre. *Christianisme et Croissance économique*. Paris: Parole et Silence, 2008.

———. *L'économie et le christianisme*. Paris: Francois-Xavier de Guibert, 2010.

———. *L'Evangile, le Chrétien et l'Argent*. Paris: Editions du Cerf, 2004.

Dembinski, Paul H. *Finance servante ou finance trompeuse?* Paris: Parole et Silence, 2008.

———, ed. *Pratiques financières, regards chrétiens*. Paris: Editiones Desclée de Brouwer, 2009.

Denzinger, Heinrich. *Symboles et définitions de la foi catholique*. Paris: Cerf, 1996. For an English language edition, see the next entry.

———. *Enchiridion Symbolorum: Compendium of Creeds, Definitions, and Declarations on Matters of Faith and Morals*. San Francisco: Ignatius Press, 2013.

de Salins, Antoine, and François Villeroy de Galhau. *Le développement moderne des activités financières au regard des exigences éthiques du christianisme*. Vatican City: Libreria Editrice Vaticana, 1994. For an English language edition, see the next entry.

———. *The Modern Development of Financial Activities in the Light of the Ethical Demands of Christianity*. Vatican City: Libreria Editrice Vaticana, 1994

Ferguson, Niall. *The Ascent of Money: A Financial History of the World*. London: Penguin Books, 2008.

Finnis, John. *Aquinas: Moral, Political, and Legal Theory*. Oxford: Oxford University Press, 1998 and 2004.

Fontaine, Laurence. *L'économie morale: Pauvreté, crédit, et confiance dans l'Europe préindustrielle*. Paris: Gallimard, 2008. For an English language edition, see the next entry.

———. *The Moral Economy: Poverty, Credit, and Trust in Early Modern Europe*. Cambridge: Cambridge University Press, 2014.

Gavignaud-Fontaine, Geneviève. *Considérations économiques chrétiennes de saint Paul aux temps actuels*. Paris: Boutique de l'Histoire, 2009.

Giraud, Gaël and Cécile Reynouard, ed. *20 Propositions pour reformer le capitalisme*. Paris: Groupe Flammarion, 2009.

Godbout, Jacques T. and Alain Caillé. *L'esprit du don*. Paris: La Découverte/ Poche, 2000. For an English language edition, see the next entry.

———. *The World of the Gift*. Montreal: McGill-Queen's University Press, 2000.

Grabill, Stephen J., ed. *Sourcebook in Late-scholastic Monetary Theory: The Contributions of Martin de Azpilcueta, Luis de Molina, and Juan de Mariana*. Lanham, MD: Lexington Books 2007.

Greci, Roberto, Giuliano Pinto, and Giacomo Todeschini. *Economie urbane ed etica economica nell'Italia medievale*. Rome-Bari: Editori Laterza, 2005.

Green, Stephen. *Good Value: Reflections on Money, Morality, and an Uncertain World*. London: Penguin Books/Allen Lane, 2009.

Kaye, Joel. *Economy and Nature in the Fourteenth Century: Money, Market Exchange, and the Emergence of Scientific Thought*. Cambridge: Cambridge University Press, 1998/2000.

Langholm, Odd. *The Legacy of Scholasticism in Economic Thought*. Cambridge: Cambridge University Press, 1998/2006.

Laurent, Bernard. *L'enseignement social de l'Eglise et l'économie de marché*. Paris: Parole et Silence, 2007.

Le Goff, Jacques. *La Bourse et la vie: économie et religion au Moyen Age*. Paris: Hachette Littérature, 1986.

———. *Le Moyen Age et l'argent*. Paris: Perrin, 2010. For an English language edition, see the next entry.

———. *Money and the Middle Ages*. Cambridge: Polity Press, 2012.

———. *Marchands et banquiers au Moyen-âge*. Nice: PUF Que sais-je, 2001.

Long, D. Stephen. *Divine Economy: Theology and the Market*. Milton Park, Milton, UK: Routledge, 2003.

Mollat, Michel. *Les Pauvres au Moyen Age*. Brussels: Editions Complexe, 2006. For an English language edition, see the next entry.

———. *The Poor in the Middle Ages: An Essay in Social History*. Translated by Arthur Goldhammer. New Haven, CT: Yale University Press, 1990.

Perret, Bernard. *Les nouvelles frontières de l'argent*. Paris: Éditions du Seuil, 1999. For an English language edition, see the next entry.

———. *New Frontiers of Money*. London: Anthem Press, 2001.

Perrot, Etienne. *Refus du risque et catastrophes financières*. Paris: Salvator, 2011.

Pontifical Council of Justice and Peace. *Compendium of the Social Doctrine of the Church*. London: Continuum International Publishing Group, 2006.

Prodi, Paolo. *Christianisme et monde moderne*. Paris: Gallimard Seuil, 2006.

Quaglioni, Diego, Giacomo Todeschini, and Gian Maria Varanini. *Credito e usura fra teologia, diritto e amministrazione—linguaggi a confronto (sec. XII–XVI)*. Rome: Collection de l'École française de Rome, 2005.

Ramelet, Denis. "La rémunération du capital à la lumière de la doctrine traditionnelle de l'Eglise catholique." *Catholica* 86 (Winter 2004–05): 13–25.

Sen, Amartya. *Development as Freedom*. New York: Alfred Knopf, 1999.

Simmel, Georg. *Philosophie de l'argent*. Paris: Quadrige/Presses PUF, 1987/1999. For an English language edition, see the next entry.

———. *The Philosophy of Money*. Milton Park, Milton, UK: Routledge, 2011.

Tiberghien, Pierre. *Encyclique Vix pervenit de Benoît XIV*. Paris: Spes, 1914.

Todeschini, Giacomo. *Richesse franciscaine: De la pauvreté volontaire à la société de marché*. Lagrasse: Editions Verdier, 2008.

Turner, Adair, Andrew Haldane, and Paul Woolley. *The Future of Finance: The LSE Report*. London: The London Publishing Partnership, 2010.

Verrier, Ramón. *Introduction à la pensée économique de l'Islam du VIIIe au XVe siècle*. Paris: L'Harmattan, 2009.

Walter, Christian, ed. *Nouvelles normes financières: S'organiser face à la crise*. Berlin: Springer, 2010.

The encyclicals and other pontifical texts in English are taken from the Vatican website, http://www.vatican.va/content/vatican/en.html.

ABOUT THE AUTHOR

PIERRE DE LAUZUN has worked in banking and finance at many levels — from the Paris Club at the French Treasury, to acting CEO of major banking institutions, to Chairman of the International Council of Securities Associations. Throughout his financial career he has also led a life of personal reflection on philosophical, economic, political, and religious issues, resulting, to this point, in no fewer than 16 books.

Lightning Source UK Ltd.
Milton Keynes UK
UKHW011033291021
393033UK00001B/9